iOS 16, iPadOS 16, macOS V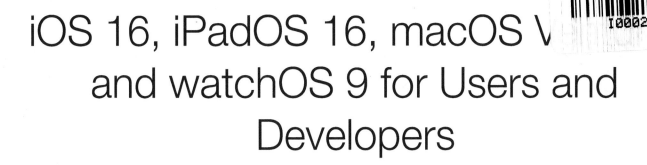 and watchOS 9 for Users and Developers

Preface

Hello and welcome to the 2022 edition of "Wayne explains why he wrote another book about Apple". This book is the 21st book about Apple's operating systems that I have written, and my 23rd book overall. I wrote two other books, one about the Playstation 4 and another about the Xbox One both back in 2013 when those products were new. Of course time has marched on and the successors to both of those consoles have been released, however, I did not write any books about their successors.

From 2013 through 2019 I wrote two books each year, one for the iOS based operating systems and another for macOS. Last year I decided to change this approach and I combined both of the books into a single book that encompassed all of Apple's platforms. Last year with "iOS 15, iPadOS 15, macOS Monterey, watchOS 8, and tvOS 15" was the first year where only a single book was written. The rationale for this was that Apple's platforms had really started to come into feature parity and it had become difficult to separate out the different operating systems due to them becoming so intertwined and having so many similar features. Furthermore, there was significant duplication between both books in the developer section. This year's releases only emphasize the similarities more than ever and reinforces my decision to combine the two books into a single one.

Given their history both iOS and iPadOS share a significant amount of their codebases, because they are in many ways just the same operating system with a few differences, like display methods, interaction types, and supported hardware.

I spent some time thinking how best to organize the book this year and I think I have come with an approach that makes sense. Given that all of Apple's operating systems share a lot of code and features, I have broken down the book by feature or topic. There are chapters that are dedicated to specific features like "Stage Manager" and "Safety Check". At the same time there are also chapters that cover a bunch of features that all fall into their own topic. A couple of examples of these are "Communication & Collaboration" and "Health and Fitness", just to name two.

Even though everything is organized by topic or feature there still do need to be platform specific chapters because there are some items that only affect a single operating system, so those need to be delineated separately.

The intention of the book is to appeal to as many people as possible as well. This could be someone who has only been using iOS, iPadOS, macOS, or watchOS for a short while to those, like myself, who have been using Macs, and computers in general, for most of my life. Similarly, the developer section is aimed towards both novices and long-time programmers and attempts to provide information for all levels. To that end there may be some information that some might consider "basic" and that everyone should know, but not everybody is working at the same level of knowledge, and this is accounted for.

There are some topics which are covered in-depth and others that are more superficial. For instance, the WeatherKit web service information is quite in-depth because web services is an area that I know really well, the same applies to Apple Silicon, purely based upon my interest in the architecture. To quote one of my favorite movies, "RISC is good".

On the other hand, topics like Machine Learning with CoreML, as well as Apple's graphics rendering engine, Metal, are two areas where my understanding is definitely more limited. I can understand the basics of these two areas, and grasp some concepts, but there does come a point where it ends up being beyond my comprehension.

The lack of depth for those topics is not an indication that those areas are not important, clearly they are important, in a variety of ways, but it is more a limitation in my own personal knowledge of the subject. In addition, there is only so many hours that one can devote to attempting to learn something before they realize that the entire subject matter is clearly beyond their understanding. For these areas, I attempt to provide a broad overview of the basic changes that have occurred.

This is one of the longest books that I have written. It is over 100,000 words and without any images it is over 230 pages in length. This is not what I had anticipated going into Apple's 2022 World Wide Developer Conference. Initially, I thought this year's book would about the same as last year's, but it turns out it is approximately 30% longer. I guess I had a lot more to say, and more to cover, than I thought.

As always, feel free to provide any feedback regarding any aspect of the book. You can do this either via email or you can send me a message on Twitter or Mastodon.

Wayne Dixon
books@waynedixon.com
Twitter: @waynedixon
Mastodon: mastodon.social/@waynedixon

Introduction

When Apple was established in 1976 in Steve Jobs' parent's garage, it would be impossible to see where the company would end up. Over the last 46 years the company has seen many shifts and changes. The Apple I was their first computer, but the Apple II is what made them a success. In 1984 a big shift occurred from a command-line interface to a graphical and mouse-based interface. The Mac would become the basis and focus of the company. In 1985 after Steve Jobs was pushed out of the company he founded, he created a new company, NeXT Computers. NeXT would ultimately be acquired by Apple in 1997, but the acquisition of NeXT brought another change, the basis for what today is called macOS, but had been previously called Mac OS X.

Modern macOS began in 2001 with the release of Mac OS X 10.0 Cheetah. At its initial launch it was not nearly as speedy as the previous Mac OS 9, but over the next few years it gain additional speed improvements and feature enhancements.

Apple could have just cruised along with the iPod and Mac, but instead, starting in 2005 they began working a new project. That project would ultimately be such a fundamental change in technology that nobody would be suspecting, at least not from Apple. The resulting product was the iPhone.

The iPhone's operating system used many of the underlying pieces from Apple's work on the Mac, but added its own multi-touch interface. The interaction model on iPhone was a fundamental shift in what the future of computing would look like that it was dismissed by many at the time. At this point Apple had two operating systems, iPhoneOS and macOS. While they had some commonalities, they began to drift apart. This became exacerbated with the introduction of another device in 2010, the iPad.

The iPad used the same operating system as the iPhone and in 2010 with the release of the next versions of the operating systems in the summer of 2010, the iPhone and iPad would be using the same operating system, iOS 4. Now, Apple was back down to two distinct operating systems, again with some underpinnings the same, but still divergent.

Beginning in 2011 Apple began the initial steps of bringing all of their operating systems into alignment. This began with a simple changing of names, but this was just merely the beginning. That simple shift began a long process of bringing all of the underlying technologies together so all of Apple's operating systems could use a common set of foundational frameworks. On top of these frameworks would come the actual interface.

All of this effort would eventually culminate in the ability for Apple to create applications that run on a lot of their platforms. These would not just similar apps, but the exact same apps. Some examples of this include Messages, the Home app, Podcasts, Voice Memos, and Stocks.

These common underpinnings ultimately allowed Apple to create a new modern programming language called Swift. Swift brought many features like type safety to the Apple platforms. Swift is also open source, which allows the community of Swift to provide enhancements and new features to the language.

Swift is the language that Apple has indicated is the future of Apple's platforms, but a programming language alone is not enough, you also need a user interface framework. That framework is SwiftUI. SwiftUI is built on top of all of the features of Swift and is an entirely different way of programming, as compared to UIKit or AppKit. Instead of telling the app exactly what to do you describe how you want it to work.

For what began in 2011 with Mac OS X 10.7 Lion, all of this work has culminated in Apple's platforms now being more similar than ever before, at least under the hood. The interface for each of Apple's devices still remains unique to that platform. SwiftUI provides a "learn once apply everywhere" mentality, in that once you learn SwiftUI you can apply it all equally to each of Apple's platforms. This is a significant change away from using previous user interface frameworks. Ultimately, this means that developers can bring their apps to the platforms where it makes sense and when they do there will be consistency between all of the apps on the platform.

This is the current state of Apple's platforms and this year's releases bring a slew of new features. Even though Apple previously had only two operating systems, that has expanded to include one operating system for each of its platforms and devices. There is iOS for iPhones, iPadOS for iPads, watchOS for Apple Watches, tvOS for Apple TV and HomePods, and macOS for Macs. Each of these has its own unique interaction types, ways of displaying information, and its own paradigms. However, underneath each of them is a common set of frameworks that all of the apps on each of the devices are built upon.

One thing you may notice about this book, that differs from last year, is that it does not include tvOS. There is a reason for that. tvOS has not seen significant meaningful improvement from Apple the last couple of years. It is still supported and it does get an occasional new feature, but it is not as prominent as it was in 2015 when it was introduced. tvOS 16 is new, but there is not much to it. It has received all of the same bug and security fixes that all of the other platforms have received.

Even though tvOS is not included, there are still all large number of changes that have occurred among the rest of the operating systems. Some of these features will come to all of the devices, while others will not. Likewise, some of the previously supported devices are no longer supported. Let us now dive into all of these changes, by starting with device compatibility.

Device Compatibility

Each set of new operating systems has its own set of requirements. Some years devices are no longer supported on the newest operating systems. It should be noted that even though a device may be supported with a specific operating system, that does not mean that it will be able to run all of the features. There are some instances, particularly with this year's operating systems, where some features will only be available on specific models of devices. Let us look at each of the list of compatible devices for each operating system, starting with iOS.

iOS

There are a total of 19 different iPhone models that are compatible with iOS 16. The list of supported devices includes:

- iPhone 14 Pro Max (A16) - 2022
- iPhone 14 Pro (A16) - 2022
- iPhone 14 Plus (A15) - 2022
- iPhone 14 (A15) - 2022
- iPhone SE (3rd Generation) (A15) - 2022
- iPhone 13 (A15) - 2021
- iPhone 13 mini (A15) - 2021
- iPhone 13 Pro (A15) - 2021
- iPhone 13 Pro Max (A15) - 2021
- iPhone 12 (A14) - 2020
- iPhone 12 mini (A14) - 2020
- iPhone 12 Pro (A14) - 2020
- iPhone 12 Pro Max (A14) - 2020
- iPhone 11 (A13) - 2019
- iPhone 11 Pro (A13) - 2019
- iPhone 11 Pro Max (A13) - 2019
- iPhone SE (2nd generation) (A13) - 2019
- iPhone XS (A12 - 2018)
- iPhone XS Max (A12) - 2018
- iPhone XR (A12) - 2018
- iPhone X (A11 - 2017)
- iPhone 8 (A11) - 2017
- iPhone 8 Plus (A11) - 2017
- iPhone SE (2nd generation) (A11) - 2018

iPhone 13 Pro Max in Alpine Green

iOS 16 has dropped support for a few devices, specifically the iPhone 6s, iPhone 6s Plus, iPhone 7, the iPhone 7 Plus, and the 1st generation iPhone SE are all no longer supported. These devices had either an A8, A9, or A10 Fusion processor. The new baseline for iOS is an A11 Bionic or newer. Before we leave iOS there is another device that needs to be discussed, and that device that is missing from the list above. Of course, that device is the iPod touch.

iPod touch

The original iPod touch was introduced in September of 2007, and the 7th generation iPod touch was introduced on May 28th, 2019. The iPod touch remained "an item in the lineup" until May 10th, 2022 when Apple announced that the iPod touch had been discontinued.

The iPod touch line up remained largely the same throughout its entire life. At first the device had a 3.5-inch, but moved to a or 4-inch screen screen in 2011. The iPod Touch also had a home button, and headphone jack, along with various quality of cameras. The iPod touch was a great device to give to a kid or to use if you wanted a light and easily portable device, or if you really just wanted "an iPhone without the phone". Alas, it is no longer being sold. The original iPod line of products, while still popular when the iPod touch was introduced, has declined in usage and popularity. In its place are hand-me-down iPhones and the iPad. These have largely been used in place of the iPod touch. It truly is an end of an era, but time marches on. It is not likely that iPod touch will have as much fondness, nor as still be as usable in a decade as the iPod has been, but only time will tell. Now, let us move onto iPadOS and the devices that are compatible with iOS 16.

iPadOS

Similar to iOS, the list of iPads that support iPadOS 16 is a long one. There are 20 iPads that are compatible with iPadOS 16. The oldest devices that is supported with iOS 16 is the first-generation 12.9-inch iPad Pro, which was released on November 10th, 2015. The list of supported iPads for iPadOS 16 is:

- iPad Pro 12.9-inch (5th generation) (M1) – 2021
- iPad Pro 11-inch (3rd generation) (M1) – 2021
- iPad Pro 12.9-inch (4th generation) (A12Z Bionic) –2020
- iPad Pro 11-inch (2nd generation) (A12Z Bionic) – 2020
- iPad Pro 12.9-inch (3rd generation) (A12X Bionic) – 2019
- iPad Pro 11-inch (1st generation) (A12X Bionic) – 2019
- iPad Pro 12.9-inch (2nd generation) (A10X Fusion) – 2017
- iPad Pro 12.9-inch (1st generation) (A9) – 2015
- iPad Pro 10.5-inch (A10X Fusion) – 2017
- iPad Pro 9.7-inch (A9X) – 2020
- iPad (9th Generation) (A13 Bionic) – 2021
- iPad (8th generation) (A12 Bionic) – 2020
- iPad (7th generation) (A10 Fusion) – 2019
- iPad (6th generation) (A10 Fusion) – 2018
- iPad (5th generation) (A9) – 2017
- iPad mini (6th Generation) (A15 Bionic) – 2021
- iPad mini (5th generation) (A12 Bionic) – 2019
- iPad Air (5th generation) (A15 Bionic) – 2022
- iPad Air (4th generation) (A14 Bionic) – 2020
- iPad Air (3rd generation) (A12 Bionic) – 2019

5th Generation 12.9-inch iPad Pro

As you might suspect, the older iPads may not be able to use some of the latest features. Some devices are no longer supported on iPadOS 16, specifically the iPad mini (4th Generation) and the iPad Air 2. Both of these were running the A8 processor. The new baseline for the iPadOS is the A9. Next, let us look at watchOS.

watchOS

watchOS 8 has a list of five compatible devices. These devices are:

- Apple Watch Ultra (S8) – 2022
- Apple Watch Series 8 (S8) – 2022
- Apple Watch SE (S8) – 2022
- Apple Watch Series 7 (S7) – 2021
- Apple Watch Series 6 (S6) – 2020
- Apple Watch SE (S5) – 2020
- Apple Watch Series 5 (S5) – 2019
- Apple Watch Series 4 (S4) – 2018

Series 7 Apple Watch in Midnight

The list of compatible devices is similar to that of watchOS 9 as it was watchOS 8. The only exception to this is the Apple Watch Series 3, which is not supported on watchOS 9. Many remarked that the Series 3 Apple Watch should not have been supported with watchOS 8, but it was. Next, let us turn to tvOS.

tvOS

tvOS has the smallest list of compatible devices with just three, with the oldest being the first device that supported tvOS, the Apple TV HD. tvOS 16 is compatible with all devices that support tvOS, including:

- Apple TV 4K (2nd generation) - 2021
- Apple TV 4K - 2019
- Apple TV HD - 2015

This is the same list of devices that were supported on tvOS 15. This is a bit surprising since the original Apple TV HD is running an A8 processor. Even though it is running an older processor, it is still easily capable of being able to handle 1080p content. Let us now look at compatibility for the last operating system, macOS.

macOS

Apple has had codenames for their versions of macOS since the beginning of its run. The first codename was Mac OS X 10.0 Cheetah, which was introduced in March of 2001. Starting in 2013 with the release of Mac OS X 10.9, the naming scheme changed from "Big Cats" to places in California. So far, the list of place names has been:

- Mac OS X 10.9 Mavericks – 2013
- Mac OS X 10.10 Yosemite - 2014
- Mac OS X 10.11 El Capitan - 2015
- macOS Sierra (10.12) - 2016
- macOS High Sierra (10.13) - 2017
- macOS Mojave (10.14) - 2018
- macOS Catalina (10.15) - 2019
- macOS Big Sur (macOS 11) - 2020
- macOS Monterey (macOS 12) - 2021

In fact, with this year's release of macOS 13, there are now officially more California place names than there were "Big Cat" names. This year's code name is "Ventura", which is named after the city of Ventura, which is a big tourist destination with beaches and historical landmarks.

As with other macOS releases, macOS Ventura does have its own set of requirements. From time to time macOS drops support for devices, and macOS Ventura is no different. The requirements for macOS Ventura are a bit more aggressive than one might have expected. Any devices that are 2016 or older are no longer supported. This means that the supported device list includes:

- iMac 2017 or later
- iMac Pro 2017 or later
- MacBook 2017 or later
- MacBook Pro 2017 or later
- MacBook Air 2018 or later
- Mac mini 2018 or later
- Mac Pro 2019 or later
- Mac Studio 2022 or later

Last year, devices as far back as early-2015 were supported, so this seems like a significant reduction in the number of supported devices. Even so it is not too surprising given the features within macOS Ventura, which will all be covered more in-depth as we go on. However, before we start diving into specific features, we do need to turn to a particular aspect of macOS, macOS Server, because there have been some changes around that product.

macOS Server

Since the introduction of the first version of Mac OS X, Mac OS X 10.0 Cheetah, on March 24th, 2001, there has been a "server" counterpart. The reason that there was a server version is because the core of macOS, even today, is a flavor of Unix, specifically BSD Unix. Unix has a long history of being used for hosting servers. An open-source unix-like system, called Linux, is by far the most popular platform for running servers.

macOS Server had a slew of features between the 10.0 and Mac OS X 10.6 Snow Leopard Server releases. This list included features like:

- Web server
- Calendar Server
- MySQL Server
- DNS Server
- RADIUS Server
- X-Grid Server
- Wiki Server
- Mail Server

macOS Server app icon

And those were just a few of the features that it provided. Mac OS X 10.6 Snow Leopard was the last version of macOS that had a distinctly separate server version of the operating system. Pricing for server versions of macOS changed over time as well. From Mac OS X 10.0 Cheetah to Mac OS X 10.5 Leopard, there were two versions of Mac OS X Server, a 10-user license for $499, and an unlimited license for $999.

The 10-user license was dropped with Mac OS X 10.6 Snow Leopard Server and only the unlimited version was available. With the reduction to one version, the price was also reduced to $499 for the unlimited licenses. It should be noted that the licensing only applied to the number of simultaneous connections when it came to file sharing. It never applied to the other services, like the web server, Wiki, DNS Server, or any other service offered.

The release following Snow Leopard introduced a significant change to the way the server version of macOS was handled.

Mac OS X 10.7 Lion Server to macOS High Sierra

Starting with Mac OS X 10.7 Lion, released in July of 2011, the entire paradigm for macOS Server changed. Instead of being separate versions, al of the server functionality was moved into a separate downloadable app. This app was purchased using the then new, Mac App Store.

The shift to using the Mac App Store also represented an opportunity to change pricing, which is exactly what Apple did. Instead of being $499, the new price for macOS Server was just $49.99.

You might think that a shift in pricing, and distribution models, for Mac OS X 10.7 Lion Server would provide Apple an opportunity to reduce functionality. However, they did not do that. Instead, they added the ability to manage devices, through a new service called Profile Manager.

Profile Manager would allow you to connect devices to a Mac OS X server and manage them. This is what today, would be known as Mobile Device Management, or MDM.

Mac OS X 10.8 Mountain Lion introduced another change to macOS Server, this one again with the price. Instead of being $49.99 it was now just $19.99, a 60% drop in the price. The $20 price tag put macOS Server squarely into hobbyist territory, and was inexpensive enough for most to purchase and investigate the offerings of macOS Server. Furthermore, macOS Server would no longer need to be a paid upgrade for future versions, meaning that you could upgrade at your own pace without needing to worry about paying again for server.

macOS Server remained largely the same, albeit with updated versions and expanded Profile Manager capabilities up through macOS High Sierra, which was released on September 25th, 2017. The next version, macOS 10.14, would introduce another big shift in macOS Server.

macOS Mojave Server

Starting with macOS Mojave (10.14), released on September 28th, 2018, the functionality of the corresponding server version was significantly reduced. The functionality that would be included would be reduced to be just two services, Profile Manager and Xsan. The other services, calendar, web server, DNS, and others were all including with every installation of macOS. The big shift is that they would not be manageable via a user interface.

This shift made sense given the landscape of the wider server world. Using macOS as a server had slowly been dropping in favor of hosted services, and even more in favor of server-less servers like CloudFlare and other server-less providers. The server functionality remained consistent up through macOS Monterey (macOS 12). Even though it remained stable in terms of support, it was clear that macOS server was no longer a priority for Apple. This was made clear in April of 2022.

macOS Ventura Server

On April 21st, 2022 Apple quietly discontinued macOS Server. The discontinuation of macOS server is, honestly, not much of a surprise. The life of macOS server has been an interesting one. It initially started as a wholly separate version of macOS, progressed to an app with Mac OS X 10.7 Lion, and now with version 5.12 being the last version, and is only compatible with macOS Monterey.

The reason that Apple has discontinued the macOS Server app is because the features it offered, Profile Manager, is now available through Apple's recently introduced service, "Small Business Essentials".

Small Business Essentials is a subscription service that is designed for small and medium businesses. Small Business Essentials allows you to manage, deploy, and support all of your devices for a monthly fee. Small Business Essentials can include iCloud storage, device support, and more.

Even though macOS Server is no longer supported, there are still a few features built into macOS that you can use. The Apache web server is still bundled with macOS Ventura. Therefore you can still run a web server from macOS, but you will need to handle the management yourself. You will need to download any languages, as well as make sure you enable the modules, like Python3, PHP, and other command-line tools yourself. Do not forget to sign them as well, because Apache will refuse to load modules if they are unsigned.

For many, it is sad to see macOS Server no longer be an option, but the writing has been on the wall for a while, but now, it has been formally announced. Even though many of the services have been removed, there are a couple services that are still included, just not manageable through an interface. macOS Server and its iterations had a long life, just about 21 and a half years. Yes it changed significantly during that time, but that is to be expected.

One thing that has happened during the lifetime of macOS is that you have been able to run it on three different hardware platforms, with the latest being Apple Silicon. Let us cover those changes in the next chapter.

Apple Silicon

Apple has used three different platforms for its devices in the last 25 years, in particular this is for the Mac. These have been Power PC from 1998 to 2006, Intel from 2005 to 2020, and beginning in 2020 Apple Silicon.

The Apple Silicon transition actually started in 2008 when Apple purchased a company called PA Semi. At the time many wondered what Apple could want with a semiconductor company. Some speculated that they would use it in their iPhones and iPod touches, and Apple would indeed do that, but that was not all. The first Apple-designed chip, the A4, was introduced with the first generation iPad in April of 2010. This same chip would also be used in the iPhone 4 that June.

Everything that was learned from the acquisition in 2008 through 2019 all lead to Apple being able to create its own custom silicon that could scale from the smallest devices all the way to its most powerful devices.

Apple has built the software that runs on its platform from its founding on April 1st, 1976, and its first product the Apple I, all the way through today. Today the hardware and software are so tightly integrated that Apple can build processors to suit the capabilities and functionality that it wants. It can then build the software to take full advantage of those features and take advantage of every single ounce of power it can.

At its World Wide Developer Conference in 2020 Apple announced that they would be introducing a whole new processor architecture for its oldest platform, the Mac. They called this architecture Apple Silicon. At the announcement, Apple did not provide a name for what they would be calling these processors, but indicated that they would begin the transition later in 2020 and that it would take about two years to complete.

Apple Silicon differs significantly from Intel and Power PC processors in that it utilized an entirely different architecture. In some other processor architectures, there is a clear separation between the Central Processing Unit, or CPU, and the Graphical Processing Unit, or GPU. This separation means that if a task needs to be done on the CPU and that result passed to the GPU, the memory that is used by the processor must be handed off to the GPU, which has is own dedicated memory. This passing of memory can cause some processes to take additional time to complete. Today, this process is very fast and efficient, but there is still some cost in terms of time and energy.

Apple Silicon has a different architecture. It utilizes a "unified memory" architecture. What this means is that the CPU and GPU do not have different pools of memory, they have one shared pool of memory and both have access to the entire pool of memory. This design allows for transferring tasks between the CPU and GPU to occur much faster. This transferring is so fast, that it is nearly instantaneous. There is virtually no lag time between the CPU and GPU.

This approach has a couple of big implications. The first is that if there is a task that the GPU can handle a lot more efficiently than the CPU, the GPU can do its processing and then immediately hand the results back to the CPU. Furthermore, this means that if data needs to go back and forth between the CPU and GPU this happens at a much faster rate.

The second implication is that there is a noticeable speed increase by the user, including responsiveness to events, and more significant, less lag time when performing actions, which is always welcome.

The third implication is when it comes to battery life. The drain on a device's battery is a combination of power usage and heat. Due to the fact that there is no need to transfer memory between the CPU and GPU, the GPU does not need to work nearly as hard. Because the CPU and GPU do not need to work nearly as hard, this results in less heat, which means that the fans do not need to spin nearly as much, ultimately resulting in a reduction of power usage, which leads to longer battery life.

Apple M1 CPU Layout

M1 Max Chip

When Apple announced Apple Silicon, many speculated what they would call their first processor. With the fact that the processor would be used on the Mac, many speculated that it would use the same general naming scheme as Apple's other processors, like the A13. Many speculated that it be called the "M1", not only because it was for the Mac, but also because Apple stopped mentioning the "Mx" series of motion co-processors.

Apple did indeed start the transition to Apple Silicon in November of 2020 with the introduction of the first processor, the M1.

M1 Family

The M1 was introduced on three devices, the MacBook Air, The 13-inch MacBook Pro, and the Mac mini. These devices did not differ in terms of physical form factor, but the internals were entirely different. This decision was deliberate. By not changing the outside casing of these devices, Apple could develop Apple Silicon and keep its development a secret as long as possible.

The next device to get an M1 processor was the replacement for the 21.5-inch iMac. The all new and completely redesigned 24-inch iMac. This was introduced in April of 2021. The M1 allowed Apple to completely redesign the internals of the iMac so that it no longer needed a bulge on the back of the machine. This redesign allowed for a very thin display.

The M1 was the only "M1" series processor until October of 2021 when Apple unveiled the second round of M1-based devices, the 14-inch and 16-inch MacBook Pros. These devices were capable of using one of two variants of the M1, the M1 Pro or the M1 Max. This brought the total number of M1 series of processors up to three.

Side Profile of the 24-inch iMac (2021)

In March of 2022, Apple unveiled a brand new machine, the Mac Studio. The Mac Studio is a desktop machine and is the replacement for the 27-inch iMac. The introduction of a new desktop machine is possible because at the same time that Apple introduced the Mac Studio, they also introduced a new stand-alone 27-inch display, aptly named the Studio Display. The Mac Studio also introduced a whole new chip, the last in the M1 family, the M1 Ultra. The M1 Ultra is a special kind of chip, because it is actually two M1 Max processors that are attached together with a special connector, called the UltraFusion connector. This interconnect allows the two M1 Max System on a Chips to act as a single processor, which means developers do not need to do anything special to take advantage of the processor.

It is a good time to look at the variations of all of the M1 family of processors to try and illustrate the differences amongst all of them. However, that might get wordy and might not do the job. Instead, to be able to easily see the capabilities, differences, and specifications of all of M1 family or processors, it is better to arrange all of it in a table.

M1 Family of Processors								
Variant	CPU cores (P+E)	GPU cores	GPU EU	Graphics ALU	Neural Engine Cores	Memory (GB)	Memory Bandwidth	Transistor count
A14	6 (2+4)	4	64	512	16	4 or 6	42.7GB/s	11.8 billion
M1	8 (4+4)	7	112	896	16	8 or 16	50GB/s	16 billion
M1	8 (4+4)	8	128	1024	16	8 or 16	50GB/s	16 billion
M1 Pro	8 (6+2)	14	224	1792	16	16 or 32	200GB/s	34 billion
M1 Pro	10 (8+2)	16	256	2048	16	16 or 32	200GB/s	34 billion
M1 Max	10 (8+2)	24	384	3072	16	32 or 64	400GB/s	57 billion
M1 Max	10 (8+2)	32	512	4096	16	32 or 64	400GB/s	57 billion
M1 Ultra	20 (16+4)	48	768	6144	32	64 or 128	800GB/s	114 billion
M1 Ultra	20 (16+4)	64	1536	8192	32	64 or 128	800GB/s	114 billion

As you can see from the table, as you go down the table, the capabilities of the processor increase, culminating in the M1 Ultra which, as described above, is two M1 Max processors directly connected with the UltraFusion interconnect. The fact that they are directly connected together is why you get a doubling of the specifications for each variant of the M1 Ultra, when compared to the M1 Max.

Apple is designing the Apple Silicon chip entirely on its own. This means that it can implement hardware features that might not be available otherwise. There are two examples within the M1 processor family, the Neural Engine, which came to the Mac for the first time with the M1, and a set of dedicated hardware encoders and decoders on the M1 Max and M1 Ultra.

These dedicated video encoding units means that many of the tasks that would previously need to be handled by the CPU and GPU can be handled by these video units, leaving the CPU and GPU to continue to be responsive for other tasks. Because these devices are designed and tuned for video, they are super fast when it comes to these tasks.

You may notice an additional item in the table above, the A14. No, this not actually part of the M1 family of chips, but the M1 architecture is built using the same manufacturing process as the A14. Therefore, they are very closely related. The entire introduction of the M1 family of processors took approximately 16 months, from November of 2020 to March of 2022.

The M1 was only the beginning of the Apple Silicon transition. At their 2022 World Wide Developer Conference introduced the first successor to the M1 family of chips, the M2.

M2

The M2 processor was introduced on June 6th, 2022 at Apple's World Wide Developer Conference. There were only two machines announced at the event. These are the MacBook Air and the 13-inch MacBook Pro. The M2 processor improves upon the M1 in a number of ways. Again, let us do a comparison with a table, but this time just with the M1 and M2.

M2 Chip

M1 Compared to M2				
Feature	M1	M1	M2	M2
CPU cores (P+E)	8 (4+4)	8 (4+4)	8 (4+4)	8 (4+4)
GPU cores	7	8	8	8
GPU EU	112	128	256	320
Graphics ALU	896	1024	2048	2560
Neural Engine Cores	16	16	16	16
Memory (GB)	8 or 16	8 or 16	8, 16, or 24	8, 16, or 24
Memory Bandwidth	50GB/s	50GB/s	100GB/s	100GB/s
Transistor count	16 Billion	16 Billion	20 Billion	20 Billion
Lithography	5nm Gen1	5nm Gen1	5nm Gen2	5nm Gen2

There is a significant increase in the graphics processing capabilities of the M2, when compared to the M1. Similarly, the memory bandwidth has been doubled to 100 Gigabits per second. Both of these changes allow for an 18% increase of the CPU performance, while using the same amount of power. The memory bandwidth and increased transistor count also allows for the GPU portion to perform significantly better, being 35% faster than the M1.

The M2 is just the first of the M2 processor family, so it is likely that additional processors will be released in the near future, likely for new products including the Mac mini, 14 and 16-inch MacBook Pro, and other devices.

While the M1 Processor family was designed for the Mac, but it has been expanded beyond that to be used on three other devices. These are the 5th generation 12.9-inch iPad Pro, and the 3rd-generation 11-inch iPad Pro, as well as the 5th generation iPad Air.

The introduction of the 11-inch and 12.9-inch M1 iPad Pros and the 10.9-inch 5th generation iPad Air is significant. These introductions marked the first time that the M1 processor would be used in a device other than a Mac. The fact that these two devices are powered by an M1 allows for these two devices to run a particular feature that is new in iPadOS 16 and macOS Venture. That feature is called Stage Manager, let us look at that in the next chapter.

Stage Manager

Feature Availability: macOS, iPads with an M1 System on a Chip

Within computers of all types, there is a concept called Windowing. A window within computing is a view into another aspect of an operating system, or a view into an app. This window could be the main screen of an app, an axillary window, or any other view of the app.

In order to be able to view multiple windows, you need what is called a Window Manager. On macOS this is Quartz, while on iOS and iPadOS this is called Springboard. Each of these platforms has its own ways of being able to manage windows. Let us look at each of these, starting with macOS.

macOS

On macOS you have a number of ways of managing windows. You can manage them manually or in Spaces, Full Screen Mode, or even in Split View depending on your preference, task, and support from the app. Each of these has their own unique abilities.

Spaces allows you to separate apps into different virtual screens. For instance, you could pair Safari and Notes together in a single space so you could easily focus on the task that you need to. While in another Space you could have social media apps, so you are not tempted while focusing on a task. What apps you put in which Space is entirely up to you.

Full Screen Mode, introduced in 2011 with Mac OS X 10.7 Lion, allows you to make a single app take up the entire screen, hence the name Full Screen Mode. When an app is in Full Screen Mode, it removes all other items from the screen, except for the app and it even hides the Menu Bar, but it is still accessible. This is a great mode should you want to be able to focus on a single app without other distractions. For the longest time, this is how the iPhone and the iPad operated, with only a single app ever being shown at a time. In fact, the idea for Full Screen mode came from iOS.

Split View mode is very similar to Full Screen Mode, in that you can actually use two apps simultaneously, side by side. With Split View Mode you have the ability to adjust the two apps to use any where between one-third of the screen to two-thirds of the screen. You can adjust the size by dragging the app divider to where you would like it to be for each app.

When in Full Screen or Split View Mode, the Menu Bar is hidden by default, but you still have access to it. You can access it by moving your mouse to the top of the screen and after a second, the Menu Bar will be displayed so you can still have full access to the tools that you need.

There are some similar approaches on iPadOS, but there are some differences as well. Let us look at those next.

iPadOS

Similar to macOS, iPadOS has had a history of different ways of being able to manage windows. When the iPad was originally introduced, it used iPhoneOS 3.2. Unlike on macOS, which has been built on a multi-tasking paradigm since the first Mac in 1984, iPhoneOS 3.2 did not have any form of multitasking. Starting with iOS 4, introduced in 2010, multitasking came to both iPhone and iPad. Even though there was the ability to have apps run in the background with multitasking, you could still only have a single application on the screen at a time. This behavior remained the same until the introduction of iOS 9 in 2015, when a whole new multitasking paradigm was introduced, true Multitasking.

Multitasking on iOS 9

iOS 9 introduced two new multitasking modes. These were Slide Over and Split View. Each of these has their own abilities and use cases. Let us look at both, starting with Slide Over.

Slide Over

Slide Over is a feature that allows you to place an app on top of other apps. When you put an app into Slide Over, it will, as the name suggests, allow the specified app to slide over on top of other apps. You can quickly move the app in and out of Slide Over and use it as needed.

You can easily see if there is an app placed in Slide Over by swiping slowly from the right side of the screen to the left, or if you have a keyboard attached, you can use the press the Globe + \ keys to show or hide Slide Over.

Apps in Slide Over only slide over from the right side of the screen, and you can only have one app in Slide Over at a time. Slide Over is great if you need to quickly reference something or only use it intermittently and do not need it to be shown all the time.

Split View

Split View on iPadOS is exactly the same as Split View on macOS, with a couple of minor differences. The biggest difference is that on iPadOS you can still have only two apps in Split View on the screen at one time. However, there are limitations on the portion of the screen that an app can utilize. Instead of being arbitrarily between one-third and two-thirds, an app can use one-third, one-half, or two-thirds of the screen, with the second app taking up the remainder of the screen.

With iPadOS 16 and macOS Ventura, there is a whole new way of being able to manage and use apps. That is called Stage Manager.

Stage Manager on iPadOS 16 and macOS Ventura

As people use their devices their usage patterns may remain the same, but it is actually more likely to change. Stage Manager introduces a new way of being able to use your apps on iPadOS 16 and macOS Ventura. Stage Manager provides you with a way of being able to keep your working area clean while still providing you quick and easy access to your other open applications.

When you activate Stage Manager your currently active app will take focus and the windows for your most recent apps will be moved to the left side of the screen. Only your most recent 4 app groups will be shown. If you want to switch to one of those apps you can simply click on the app and it will be moved to the front, and your just used app will be moved to the left side.

Sometimes you just want to jump right in and start using a feature, so let us look at how to activate Stage Manager.

Activating Stage Manager

Stage Manager is an entirely optional feature that you can enable. It is entirely possible that you could use iPadOS 16 and macOS Ventura and never enable the feature. However, if you want to enable Stage Manager this can be done in Control Center.

On iPadOS this is done by swiping down from the upper right corner to display Control Center and then clicking on the "Stage Manager" icon. On macOS, you click on the Control Center menu bar item and then click on Stage Manager.

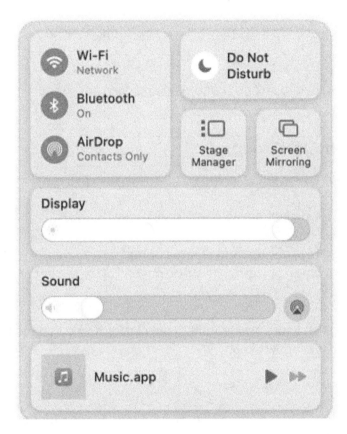

Control Center with Stage Manager button

App Groups

When using Stage Manager you are not restricted to using just a single app. You can actually group multiple apps together as a single group. You can easily create a group by simply clicking on an app, or app window, and then drag it on top of your current app. Similarly, you can also drag an app, or app window, out of an app group by simply dragging the app to the left side of the screen.

App Group Limits

One thing to be aware of with Stage Manager is that on iPadOS you do have a limit to the number of apps that can be within an app group. That limit is four apps, per screen, but more on that in a bit. If you attempt to add a fifth app, the oldest unused app, in the current app group, will be moved to the left side. This limitation does not apply on macOS.

Adding Apps to an App Group

There are a couple of different ways of adding an app to an app group. The first way is to drag and drop the app into the current app group on the left side of the screen.

The second way is to use the following steps:

1. While in Stage Manager tap on the "**...**" button at the top of an app. Doing this will bring up a Stage Manager menu with three icons a full screen button, an Add App button, or Remove App button.
2. Tap on the **Add App** button. When you tap on the button the apps in the app group will move out of the way and the Home Screen will appear.
3. **Navigate** to the proper app and tap it to open it. If the app supports window and resizing it will be added to the App Group.

Not all apps will support being added to an App Group. If an app does not support multiple windows, it will not work with Stage Manager.

Removing Apps from an App Group

Removing an app from an app group is similar to adding one. You can use the following steps:

1. Locate the app you want to remove from an App Group.
2. Tap on the "**...**" button at the top of the app window.
3. Tap on the "**-**" button to remove the app from the App Group.
4. When you remove an app from an app group it will be pushed off to the left side where the recent app groups are shown.

Stage Manager on iPadOS brings an entire new feature to the platform, one that many power users have been wanting for awhile. That feature is window tiling.

Tiled Windows

As outlined earlier, macOS has long had the ability to have multiple windows on the screen simultaneously and the iPad has only had the ability to have multiple apps on the screen since 2015. The one thing that macOS has always had, that iPadOS has not, is the ability to have windows that overlap. The ability to have multiple overlapping windows on the screen at once is called, tiling.

As mentioned above, you can have multiple apps grouped together to create an app group. When you drag an app into an App Group, its window will overlap the existing windows. You can then move the app windows around to suit your working needs. Having tiled windows is a good enhancement for the iPad, but it also includes another capability on iPadOS, resizing windows.

Resizing Windows

When you add an app to an App Group you want to be able to organize the apps as needed. You might expect that all apps in an app group would have the same physical size and each of the four apps would be in one of the four corners. If Apple had gone with this approach, many would have indicated that this was an acceptable limitation for the first iteration of the feature. However, luckily for power users, Apple chose not to implement tiled windows in this manner.

Stage Manager on iPadOS with two applications that can be resized

There are those instances when using an iPad that you might need to be able to adjust the size of an app's window. You are able to resize each application window to the size that you need. This can be done by using one of the window adjustment handles that is on the corner of each app window. Alternatively, if you have a pointing device attached to an iPad, you can also hover over any of the edges of a window and a re-adjustment arrow will be shown. When the adjustment arrow is shown you can tap and drag on the arrow and it will re-adjust the app window accordingly.

There are some limitations to the size that you can make a single app window. For instance, the smallest width you can make an app's window is about the same as when it is in slide-over. Similarly, you can only make the height about half of the size of the screen of the iPad.

There's also a maximum size that you can make an app on iPadOS when using Stage Manager. You can make it almost full-width. There's still about a 5% border around the window. When you make a window its full width, the Recent App Switcher, on the left side of the screen, will be hidden so you can focus on the apps that you are using. You can easily make the Recent App Switcher re-appear by making the width of the window slightly smaller.

That is the default behavior of Stage Manager, but this may not be what you want. There are a couple of customizations that you can make to the default behavior.

Customizing Stage Manager

As stated, Stage Manager does have some default behaviors that will be suitable for most users. However, you can make two customization options. These are whether to show Recent Apps by default and whether to show the Dock by default.

To customize Stage Manager on iPadOS perform the following steps:

1. Open **Control Center** by swiping down from the top right corner of the screen.
2. Enable Stage Manager by tapping on the **Stage Manager icon**.
3. **Tap and hold** on the Screen Manager icon to bring up the options.
4. **Enable** or disable, showing the Recent Apps.
5. **Enable** or disable, showing of the Dock.

To customize Stage Manager on macOS, perform the following steps:

1. Open **System Settings**.
2. **Scroll** down to Desktop & Dock.
3. Click on **Desktop & Dock** to open the settings for the Desktop and Dock.
4. **Scroll down** to Stage Manager.
5. Click on the **Customize** Button
6. Click on **Show Recent Apps** or **Hide Recent Apps** to show or hide recent apps while using Stage Manager.

Once you make a change, it will be saved on both macOS and iPadOS. The option to not show the Dock is only available on iPadOS. but not on macOS. This is because the Dock has its own preferences on macOS, so you can independently manage the hiding functionality on the Dock through the Dock's preferences.

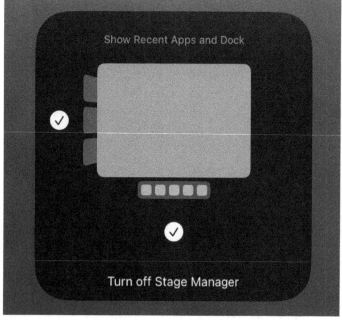

Stage Manager options on iPadOS 16

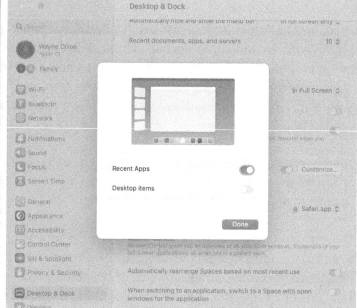

Stage Manager settings on macOS Ventura

On macOS there is also an option to add Stage Manager to the Menu Bar. When you do this, you can easily access the settings for Stage Manager from the Menu Bar item. Each of the supported platforms has some requirements.

Supported Devices

All Macs that support macOS Ventura will be able to use Stage Manager. However, on the iPad Stage Manager is limited to iPads with an M1 processor. All iPad Pro models that have an M1 processor are supported. The iPad Air with M1 processor is supported, provided it is configured with 256GB of storage. The reason that the feature is limited to the iPads with M1 is because of another new feature that is exclusive to the M1 iPads, that feature is called Virtual Memory.

Virtual Memory

All computing devices have limitations in the amount of physical memory that is usable. In almost every case, the amount of physical memory is significantly less than the amount of physical storage. As an example, of this disparity, the amount of memory available on Apple's iPads, at least as of this writing, can range between 3GB up to 16GB, depending on device and storage configuration. The amount of storage can range between 64GB to 2TB, again depending on device.

For instance, you can configure a 9th generation iPad with either 64GB or 256GB of storage. At the lowest configuration there is 21.3x as much storage as memory. In the 256GB configuration, there is 85.3x more storage than memory.

Similarly, all iPad Pro models come with 8GB of physical memory, unless it is a 1TB or 2TB model. In those instances, there is 16GB of memory. Therefore, an iPad Pro with 128GB of storage has 16x more storage than physical memory. The highest-end configuration of 2TB of storage has 128x more physical storage as compared to memory.

iPadOS is designed to keep as much information readily accessible in its memory as possible. However, as you load up additional apps, more and more memory is consumed. If you open enough apps, at some point all of the available memory is consumed.

From the first generation iPad introduced 2010, and even with the iPhone, if an iPad or iPhone runs out of physical memory iPadOS, and iOS, will begin to terminate apps and processes in order to free up enough memory for the current application to run efficiently and smoothly. Typically, you do not notice because the system does this in the background. The only indication that an app's process was ended, or that memory was cleared, is when you reopen the app and it has to relaunch everything.

Regardless of the platform when the amount of physical memory is exhausted, and if the device still needs additional memory, some of the least recently used data can be placed temporarily into a dedicated portion of physical storage. This type of memory is called Virtual Memory, or can also be called swap.

macOS has long had support for virtual memory, and it uses it regularly. When data is moved to Virtual Memory on macOS, you may notice a slight slowdown when that memory is transferred back from Virtual Memory to physical memory.

As mentioned earlier, Virtual Memory is only enabled on devices with an M1 processor. The reason for this is due to the architecture of the M1, specifically, there is is enough storage and memory bandwidth to be able to easily handle the amount of data to transfer between storage and memory. As outlined in the **M1 Family of Processors** table in the previous chapter, the A14 has a maximum bandwidth of 42.7 Gigabytes per second, this is not close enough to the 50 Gigabytes per second that is in the M1. Similarly, the A15 processor in the 6th generation iPad mini, has the same bandwidth as the A14, at 42.7 Gigabytes per second.

Beyond this, the iPad also has significantly enhanced support for external displays, more on that in a bit,. The M1 iPads all have a Thunderbolt connection, which can support transferring data between the iPad and the external display. There is a lot of data being sent between the iPad an an Apple Pro Display XDR, which can support 6K resolution. The amount of data needed for the highest resolution on the Pro Display XDR is 78.61 Gigabits per second, or about 9.83 Gigabytes per second. That is a lot of bandwidth that is being transferred between an M1 iPad and a Pro Display XDR.

There are a couple of things to note about Virtual Memory on the iPad. In computing there is the concept of wired memory. Wired memory is the idea that a process will always use physical memory and never be moved to virtual memory. The reason that this type of memory exists is due to the need to make sure that some processes always remain live, like the process for moving items between physical memory and virtual memory. If that process is moved to virtual memory, then it will likely crash. On iPadOS all system processes are considered wired memory. This means that only applications will be swapped using virtual memory. System processes, like Springboard (home screen), the Lock Screen, Notification Center, and other system processes will never be swapped using Virtual Memory. Virtual Memory does have a side effect, one that iPads have not had to worry about previously, and that is SSD wear.

Solid State Device Wear

As outlined above, Virtual Memory is designed to use physical storage to temporarily store data. This type of use can have an impact on the physical storage. All physical storage will eventually wear out, including SSD storage. SSDs have a limited number of times that they can be written to before the data may no longer be read. When this happens this can result in data loss. macOS has long had the idea of virtual memory built-in, so any storage devices that are designed specifically for use with the Mac will have this accounted for.

All iPhone and iPad devices have only had a limited amount of physical memory and once that memory is used up any unneeded memory is removed. This is typically done by stopping apps from running so the current apps can run smoothly and efficiently. Physical memory is designed to be in constant use. Therefore, it is designed to be able to withstand this type of usage. Solid State Devices, or SSDs, are not generally designed for this. They are designed to be read from, more often than they are written to.

However, on the iPad this is entirely new. Previous chips in the iPad, like the A12Z, and even the A14 Bionic, and A15 Bionic were not designed to have storage that would be able to have a significant increase in the number of read-write cycles that occur on the SSD. On the other hand, the M1 was designed with this in mind because it was designed to go into the Mac, the wearing of SSDs was taken into consideration when it was developed. Therefore, it does make sense as to why Stage Manager has been limited to iPads that have an M1 processor. Virtual Memory was added to they M1 iPads for a new feature, improved external display support.

External Displays on iPad

Many people use their iPad as their primary computing device and in a vast majority of instances the screen resolution on an iPad may be plenty for what they need to do. However, there may be instances when they need just a bit more space. This is where an external display might be useful.

The only downside to using an external monitor on an iPad is that when you connect an external display, its usefulness is quite limited. With iOS 15 it is possible that an app might be used on an external display, but the would need to be explicitly designed to accommodate a second display. When you connect an external display on an iPad running iPadOS 15 your iPad screen will mirror what is being shown to the monitor, possibly with a black border around the edges, depending on the resolution of the iPad and the external display being used. This changes with iPadOS 16.

On an M1 iPad with iPadOS 16 you can also use Stage Manager on external displays. In fact, when you plug in an external display, the external display will be put into Stage Manager mode. The external display Stage Manager is a wholly separate instance of Stage Manager and will act independently of the built-in Display.

In the default configuration, your iPad will be usable as an iPad not in Stage Manager mode, and the external display will be in Stage Manager Mode.

There is one exception to all of this mentioned above. If an app has explicit support for an external display, it will continue to act the same way. As an example, the app Screens, which is used to connect to other devices like Macs, Windows, and Linux computers, will show the computer you are connected to on the external display. When you switch to another app, the second display will return to Stage Manager mode.

Having an external display connected means that you can move apps between the built-in iPad display and the external display. Furthermore, you have additional options. For instance, if you want to use the built-in iPad display as you would normally but also use Stage Manager on the external display, that is entirely possible. Of course, if you want, you can have Stage Manager enabled on both the built-in display as well as an external one.

Non-M1 iPads and External Displays

As outlined above, only iPads with an M1 processor support Stage Manager. Therefore, you might be wondering what is the behavior of non M1 iPads on iPadOS 16. The behavior is the exact same as under iPadOS 15. This means that the display will be mirrored, just as it was under iPadOS 15.

Closing Thoughts on Stage Manager

Stage Manager is a new way of being able to easily focus on your current task on both iPadOS 16 and macOS Ventura. With Stage Manager you can group applications together into an App Group, resize windows, add apps, and even remove apps. Stage Manager supports external displays as well, including being able to have Stage Manager enabled on an external display, and still use your iPad normally.

Apps are now able to use up to 16GB of memory, which is only possible with the new Virtual Memory support. Virtual Memory support is only supported on M1 iPads due to the amount of memory bandwidth available with the M1. On the 5th generation iPad Air, you do need 256GB of storage for this feature to be available.

Now that we have covered a big new feature on both macOS and iPadOS, let us turn to the biggest feature of iOS, a redesigned Lock Screen.

Redesigned Lock Screen

Feature Availability: iOS

As much as everyone might try to argue, people pick up their phones quite a bit throughout the day. It is not possible to get a consensus on a daily average. Luckily, Apple does have a feature called Screen Time that can keep track of this for a person. For me, the average number of daily pickups is around 130 across all my devices. According to my Apple Watch on average I am asleep for about 7 hours every night, If you combine these two pieces of information, that means that I have around 7.65 pickups per hour, or approximately one pickup every 7 minutes and 50 seconds while I am awake. This is across all of my devices, an iPhone, and iPad, and three different Macs.

Often, when I pick up my phone it is with the intent of just "checking one thing", but it turns out that this can easily turn into a "let me check email" and a "Oh, while I am here, let me check Twitter too". Sometimes, I actually forget the entire reason why I even unlocked my phone to begin with. This happens a lot more often than I care to actually admit. In some other instances, this is not a problem, but in others I just really wanted to check that one thing.

Most often, for me, when I pick up my phone, or even just wake it up, it is to switch the song that I am listening to. Other times, it is for another purpose entirely. There are instances where some information can be quickly glanced at, like notifications. At the same time, other things might take some time, like watching a longer video. There are those times when you know what information you are looking for but not be able to easily see the corresponding app.

For some, if all you need is to quickly glance at information the Apple Watch can help, due to the complications on the Apple Watch and their inherent glanceable nature. What might make things a bit easier would be the ability to have glanceable information right on the Lock Screen of the iPhone. With iOS 16, this is now possible with the redesigned Lock Screen.

There are a number of new features on the Lock Screen. Some of these include, Widgets, Live Wallpapers, Live Activities, and slight changes to notifications. Let us look at each of these in turn, starting with Widgets.

Widgets

Widgets are not new to the iPhone, they were introduced in 2019 with iOS 14, but they are new on the Lock Screen. Widgets on the Lock Screen on the iPhone are very similar to Complications on the Apple Watch, in that they provide you with a way of being able to easily glance at information right on the Lock Screen, without needing to leave the Lock Screen. Widgets on the Lock Screen also have limited functionality, where they can provide updated information but cannot allow any interactions, excluding opening your app. In fact, Widgets on the iPhone Lock Screen may be the exact ones as on the Apple Watch, given that they use the same technology.

There are three possible widget types that can be shown on an iPhone Lock Screen. These are Circular, Rectangular, and Inline.

Circular Widget

A Circular widget is one that will show information in a circular fashion. A couple of good examples of this are the Apple Watch Battery widget, the Activity Rings, and the Current Temperature widget from Weather.

Rectangular Widget

The Rectangular Widget, as the name indicates, is rectangular in nature. The Rectangular Widget occupies two of the four possible Widget locations and is good for displaying a bit more information than could be shown in the circular widget.

A couple of examples of this are the Activity widget, which shows your current activity for the three ring types, move calories, move minutes, and stand hours. A second example of the Rectangular Widget is the Indoor Climate widget from the Home app.

Inline Widget

The last Widget type, called Inline, is designed to provide you with a line of text. One example is the default inline widget, which shows the current date, while another is Reminders widget, which will show you any reminders that you have to do for the day.

Widget Locations

There are two spots available for widgets, The first spot is strictly for the Inline widget type, which is above the current time, and the second spot is directly below the current time. On this second section you can mix and match the Circular and Rectangular widget types. In this you can have up to four complications configured at a single time.

iOS Lock Screen Widgets

Being able to configure your Lock Screen with a number of widgets at the same time is great, but the information for these are updated on a schedule, as determined by the system. What would be really convenient would be the ability to be to receive up to date information. This is possible, with a new feature called Live Activities.

Live Activities

Often when there is a big game you may want to have the most up to date information. This could be accomplished by push notifications or even texts messages. The number of push notifications could vary wildly depending on the sport. For instance, if you are watching a Soccer match, you might only get a half dozen notifications throughout the entire 90 minute game. Conversely, if you are following a basketball game, you could easily get a couple of hundred, if a push notification was sent each time the score changed.

While this would indeed work, it is far from an ideal situation. Instead, there is a different way of being able to stay up to date on information. That technology is called Live Activities. Live Activities is a wholly new widget type that will provide you with near real time updates for certain types of data. The biggest usage case is one that Apple highlighted, Sports Scores, but that is not the only usage.

When there is a playoff game on the line that could decide whether your favorite team continues onto the next round, you will want to keep up to date. With Live Activities you will be able to do so. Instead of receiving a slew of push notifications or text messages, you will be able to see the current score of your team right on the Lock Screen. Live Activities is not limited to just sports scores, but it can also be used for tracking things like an estimated arrival for a ride sharing car, or a delivery from a restaurant. These are just a few examples of the possibilities of Live Activities.

Now that we have covered some of the new features of the Lock Screen, and the fact that you can customize the Widgets on the Lock Screen, there is more that needs to be covered. Pointedly, the biggest item that needs to be discussed is exactly how to customize your Lock Screen. Before we delve into that, let us look at how to add a Lock Screen.

Adding a New Lock Screen

Under iOS 15 and earlier versions you were able to actually have two different wallpapers, one for the Lock Screen and another for the Home Screen. This method is still available, but it is handled differently. In fact, the first Lock Screen that you should have is an upgrade of your current Lock Screen Wallpaper and Home Screen Wallpaper.

This default Lock Screen will not have any Widgets on it. There is only one customization option, Focus selection, but that will be covered in depth a bit later in the chapter. You might think that you could use the old method of customizing the Lock Screen and Home Screen wallpaper. Technically you can, but the way that you accomplish this is a bit convoluted, and it will be covered in a bit. But first, let us look at how to add a new Lock Screen. If you are ready to add a new Lock Screen, use these steps:

1. **Swipe down** to show the current Lock Screen.
2. **Tap and hold** on an empty area. This will bring you into the Lock Screen Switcher.
3. Tap on the "**+**" button in the lower right. This will bring up the Add New Wallpaper screen.

The **Add New Wallpaper** screen has eight different sections to it. The first section is just a shortcut to each of the other sections. Each of the remaining seven sections has its own set of different wallpaper types. The remaining sections are:

1. Featured
2. Suggested Photos
3. Photo Shuffle
4. Weather & Astronomy
5. Emoji
6. Collections
7. Color

Let us look at each of these in turn, starting with Featured.

Add New Wallpaper   Add New Wallpaper screen

Featured

The **Featured** section are various Wallpapers that Apple wishes to highlight and are generally individual selections from the other wallpaper sections.

Featured Wallpapers

Suggested Photos

The **Suggested Photos** section are various photos either from your own Photo Library that might make for a good wallpaper. Each of the various suggestions will have its own suggested widgets that complement the wallpaper and are suggestions.

You have complete control over which photo is used. You can use a suggested photo or you can tap on the Photo button, which will bring up a photo picker. The photo picker will have the Featured tag enabled by default, but you can use another one of the tags, like People, Nature, or Urban. At least those were the tags that were shown for me. It is possible you might have other tags depending on your Photo Library.

Alternatively, you can search through all of your photos for people, places, objects, or any other keyword. If you have a variety of albums you can tap on the Albums button at the top to browse through your albums to find the right photo.

Once you have selected your photo, you then have an option for one of four filters. These filters are:

- Natural
- Black & White
- Duotone
- Color Wash

The **Natural** option will keep the photo just as it is without any changes. **Black and White** will make the photo become black and white. **Duotone** will give the photo two different shades. The **Color Wash** option removes all but one of the colors from the photo. The default colors chosen for Duotone and Color Wash will be different depending on the actual image used.

Suggested Wallpapers

For both Duotone and Color Wash you can actually select the color you would like by tapping on the "**...**" button in the lower corner and then selecting one of the color options provided.

You can swipe between the various filters by swiping from right to left to see your currently selected photo using each of the various filters.

With the Photos you also have the ability to pan and zoom. You can zoom in fairly far, using the standard pinch gesture. The same applies to zooming out. There is a limit to how far you can zoom out, because the entire screen must have some portion of the photo in it, meaning that you cannot have any black bars around the image, unless the image already has some black bars around it.

Photo Shuffle

The **Photo Shuffle** wallpaper is one that will allow you to see your favorite photos throughout the day, with a new one appearing each time you raise to wake up the display. This can be a good option to see a variety of photos throughout the day.

When you tap on the Photo Shuffle option, you will be presented with the photo picker, exactly like the one in the Photo wallpaper. But instead of selecting just a single photo, you can select a number of photos.

There is one thing to note about this wallpaper. The more photos that you select, the longer it will take to save the wallpaper. This is because each of the photos must be rendered to fit your iPhone. However, you can select as many photos that you would like. You can also change the photos at any point.

After you have selected the photos, the Photo Shuffle wallpaper has an option called Shuffle. This will shuffle your selected photos so that they will not appear in the order that you selected nor in the order that they appear in your Photo Library.

Photo Shuffle Wallpaper

Photo Shuffle Wallpaper Examples

Weather & Astronomy

The **Weather & Astronomy** wallpapers will show the current weather conditions or an Astronomical item. The Weather wallpaper is one that will update throughout the day as weather conditions change. This means that if it is cloudy, the Weather wallpaper will be shown with clouds in the sky. Similarly, if it is raining the Weather wallpaper will be updated with rain. Likewise, if it is sunny, you will get a Wallpaper with the sun shining. This wallpaper also changes as the day progresses. As an example, if it is early in the morning the colors on the Weather wallpaper will mimic a sunrise, the same applies to sunset.

There are five Astronomical wallpapers. These are Earth, Earth Detail, Moon, Moon Detail, and Solar System. The Earth wallpaper will show the entire Earth, centered over your current location, including the current position of the Sun. The Earth Detail is just like Earth, except zoomed in on your current location.

The Moon wallpaper will show the entire moon, with sunlight on it. The Moon Detail wallpaper will show a zoomed in view of the moon.

The Solar System wallpaper will show the entire solar system as if you were looking down at it from above.

For all of the Astronomical Wallpapers, the suggested widgets are all weather and astronomical in nature. They could include the current weather, including high and low, the Sunset time, the Moonrise time, as well as the current phase of the moon.

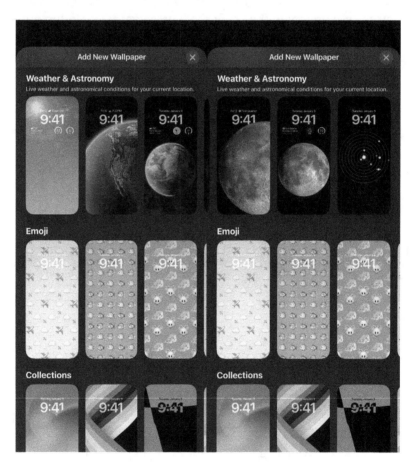

Weather and Astronomy Wallpapers

Emoji

The **Emoji** wallpaper will allow you to select up to six different emojis to show in a number of designs. The available designs are:

- Small Grid
- Medium Grid

- Large Grid
- Rings
- Spiral

As you customize this wallpaper, the preview will change. And as you may notice while doing customizations, the order of the emoji will affect how the wallpaper looks.

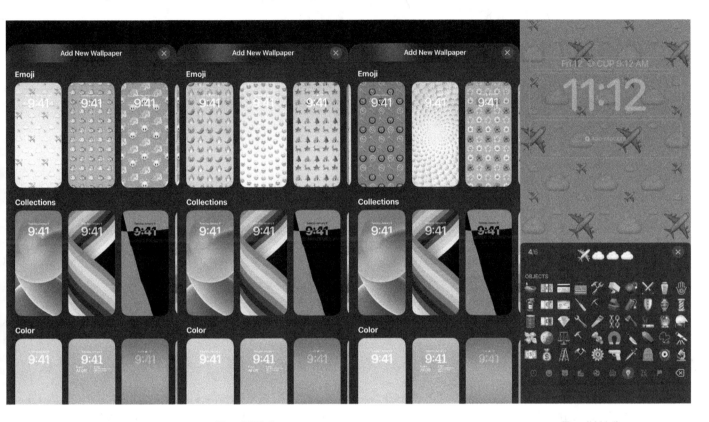

Emoji Wallpapers

Emoji Wallpaper
Customization screen

Collections

The **Collections** wallpapers are, as the name suggest, collection of various wallpapers that fit into a theme, or are just a collection of similar wallpapers. Some of the Collection options have their own customization options.

As an example there is a **Bokeh** collection, which consist of nine different colors, including; Green, Yellow, Orange, Red, Purple, Blue, Warm Silver, Cool Silver, and Multicolored. On each of these you can set the appearance to be Dark, Light, or Automatic, where automatic will change to dark at sunset, and light at sunrise. These also have the option of enabling **Perspective Mode**.

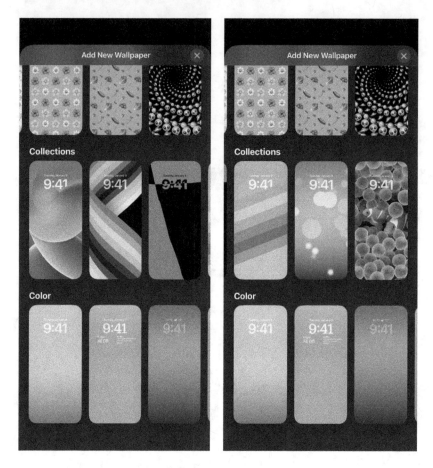

Collections Wallpapers

Color

The **Color** wallpaper will show a gradient of a selected base color. With the Color wallpaper you can choose just about any color as your selected base color. Once you have selected the color, you have six different display modes. These are Vibrant, Tone, Deep, Vapor, Bright, and Solid. Each of these will change the base color slightly to reflect the type that you have selected. With these modes, you can create just the right look for your wallpaper.

Wallpaper Pairs

When you have selected a Lock Screen Wallpaper a popup will appear, it will look similar to the image below.

Here is where you can decide whether to use the same wallpaper for both the Lock Screen and the Home Screen, or you can choose to have a separate Home Screen wallpaper, similar to the way that it was under iOS 15. If you are happy with your selection, you can choose **Set as Wallpaper Pair**. If you would prefer to have a different Home Screen wallpaper, tap on **Customize Home Screen**.

Customize Home Screen

Not all photos will work as a wallpaper for a home screen. Sometimes the colors on a photo may interfere with the text for certain elements. This is where the Customize Home Screen options might be helpful.

When you tap on the Customize Home Screen button you will have some additional options for the Home Screen. The available options are:

1. Legibility Blur
2. Gradient Background
3. Color Background
4. Photo Selection

Set Wallpaper pair screen

Legibility Blur

If enabled, Legibility Blur will add a blur to your selected background. When this is applied features will, as you might expect, be more blurred, but the colors will still show through. It will not be opaque, but will have more of a frosted glass look to them. You can see the differences between the two by tapping on the Legibility Blur button.

Gradient Background

In the event that you would prefer to have a gradient for the background, you can enable this by tapping on the Gradient option, which is the second button at the bottom of the screen. You can adjust the colors of the gradient by tapping on the Configure button.

When you do this, a Choose Gradient sheet will appear. On this sheet will be a choice of 18 different colors. You can tap on one of these and then select the exact color for the gradient that you would like. If none of the preselected colors are what you are looking for, in the upper left of the Select Gradient sheet, there is the color selection tool.

This is the standard iOS color selection sheet. Here you can use the grid selection, spectrum selection, the sliders, or even any of your favorites which you have previously defined. When you are finished, you can tap on **Done** and that color selection will be applied as a gradient.

Color Background

The Color Background option works just like the Gradient option, except instead of having a gradient on the background, the entire background will be a solid color. This is accessed by tapping on the third button at the bottom of the Customize Home Screen screen.

Photo Selection

The Photo Selection option is where you can replicate the experience of having a separate Lock Screen wallpaper and Home Screen wallpaper. This is done by tapping on the **Photos** button, which is at the bottom right of the screen.

When you tap on this button the Image Picker will appear. When loaded, the option of Featured Images will be selected. These are the images that you have taken that might work the best for the Home Screen Wallpaper. You can use one of these suggestions or you can use the other filters, search for a photo, place, person, or you can just browse all of your albums.

One thing to note about this option. If you choose a photo you cannot add a Legibility Blur, this means that the background shown will be the actual image as it was originally taken.

Once you have made your final selections, you can tap the **Done** button and your selected changes will be saved to the Lock Screen. You can then select that Lock Screen to use.

Customizing Your Lock Screen

Discussed above were the different aspects of the Lock Screen and the various options you have for different wallpapers. Now, we need to cover the customization options, and how to customize the Lock Screen. If you have an Apple Watch and have customized an Apple Watch face, you may find customizing the iOS Lock Screen to be very familiar.

As outlined above, there are four distinct aspects of the Lock Screen that can be customized. These items are:

1. The Inline Widget
2. The Current Time
3. The Circular/Rectangular Widget section
4. Wallpaper

In order to customize a Lock Screen, perform the following steps:

1. **Swipe down** to show the current Lock Screen.
2. **Tap and hold** anywhere on the Lock Screen. This will bring you into the Lock Screen Switcher.
3. **Swipe to the Lock Screen** you wish to customize.
4. Tap on the **Customize** button to begin customization.

Once you have tapped on the **Customize** button you can begin customizing the screen.

Inline Widgets

Customizing the Inline Widget or the Circular/Rectangular widget areas are the same. As soon as you tap on either area, an Add Widgets sheet will appear from the bottom.

Here you can select the appropriate widget, or widgets. To add a widget to the Circular/Rectangle widget section, you can simply tap on a widget and it will be added. You also have the option to drag a widget to the area and place it in the position that you prefer.

There is one thing to note, unlike with the primary widget area, you cannot leave the Inline Widget area blank, there must be something in that line. Furthermore, if you put anything other than the default Inline Calendar widget into the spot, the current day will be shrunken, so the date will always be shown when you look at your Lock Screen. Next, let us look at customizing the Time.

Customizing the Time Section

The last section that you can customize is the Time. When you customize the Time, you will notice that you have a bunch of different customization options. In fact, you can customize the font and the color of the time.

You have size different font options, including Standard, Rounded, and Outline, to name a few. The second item you can customize is the color. By default when you select the background for your Lock Screen, a color that is very complementary to the background will be chosen for you. However, you can choose any color that you want.

When you look at the colors, you will see the default color on the far left, with suggested colors along the bottom of the sheet. When you tap on any of the colors, a slider will appear where you can dial in the exact shade of that color that you want. On the right of the list of colors is a multicolor option. Tapping on this will bring up a the System Color Picker where you can get the exact color you want, including any of your favorites that you have saved.

No matter which color you select, that color will be applied to each of the three elements, the Inline Widget, the Time, and the Circular/Rectangular Widget area. There is one last customization item strictly related to the time to discuss, and that is the type of numerals used for the Time.

Time Numerals

A majority of the world uses Arabic numerals for displaying time, but these are not the only type of numerals throughout the world. The Time on the Lock Screen also supports three script types for numbers, Arabic, Arabic Indic, and Devanagari.

You can select any the three types of scripts by tapping on the Globe icon. This will present a menu where you can select Arabic, Arabic Indic, or Devanagari. Once you select the script, the time will change to be that script.

Circular/Rectangular Widget Area

This third area you can configure is the Circular/Rectangular Widget Area. Here you can place up to four different small widgets, two rectangular widgets, or two small widgets and one rectangular. You can configure the Lock Screen as you desire. To add a widget to this area, perform the following steps:

1. **Swipe down** to show the current Lock Screen.
2. **Tap and hold** anywhere on the Lock Screen. This will bring you into the Lock Screen Switcher.
3. **Swipe to the Lock Screen** you wish to customize.
4. Tap on the **Customize** button to begin customization.
5. Tap in the **Widget Area**. The Add Widgets sheet will appear.
6. Locate the widget you want to add either from the suggestions or by browsing the items widgets.
7. Once located **tap on the widget** you want to add. It will be added to the widget area.

After you have added the widgets you would like, you can rearrange them to be the in order that you would like. To do this, simply tap and hold on any of the widgets and drag it to the location you would like it to be placed. Next, let us look at pairing a Home Screen and a Focus Mode.

Integrating Home Screens and Focus Modes

Last year with iOS 15, Apple introduced a new feature called Focus Modes. Focus Modes are ways of being able to limit who can contact you, what apps are shown, and even which Home Screens are shown, all based upon the current Focus Mode that you have enabled.

Focus Modes have gotten a few new features, but those will be covered later in the book. For now, we will cover just a single feature related to Focus modes, and that is the ability to connect a Lock Screen to a specific Focus mode. To customize a Lock Screen to be automatically enabled with a particular Lock Screen, perform the following steps:

1. **Swipe down** to show the current Lock Screen.
2. **Tap and hold** anywhere on the Lock Screen. This will bring you into the Lock Screen Switcher.
3. **Swipe to the Lock Screen** you wish to link to a Focus Mode.
4. Once you have located the Lock Screen tap on the **Focus** button at the bottom of the wallpaper. This will bring up a Focus Mode popup list.
5. In the Focus Mode popup list **select** the specific Focus Mode that you wish to link to the Lock Screen.

Wallpaper selection screen   Link Focus selection screen

When you link a Lock Screen to a Focus mode, and when that Focus mode is enabled, the linked Lock Screen will be shown automatically. You can test this by switching to a Lock Screen that is not linked to a Focus mode, or linked to another Focus Mode, and then enabling a particular Focus Mode. When you do this the Lock Screen should automatically be switched to its linked Lock Screen.

Even if you do link a Lock Screen and a Focus mode, you can still manually switch to any Lock Screen you want to use. The idea of linking a Lock Screen and Focus mode just provides automatic behavior, so you do not have to manually switch each time that you enable a Focus Mode, or when a Focus Mode is enabled automatically.

Customizing The Home Screen at a Later Time

It is possible that as you use a particular lock screen you may want to modify the Home Screen again at a later time. You would think that this might be possible through the Lock Screen, but it is not. Instead, in order to customize the Home Screen after you have initially configured it, perform the following steps:

1. **Swipe down** to show the current Lock Screen.
2. **Tap and hold** anywhere on the Lock Screen. This will bring you into the Lock Screen Switcher.
3. **Swipe to the Lock Screen** for which you want to customize the Home Screen.
4. **Tap** on the Lock Screen to set it as the current Lock Screen.
5. **Swipe up** from the bottom to unlock the iPhone.
6. Open the **Settings** app.
7. Scroll down to **Wallpaper**.
8. Tap on **Wallpaper** to bring up the Wallpaper settings.
9. Underneath the Home Screen wallpaper tap on **Customize**. A popup will appear.
10. Tap **Customize Current Wallpaper** to begin customization.
11. **Customize** the Home Screen as you would like.
12. Tap **Done** to save your changes.

It seems a bit strange that you cannot modify the Home Screen at the same time that you customize a Lock Screen, but that is the current procedure. Let us now see how you can Remove an already configured Lock Screen.

Removing a Lock Screen

It is likely that at some point you will want to delete a Lock Screen. This can be done by performing the following steps:

1. **Swipe down** to show the current Lock Screen.
2. **Tap and hold** anywhere on the Lock Screen. This will bring you into the Lock Screen Switcher.
3. **Swipe to the Lock Screen** you wish to remove.
4. **Swipe Up** from the bottom. A Trash icon will appear.
5. Tap on the **Trash Can** Icon to delete the item. A confirmation dialog will appear.
6. Tap on the **Delete** to confirm that you want to delete the Lock Screen.

As is the case with other delete actions, once you have deleted the Lock Screen it will be removed and cannot be retrieved. This means all of your widgets, font choices, color selections, for both the Lock Screen and Home Screen will be removed. It is not unexpected the this would be the case, but it is something to be aware of.

There are a myriad of methods that people employ to try and stay up to date on information. This can be by checking social media, receiving push notifications from apps, or even just via text message or email. Regardless, any notifications that you receive are likely to be displayed on the Lock Screen.

Notification Changes

The last section to be covered regarding the redesigned Lock Screen on the iPhone is regarding notifications. Notifications still appear on the Lock Screen, as does the Now Playing system widget. The change to notifications is that they now roll in from the bottom. The reason for this, has been outlined above. It is for the new widgets on the Lock Screen.

The most recent notification will appear at the bottom of the screen. You can easily scroll through your notifications to see all of them, and when you do additional notifications will roll underneath. As you scroll through your notifications, the Now Playing system widget will be moved up and your notifications will scroll.

This is the new default behavior, but there are actually three different notification styles that you can choose from. These options are:

- List
- Stack
- Count

Which option you may want depends on your personal preference. The **Stack** style is the new style, where notifications will roll in from the bottom. The **List** stack is the old way of handling notifications, that will show a list of all of the notifications, similar to the way it was shown in iOS 15. The last item, **Count** will only show you a count of the number of notifications. If you use the Count stye, you will be able to tap on the count and it will display the notifications themselves.

You can customize the Notification style by using the following steps:

1. Open the **Settings** app.
2. Scroll down to **Notifications** in the second group.
3. Tap on **Notifications** to bring up the settings for notifications.
4. Tap on **Display As** it should be the first item in the list.
5. **Select the style** that you wish to use.

When you select your preferred style, the style should change immediately to your selected style. The thing with the different styles is that you can easily switch between the various styles. This is done on the Lock Screen itself.

You can hide, or display, notifications by simply swiping down on the top of the Now Playing widget. When you do this, the notifications that are below it should be hidden. Similarly, you can swipe up on the top of the Now Playing widget, and it will display the notifications.

The way that you interact with the notifications continue to work as they did under iOS 15, meaning that you can continue to manage your notifications as you did before. This includes any Notification Summaries that you have configured, because these will continue to be shown as normal.

Notification Display style options

Closing Thoughts on the Redesigned Lock Screen

The newly redesigned Lock Screen is one of the biggest changes to the Lock Screen in the history of iOS. With iOS 16 you can now create as many custom Lock Screens that you want. On each Lock Screen you can choose the wallpaper, widgets, and even customize the colors.

If you are not sure what type of Wallpaper you want to add, you can use the new Wallpaper gallery to be able to see a variety of different suggestions from Apple. Some of the options include, Photo, Photo Shuffle, Emoji, Color, and even a Bokeh effect wallpaper.

The Lock Screen is not limited to just nice wallpapers, but the Lock Screen now also supports widgets, including third-party ones. You have two different sections for widgets, the Inline widget area, where a single line of text can be shown, as well as the Circular/Rectangle widget area where you can have up to four different widgets that will allow you to see glanceable information.

Another new feature of the Lock Screen is the new Live Activities API. This API will allow you to get near real time information right on your Lock Screen. This information could be how long until your ride share arrives or, more likely for many, is real time score updates.

The last new feature is a slight change to notifications. By default, notifications will now scroll in from the bottom, including the system Now Playing controls, which will always be shown if audio is playing. However, you can customize the way notifications are displayed by using any of the available styles, Count, List, or Stack, depending on your preference.

You can still replicate the iOS 15 style of having one photo for the Lock Screen and a different photo to for the Home Screen. While you can choose your initial configuration from the Lock Screen, you will need to go through Settings to make any changes to the Home Screen wallpapers in the future. This is a minor inconvenience, but this is the same behavior as under iOS 15.

When you do link a Wallpaper to a Focus mode, whenever you enter into the linked Focus mode, your Wallpaper will automatically switch to that Lock Screen. At first, this might seem like a waste to link a Wallpaper to a Focus mode, but Focus modes have gotten some great enhancements. And on the subject of Focus Modes, let us look at those changes in the next chapter.

Focus Mode Enhancements

Feature Availability: iOS, iPadOS, macOS

The last chapter was focused on the changes around the Lock Screen changes on iOS 16. The Lock Screen can actually be integrated into a feature introduced in iOS 15, called Focus. Focus was introduced in iOS 15 and is a way of being able to reduce distractions and concentrate, or focus, on the task at hand.

Under iOS 15 and iPadOS 15 you had a few options, including being able to select which Home Screens, apps, and even have a Focus mode automatically enabled based upon using an app or even a time of day. Focus Modes in iOS 15 were a great start, but there are some new features introduced in iOS 16, iPadOS 16, and macOS Ventura. These features include, pairing Lock Screens and Focus modes and Focus Filters. One method of linking Lock Screens to Focus modes was covered in the previous chapter, but there is a second way of linking Lock Screens and Focus modes, so let us look at that next.

Linking a Focus Mode to a Lock Screen

As mentioned above, we covered linking a Focus mode to a Lock Screen through the Lock Screen. However, there is an alternative way of linking these together, through a Focus mode. To edit your Focus modes, perform the following steps:

1. Open the **Settings** app.
2. **Scroll down** to Focus which should be the third item in the second group.
3. Tap on **Focus** to bring up the Focus settings.
4. **Locate** the Focus mode that you wish to modify.
5. **Tap** on the Focus mode you wish to link to a Lock Screen.
6. Under the Customize Screens tap on the **Choose** item on the left side. If you have a Lock Screen already configured tap on the **Edit** button. Either option will bring up the Lock Screen selection screen.

Once you have opened up the Lock Screen selection screen, you will see all of your configured Lock Screens. You can link or unlink any of your Lock Screens to the currently selected Focus. Once you have finished making your changes, tap on the **Done** button in the upper right corner.

Notification Options

There is one other slight change to mention. The Options, which used to be its own group under iOS 15 and iPadOS 15 has been moved into the Allowed Notifications area. The same options exist, hiding notifications, dimming the lock screen, and showing silent notifications on the lock screen, are all still there, they are now all just lumped together.

Next, let us turn to the biggest change to Focus in iOS 16, iPadOS 16, and macOS Ventura, Focus Filters.

Focus Filters

Under iOS 15 and iPadOS 15, you had the option of being able to allow notifications from particular people or apps. This approach definitely worked, but it was a broad brush. What many had hoped for was more fine-grained controls.

For instance, you may have a variety of calendars configured. This could be one for work, another for home, and possibly even a third for your significant other. It is possible that there are notifications for all sorts of events. Under previous iterations of Focus, you would only be able to add the entire Calendar app. When you added the Calendar app, you would end up getting all of the notifications for all of your calendars, even if they were not directly related to your current Focus. You could get notifications for work events, while on vacation, or even notifications about personal events while in your working Focus.

This all changes in iOS 16, iPadOS 16, and macOS Ventura. With these new versions you are able to drill down and

Focus Filter Options on macOS Ventura

Focus Filter Options in iOS

filter even more. With Calendar, you can now filter which calendars, and notifications of said calendars. To customize the filters for a particular Focus, use the following steps:

1. Open the **Settings** app or System Settings on macOS.
2. Scroll down to **Focus** which should be the third item in the second group.
3. **Tap** on Focus to bring up the Focus settings.
4. Locate the Focus mode that you wish to modify.
5. **Tap** on the Focus mode you wish to modify.
6. **Scroll down** to Focus Filters.
7. Tap on the **+ Add Focus Filter** button. This should show the Focus Filters screen.

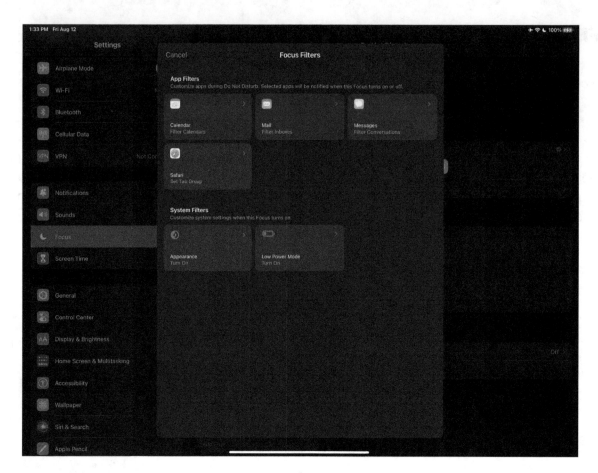

Focus Filter Options on iPadOS 16

On the Focus Filters screen you will see two types of filters, App Filters and System Filters. The System filters consist of whether or not to turn on Low Power Mode and a selection of which Appearance to show, Dark mode or Light Mode.

As for App Filters, these are filters that you can use to configure how certain apps react to a particular filter. These are not limited to Apple's apps, but instead can be configured by third parties Apple provides these four apps, Messages, Mail, Calendar, and Safari. Let us look at each of these in turn.

Messages

If you enable the Messages app filter, you can filter messages to only show those who are on your Allowed People list. With this enabled, you can filter out any unnecessary messages. This is a simple toggle, when you add the Messages filter, it is enabled. You can, of course, disable it if needed.

Mail

The Mail app filter will allow you to filter the Mail app to only show particular accounts that you want to see while the selected Focus is enabled. When you tap on the Mail app filter, a list of your accounts will be shown and you can simply tap on the account and it will be added to the filter.

The Mail app filter is a great one to enable if you have a Work focus and you want to filter Mail to only show your work email account and not get distracted by your personal or nonwork accounts.

Calendar

The Calendar app filter works similar to the Mail app filter. When you add the Calendar app filter, you can select the specific Calendars that you wish to have shown while the Focus is enabled.

Safari

The Safari app filter is an interesting one. When configured it will allow you to open a particular Tab Group when the Focus is enabled. Furthermore, you also have the option of not allowing external links to be opened when in the particular Focus mode. This option might be particularly useful if you are doing some research for a topic and do not want to allow any other website information to distract you.

Other App Filters

The Apple provided filters are not the only ones that you may see. In fact, third-party developers can also provide you with the ability to filter data within their apps. Therefore, you may see additional apps in the App Filters, that you can customize to your need.

Closing Thoughts on Focus Filters

The Focus feature was introduced in iOS 15, iPadOS 15, and macOS Montgomery and it has been enhanced under iOS 16, iPadOS 16, and macOS Ventura. All of the Focus Filter features are available on all of the platforms, while linking a Focus mode to a Lock Screen is only available on iOS 16, because custom Lock Screens are only available on iOS 16.

Focus Filters will allow you to provide custom configurations for each of your Focus modes to filter out information that you do not necessarily want to see while a Focus mode is enabled. Beyond any of the built-in Focus filters, you can also enable Focus filters in third-party apps, provided that they have added the capability. This means that you will be able to reduce unnecessary distractions even more than you could under previous versions.

Lastly, as you might expect, your Focus Filters will synchronize across all of your devices, so you can have all of the proper filters applied no matter which particular Focus and device you are using. Focus filters can absolutely help you be even more productive. On the topic of productivity, sometimes you can be super productive when working with others. So, let us look at some collaboration changes in the next chapter.

Communication and Collaboration

One thing that everyone ends up doing on the devices is communicating with people. This communication may take various forms. It could be by using FaceTime to talk via video, working on a document or spreadsheet with Pages or Numbers, and of course communicating with others throughout the day with Messages, or any other app. All of these items fall under the umbrella topic known as collaboration.

While you might not think of chatting via Messages or even having a video call with someone as collaboration, it is possible that a conversation might eventually turn into collaborating, even if you are just casually chatting. Throughout this chapter we will cover a variety of changes to a variety of apps related to communication and collaboration. Apps that will be covered include Messages, FaceTime, Notes, Mail, and a brand new app called Freeform. Let us start with FaceTime.

FaceTime

FaceTime is Apple's video calling app that allows you to initiate video calls from your iPhone, iPad, or Mac. Even though FaceTime was limited to just Apple devices, that changed last year with the ability to invite anybody to join a FaceTime call with FaceTime on the web. FaceTime on the Web works well with any modern browser or device, including Android, Windows, and even on ChromeOS.

One thing that many Apple users have long hoped for was the ability to easily move FaceTime calls between their devices. Starting with iOS 16, iPadOS 16, and macOS Ventura you can easily move any FaceTime call from one device to another, but not including Face Time on the Web.

Moving Devices

In order for a FaceTime call to be able to transfer from one device to another, both devices must both be on iOS 16, iPadOS 16, or macOS Ventura, and they must be signed into the same iCloud account.

There are a variety of reasons that you might want to do move your FaceTime call. One could be that you want to be able to easily share something on your Mac, but you started a call on your iPhone. Another possibility is that you may want to be begin a Share Play session and watch a movie at the same time as someone, but want to use another device to watch the movie. Whatever the reason, it is now possible to do. Let us look at how to do this.

When you are in a FaceTime call with someone else, your other devices will show a FaceTime icon in the Menu Bar area at the top of the screen. You can then tap, or click, on the FaceTime icon. This will bring up a message from the top of the screen verifying that you want to switch devices. Once you tap on **Switch** the destination device should take over the FaceTime call.

There is one thing to note, the others that you are on a FaceTime call with do not need to be on the latest operating systems, only your devices need to be. In fact, you can even have people who are using FaceTime on the web. These users will of course see the change in video. The ability to move FaceTime calls in a fast and easy manner is a great addition, but that is not the only change. There is another feature to look at, that feature is called Live Captions.

Live Captions

If you have ever been on a phone call or video call, it is quite possible that you might need someone to repeat something because either you misheard them, or could not hear them at all. When this happens, this might be a minor inconvenience for someone. However, there are those who may be hard of hearing all of the time and some of these people may feel self-conscious about asking people to repeat themselves. What would be quite useful would be the ability to have a transcript, but this is not likely.

That is where the new Live Captions feature may come in handy. This feature is considered a "beta", meaning it is not finalized and is likely to change. Live Captions is only available in English, specifically U.S. English and Canadian English. Live Captions is not available on all devices, in fact the following devices support Live Captions.

- iPhone 11 or newer
- iPad with an A12 Bionic, or newer
- A Mac with Apple Silicon

If you have an iOS device or an iPadOS device that supports Live Captions you can enable it by performing the following steps:

1. Open the **Settings** app.
2. **Scroll** down to FaceTime.
3. Tap on **FaceTime** to open FaceTime settings.
4. Scroll down to **Live Captions**.
5. Tap on the **toggle** next to Live Captions to enable the feature.

If you have a Mac with Apple Silicon you can enable it by using these steps:

1. Open **FaceTime**.
2. Click on the **FaceTime** menu item.
3. Click on **Settings**.
4. Click on the checkbox next to **Live Captions**.

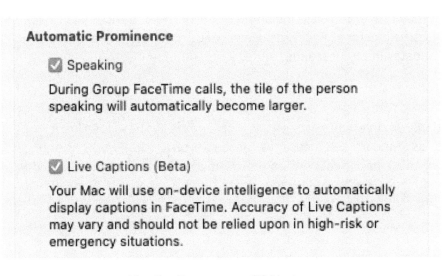

Live Captions on macOS Ventura

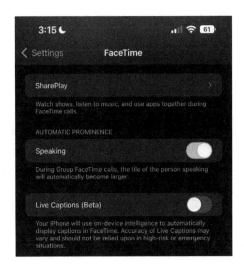

Live Captions on iOS

There are some items to note about Live Captions. First, processing is done locally, entirely on the device. Audio is not sent over the network, it is only locally processed. Secondly, everyone on the FaceTime call will be notified that Live Captions is enabled. It makes sense to alert others that the feature is enabled. The last thing to note is that Live Captions will use additional battery, since your device is processing all of the audio from the FaceTime call and then provides the captions to you.

Even with these limitations, this is likely to be a great option for users who could benefit to it. In particular, the fact that the captioning is being handled on device is a boon for privacy. There is one additional feature regarding FaceTime to discuss, and that feature is the discovery of SharePlay apps.

SharePlay App Discovery

SharePlay is a feature introduced in iOS 15, iPadOS 15, and macOS Monterey that will allow you to partake in activities at the same time in third-party apps. When you would be on a FaceTime call it might not be easy to discover what possibilities there were to use SharePlay. But that all changes in iOS 16, iPadOS 16, and macOS Ventura. Now, when you are in a FaceTime call, you can tap on the Share icon. When you do this you will have two options, Share My Screen, which will share you current screen as it did previously, but you will also see a list of apps that support SharePlay in them.

SharePlay Apps in FaceTime

This horizontally scrolling list will allow you to see all of your currently installed apps that support SharePlay. You can tap on any of them and the app will open, so you can begin a SharePlay activity from within the app. Also within this popup is a **More** button. This button will open a list of supported apps from the App Store, so you can possibly get additional apps for use with SharePlay.

Closing Thoughts on FaceTime

FaceTime has seen some pretty good improvements with both Live Captions and App Discovery. Live Captions will transcribe an audio call in near real time, and all in a privacy preserving manner by performing the caption processing right on your device.

The second new feature, the ability to easily move FaceTime calls, including video, between devices is one that has been a long-time coming and a very welcome one for all FaceTime users. Let us now switch to another communication tool which has seen a few updates itself, Messages.

Messages

Messages is one of the most used applications within Apple's ecosystem. Messages is the base for a lot of communications for both iMessages as well as standard text messages. Messages on iOS 16, iPadOS 16, and macOS Ventura have all been improved to include some great new features. One of these actually relates to the last topic covered, FaceTime. The changes with FaceTime and Messages comes with a new way of being able to start a SharePlay session, and that is right from Messages.

SharePlay in Messages

When you are communicating with someone within Messages, you may want to easily be able to start a SharePlay session. Previously, you would have to locate the app, and then start a SharePlay session. Now, from within Messages you can start a synchronized SharePlay experience right from Messages.

SharePlay is not the only new feature in Messages. In fact, you can now perform even more actions within Messages. There are four new tasks you can do, let us start with Mark as Unread.

Mark as Unread

Quite often when you receive a message you may not have time at that moment to read a message. You can just not read the message, but sometimes you accidentally end up opening a thread, which marks it as read. You can try and remember to get back to it later, but with everything that is going on these days, it is likely that you may not remember to get back to the thread.

What might be helpful would be the ability to mark a thread as Unread. With iOS 16, iPadOS 16, and macOS Ventura, this is now possible. To set a thread as unread, perform the following steps:

1. Open **Messages**.
2. **Locate** the thread that you want to mark as Unread.
3. **Swipe from left to right** to mark the thread as Unread. Alternatively, you can tap and hold on the thread and tap on **Mark as Unread**.

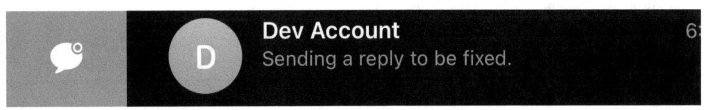

Mark as Unread on iOS and iPadOS

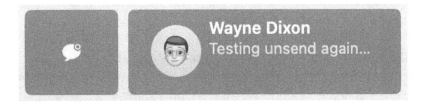

Mark as Unread on macOS Ventura

When you mark a thread as Unread, the entire thread will be marked as unread. There is something to note about this action. If you have Read Receipts enabled, if you mark a thread as Unread after reading it, a Read Receipt will still be sent to the user. Therefore, the intention of Mark as Unread is a means of being able to let yourself know you need to get back to the thread, not to try and unsend a Read Receipt. Next, let us talk about fixing messages.

Editing Messages

Testing unsend again...|

Editing a message in Messages on iOS, iPadOS, and macOS Ventura

How many times have you been typing out a message to someone, hit the send button, and then after sending it realize that you misspelled something? It is probably not a stretch to guess that it is more than once, and it is entirely possible that it happened already today.

When this happens it would be helpful to be able to edit the message text. Good news, this is now possible with iOS 16, iPadOS 16, and macOS Ventura. To edit a message that has already been sent, perform the following steps:

1. Open **Messages**.
2. **Locate the thread** that contains the message that you want to fix.
3. **Tap** on the thread with the message you want to fix.
4. **Scroll** to the message that you want to fix.
5. **Tap and hold** on the message with the mistake in it.
6. Tap on **Edit**. This will bring up the ability to edit the message
7. **Correct** the message as necessary.
8. Tap on the **checkmark** to save the changes. To cancel the changes tap the **X** button to cancel.

Once you make an edit and save it, the message will be updated on everyone's devices. There are a few things to note about editing a message. The first is that you have a limited amount of time to edit a message. As of this writing that time frame is 15 minutes. Secondly, if a message has been edited, it will be noted directly below the message on the same line as the Delivered/Read line.

The third item to mention is that you can only edit a message up to five times . The fourth thing to note is that the entire history of the edits will be viewable to everyone. This is for transparency reasons, so that someone cannot claim that something was said, that was not actually said.

The final thing to note is that editing, and any edits made, are only available on iOS 16, iPadOS 16, and macOS Ventura. Devices on older operating systems will actually be sent a follow up message that begins: **Edited to ...**, with the edited message. The last item to mention is that this only applies to iMessage users. Edits will not be sent to standard text message users, nor can standard text messages be edited. Let us now look at another new feature, unsending a message.

Unsending Messages

There are times when you are chatting when you may have inadvertently send a message to someone. Sometimes this is purely innocent, other times you regret sending it and wish you could unsend it. This is now possible to do. To unsend a message use the following steps:

1. Open **Messages**.
2. **Locate** the thread that contains the message that you want to fix.

3. **Tap** on the thread with the message you want to unsend.
4. **Scroll** to the message that you want to unsend.
5. **Tap and hold** on the message you want to unsend
6. Tap on **Undo Send**. This will immediately unsend the message.

Once you unsend a message, a message will be put in its place. It is one that states:

> You unsent a message. [NAME OF CONTACT] may still be able to see the message on devices where the software hasn't been updated.

Beyond the message above, the other restrictions that applied to editing a message also apply to unsending a message. This means that only iMessage users on iOS 16, iPadOS 16, and macOS Ventura will actually have the message unsent. You only have a limited amount of time to unsend a message, specifically you have 3 minutes. Again, this only applies to iMessage, you cannot unsend standard text messages because Apple has no control over those systems.

The ability to unsend a message is one that many users will be thankful for. The fact that a note is placed about the fact that a message was unsent is good, because it provides transparency as to what is happening in the conversation thread. Let us now look at one last item, Recently Deleted threads.

Recently Deleted

From time to time we may delete an entire thread in Messages, but then realize we actually did not want to delete that thread, but another one. When a thread is deleted in Messages, it is gone. Well, that was true under previous versions. iOS 16, iPadOS 16, and macOS Ventura all now have the ability to recover recently deleted messages. This is similar to recently deleted Photos, in that you have up to 30 days to recover deleted threads. The steps to recover a deleted thread differ between macOS and iOS or iPadOS. Let us look at both. To recover deleted messages on iOS or iPadOS perform the following:

1. Open **Messages**.
2. Tap on the **Edit** button in the upper left corner.
3. Tap on **Show Recently Deleted** to bring up the recently deleted messages.
4. **Locate** the thread that you want to recover.
5. **Tap** on the thread you wish to recover.
6. Tap on the **Recover** button in the lower right corner. A confirmation will appear.
7. Tap on **Recover Messages** to confirm you want to recover the message.

When you recover a thread, it will be placed back in with your other messages. If you are recovering the last item in the Recently Deleted list, the popup will automatically close. On the Recently Deleted screen there are two other options, you can delete your selection of messages. You can also Delete All or Recover All of the recently deleted items, if you so choose.

As mentioned above, on macOS Ventura, the process of showing Recently Deleted messages is slightly different. To recover a recently deleted thread on macOS Ventura, perform the following steps:

1. Open **Messages**.
2. Click on the **View** menu.

3. Click on **Recently Deleted**. All of your recently deleted messages will be shown.
4. **Locate** the message you want to recover.
5. Click on the **message thread** you want to recover, or delete.
6. Click on **Recover** a confirmation popup will appear.
7. Click on **Recover Messages** to confirm you want to recover the message.

An alternative way of showing Recently Deleted is to use the key combination of Control + Command + 5, and this will quickly switch you to the Recently Deleted items.

As is the case on iOS and iPadOS, you can also permanently delete the selected thread, by clicking on **Delete** and confirming you want to delete the thread. There are a couple of other screens on Messages on macOS. These screens are:

- All Messages
- Known Senders
- Unknown Senders
- Unread Messages

Each of these are accessible in the View menu item. Alternatively, you can use a key combination to access each of these:,

- Control + Command + 1 for All Message
- Control + Command + 2 for Known Senders
- Control + Command + 3 for Unknown Senders
- Control + Command + 4 for Unread Messages.

The last thing to note is that there is no Delete All nor a Recover All option in Messages on macOS.

Closing Thoughts on Messages

All of the changes in Messages are welcome ones. The new ability to start SharePlay right from messages should allow you to more easily start a SharePlay session where it makes the most sense, when you are talking to someone.

The ability to either edit or unsend an already sent message are both very welcome changes, and ones that users have been wanting for a long time. The actual unsending and edited text will only be available to be performed on, and the results will only be shown on, the latest operating systems, but this is to be expected.

Additionally, the 15 minute window for performing an Undo Send or Editing a message make sense, because otherwise it could cause significant confusion if these were allowed to happen outside of this window, it could be chaotic.

The ability to recover or permanently delete any Recently Deleted threads in Messages is a very welcome one. Lastly, on macOS Ventura you can easily filter the types of messages that are shown by using key combinations or using the View menu to show just the messages that you want.

Next, let us turn to another brand new app that is useful for collaboration, that app is called Freeform.

Freeform

During their World Wide Developer Conference Apple unveiled a whole new collaboration app called Freeform. Freeform is a collaboration app that will allow you to have a shared whiteboard. Freeform can be used for anything from diagramming projects, brainstorming, or anything else that you can imagine.

Freeform is available on iOS, iPadOS, and macOS Ventura. With Freeform you can draw directly (on iOS and iPadOS), put in text, embed PDFs, audio, and web links. Beyond this, you can start a new session from Messages.

The key to Freeform is that any edits that are made by those included in your canvas are in real time, meaning you can work in real time with anybody you need. Freeform is an app that should be available in late 2022, so minimal information is known about it at this time.

Next, let us look at some changes in another collaborative tool, Notes.

Notes

Notes has been a mainstay on iOS since the introduction of the original iPhone in 2007. In its 15 years the Notes app has grown from just being an app that synchronized with IMAP email accounts to being an app that is capable of many things.

The biggest change for Notes came with the introduction of iOS 9 in 2015. While the changes were welcome on all of Apple's platforms, the redesigned Notes had the original 12.9-inch iPad Pro in mind when it was developed. In that time, Apple has added a slew of features, like drawing support, the ability to scan images to make them into PDFs, tags for notes, and plenty more.

One of the areas where additional tweaks were made were around organization. Notes has had the ability to create folders, and even pin notes for a while, However, sometimes it would be convenient to be able to see your most recent items. Technically this is possible, because by default any note is sorted by the most recently modified. However, it is not easy to ascertain which notes were modified. It is true that the name would be helpful, but it is possible that you could name some notes verify similarly.

In iOS 16, iPadOS 16, and macOS Ventura all notes will be now be organized by date. There will be a number of possible groups including:

- Today
- Yesterday
- Previous 7 Days
- Previous 30 days
- Previous months for the current year
- Previous years

Having items broken down in this manner is a fantastic addition. With this new organization you should be able to easily find what you are looking for based upon time. It should be noted that if you do not have any notes that fall into one of the above categories, then it will not be shown, meaning you will not have an empty group for Yesterday if you do not have any notes that were last modified yesterday.

Smart Folders

Beyond organizing by date is not the only new feature for Notes. There are some enhancements to Smart Folders. Smart Folders are used to create groups of notes based on the criteria that you specify. The benefit of a Smart Folder is that it will stay up to date and any new notes that you create that match the specified criteria will be included in the folder.

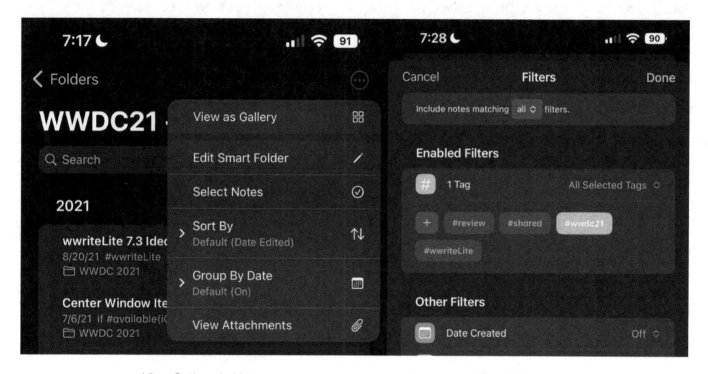

View Options in Notes   Filter Options in Notes

With iOS 15, iPadOS 15, and macOS Monterey Smart Folders were only able to be filtered using tags. Of course this is still possible in iOS 16, iPadOS 16, and macOS Ventura, but now you also have additional options. The complete list of options includes:

- Tags
- Date Created
- Date Edited
- Shared
- Mentions
- Checklists
- Attachments
- Folders
- Quick Notes
- Pinned Notes
- Locked Notes

Filter options for a Smart Folder in Notes on macOS Ventura

Let us dive into each of these, starting with Tags.

Filter options for a Smart Folder in Notes on macOS Ventura

Tags

The Tags option is similar to previous operating systems. You now have a few additional options with tags. You can include All Selected, meaning the note must have all of the tags. There is the Any Selected option, meaning that as long as any of the selected tags are in the note, it will be included. There is the Any Tag option, which means as long as there is any tag, it will be included. The last option is Untagged Notes Only, which will, as the name suggests, only include notes without any tags.

Date Created and Date Edited

The Date Created and Date Edited options provide the same filter options, just different fields. The filter options include relative dates of Today, Yesterday, Last 7 Days, Last 30 Days, Last 3 Months, and Last 12 Months. These filter options are good if you need a rolling view of notes created or edited with these values. This set of options is good if you need to view a set of relative notes, say from a conference that has occurred this year and you do not want notes from a conference the previous year.

There are also some more specific options including, Specific Range, Relative Range, On a Date, Before a Date, and After a Date. The Specific Range option will provide you with a start and end date. On a Date, Before a Date, and After a Date will all provide you with a single date which will be used for the specified filter.

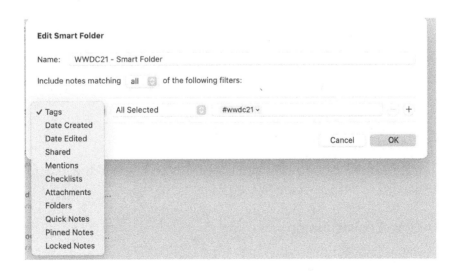

Filter options for a Smart Folder in Notes on macOS Ventura

The Relative Range option is a filter that will allow you to enter in a specific number of Hours, Days, Weeks, Months, or Years.

Shared

The Shared filter provides three options, With Anyone, Not Shared, and With Specified Users. The With Specified Users option will allow you to specify whom you want to include. It should be noted that only those users who you have shared notes with will be listed in the dropdown. You can either select All Selected or Any Selected for how to handle the filtering.

Mentions

The Mentions filter will allow you to filter based on mentions within a note, which are generally shared notes. The options are Me, Anyone, Specified Users, and No Mentions. Just like with Shared, you can include anyone you want in the Specified Users, you can add a list of users and select either All Selected or Any Selected, depending on your use case.

Checklists

The Checklists filter has only three options, Any, Incomplete, and No Checklists. This one is somewhat baffling, because what if you want to include only complete checklists? It seems like it is an oversight that there is not that option for filtering notes with only Completed Checklists.

Attachments

The Attachments filter is used to search for any media that has been added to a note. The complete list of options includes:

- Photos and Videos
- Scans
- Drawings
- Maps
- Websites
- Audio
- Documents
- No Attachments

All of the Attachment filter options are basically **If It Includes**, meaning that it has to have that item, if this filter is added.

Folders

The Folders filter allows you to either include or exclude specific folders. Any of the folders for this filter must be standard folders. Smart Folders are not able to be filtered with this filter.

Quick Notes, Pinned Notes, Locked Notes

These three filters, Quick Notes, Pinned Notes, and Locked Notes only have two options, Include and Exclude. If you opt of Include, then those note types will be included, similarly if you opt to Exclude it, then those note types will be excluded.

New Folders and New Smart Folders

A slight tweak with the New Smart Folder and New Folder popup has also been made. They are actually the same popup. Now, there is just a checkbox that indicates whether the new folder should be a Smart Folder or a standard folder. You can easily switch between the two by simply using the Make Smart Folder checkbox. If unchecked it will be a standard folder and if checked, it will be a Smart Folder.

Closing Thoughts on Smart Folders

You can add any, or all, of these to a Smart Folder's filter to be able to create a Smart folder that contains just the items that you want. There is another option that you can choose, you can either use **all** of the specified filters, which is the default, or you can use **any** of the specified. Which one you choose depends on your use case.

The new Smart Folder filter options are a fantastic addition that should allow people to create even better smart folders than you could previously. The myriad of new filters will allow users to create finely tuned smart folders to include, or exclude, whatever notes they need to be able to filter. There is one other new feature to discuss, securing notes.

Securing Notes

Most of the time when we create new notes, they likely do not contain any sensitive information. However, that is not always the case. There may be some information that you would want to keep private. The range of possible situations as to why you may want to secure a note is vast. You may have a password that you need to store but cannot store in Keychain. You may have a secret list of places that you want to go that you do not want anybody else to see. You may also use the Notes app to store your personal journal, and you would prefer not to have anybody look at it. You might even have a holiday or birthday shopping list that you would not want spoiled. Regardless of the exact reason, it is possible that you may want to to have secure notes. Previously, you could secure notes with a password. Starting with iOS 16, iPadOS 16, and macOS Ventura, it is now possible to secure individual notes, even more security than before.

Now, there are two possible ways to secure your notes. When you first enable locking of notes, you will be presented with the choice of which one to use. The first option is with your device's passcode. This means that your passcode that is used to secure your iPhone, iPad, or Mac. The second option is to use a separate password to secure the notes. There are some tradeoffs between the two options.

If you choose the device passcode option, you will not need to remember a separate password to secure the notes. This is likely the method that most people will use. However, the downside to this method is that if someone else knows your passcode, they will have access to all of your notes.

The second option of creating a separate password means that you will need to keep track of another password. However, this also means that if you forget your password, it is not recoverable and you cannot unlock the notes.

The option you choose will depend on your own personal use case. The first time you attempt to lock a note you will be presented with a screen that will provide some information about locking a note. This screen will also let you decide between which method you want to use.

If you opt for using your device's passcode, it will be a simple selection and confirmation. However, if you opt to use a different password, you will need to enter in the password, confirm the password, and then enter in a hint. The hint is optional, but recommended.

You do have the option of using biometric authentication for locking and unlocking notes. This means that you can use either Face ID or Touch ID to quickly lock or unlock notes. This is entirely optional and does not need to be enabled. When you change that status of using biometric authentication with locked notes, you will need to authenticate with your device's passcode.

Once you have made your password choice, you can then actually lock notes. So let us look at how to lock a note next.

Locking a Note

There are two different methods to lock a note, either the context menu or from the individual note's menu. Let us look at both ways. To lock a note from the context menu perform the following steps:

1. Open **Notes**.
2. **Locate the note** that you want to lock.
3. **Tap and hold** on the note to bring up the context menu. A popup preview of the note and context menu will appear.
4. Tap on **Lock Note**. The note will now be locked.

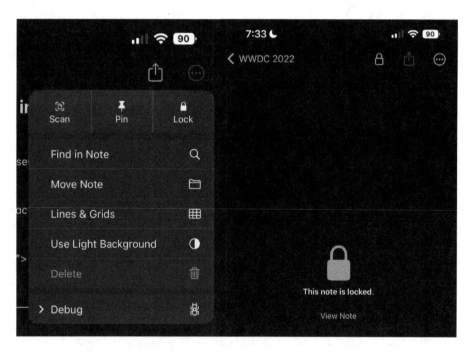

Notes popup menu to Lock a note   Locked Note example on iOS and iPadOS

The second method is to lock the note when viewing the note. To use this method use the following steps:

1. Open **Notes**.
2. **Locate the note** that you want to lock.
3. **Tap on the note** to open it.
4. Tap the "**...**" to bring up additional options.
5. Tap on **Lock** to lock the note.
6. Once you tap on **Lock**, you will need to enter in your passcode or password.

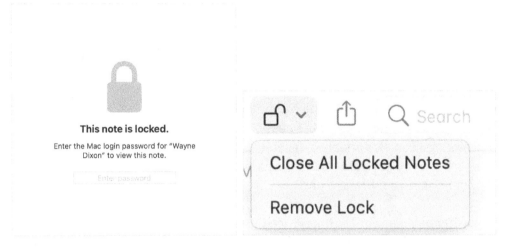

Locked Note on macOS Ventura   Close All Locked Notes Menu item

There is one thing that needs to be mentioned about locked notes. The title of the note will always be visible in the list of notes. This is so you can easily identify the note just the from title. All other content will be hidden. Next, let us look at how to unlock a note.

Unlocking a Note.

If you have locked a note and you want to look at its contents and modify it this can be done quite easily. When you open a locked note, you will only see a screen that says This note is locked with a link that says View Note.

When you click on this View Note link one of two things will occur. If you have enabled Face ID or Touch ID, you will need to authenticate. If you are only using a password, you will need to enter that. If you are using your device's passcode, you will see the standard device's password dialog screen.

If you have opted to used a custom password you will see an alert asking for the custom locked password. If you incorrectly enter in the custom password twice, your entered hint will be shown to help you remember the password.

If you want to switch the type of password that is being used, you can do this, so let us look at that next.

Switching Password Options

As mentioned above you have two different password options, using your device's passcode or a custom password. When you start using locked notes you may have opted for one solution but you may want to switch to the other. This is possible to do, simply use the following the steps:

1. Open the **Settings** app.
2. **Scroll down** to Notes
3. Tap on **Notes** to bring up the settings for Notes
4. Tap on **Password** to bring up the password options.

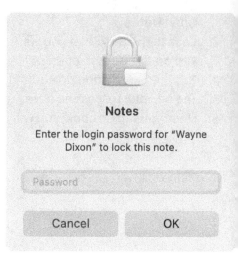

Unlock with Password on macOS
Ventura

Once the password options are shown, your current method should be selected. Similarly, if you have chosen to use Face ID or Touch ID that should be enabled as well.

To change the option, simply select the other option. For instance, if you have Use Device Passcode selected, tap on Use Custom Password, or vice versa.

If you go from using a Device's Passcode to using a Custom Password, you will receive a popup where you will need to set the password, confirm it, and add the optional hint. You can also enable or disable the use of Face ID or Touch ID here as well. Once you have entered in the password, tap on the Done button in the upper right to confirm the choice.

If you are going from a Custom Password to the Device Code, and you have Face ID or Touch ID enabled, you will simply have to use your biometrics to authenticate. However, if you do not have biometrics enabled, you will need two enter in your Device's passcode to confirm.

Regardless of which method you are going from and going to, once you have updated your password option, you will need to use that for unlocking your notes going forward.

Closing Thoughts on Notes

Notes has had a long history on iOS, iPadOS, and macOS. The new features in iOS 16, iPadOS 16, and macOS Ventura are great additions. Smart folders has been significantly enhanced with a variety of new filtering options, including Date Created, Dated Modified, Mentions, Checklists, and even the ability to filter by attachment type. With all of the new options you will be able to create even more finely tuned filters to meeting your needs.

Notes now has the ability to lock individual notes using either your Device's Passcode or a Custom Password. If you need to change the locking mechanism, you can do so within Settings and then looking for Notes. Regardless of which option you use, you can easily lock and unlock a note using either the context menu or a menu within the individual note. This is a great addition that will allow people to keep their own information even more private, no matter the reason why.

Now that we have covered Notes, let us move to the most used communication tool, Mail.

Mail

As much as many would like to eschew having to deal with email, there are some instances when it is still needed. These situations can include resetting passwords, receiving important information, or even just dealing with loathsome spam email. Regardless, of what email we receive, we have to deal with it.

There are those instances when we receive an email that we know that we do not have the time to deal with now, and know we will need to deal with it later. There are many strategies for how to tackle this. One approach is that you can flag an email for follow-up. Another approach is to mark the message as unread, so you may be likely to look at it again later. This approach only really works if you have a few unread emails at any time. The last approach, which often does not work, is to just try and remember. We all know that this last option often fails due to the nature of life. What is really needed is the ability for our mail app to remind us. Starting with iOS 16, iPadOS 16, and macOS Ventura, this is now possible.

Remind Me

There is a new feature in Mail that will remind you of an email. You have a few options for when you should be reminded. These options are:

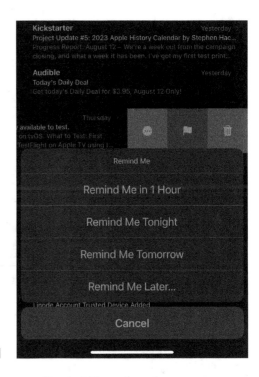

- Remind me In 1 Hour
- Remind me Tonight
- Remind me Tomorrow
- Remind me Later...

The first three options are somewhat self explanatory. The Later option takes a bit of an explanation. When you select the Remind me Later... a popup will appear. Here you can select an exact date and time for mail to remind you.

Regardless of which option you choose, the same actions will occur. The first thing that will happen is that the email message will be removed from the list of email messages. The email message is not deleted, but just hidden from your current emails. If you were to set a reminder for an email message and then were to log in to the web interface for your email provider, the email would still be shown.

Remind Me options for message

In order for Mail to be able to remind you, you need to tell Mail to do so. Let us look at how to do that.

Setting a Reminder on an Email

Telling Mail that you want to be reminded of an email is a straightforward process. You simply perform the following steps:

1. Open **Mail**.
2. **Locate the message** that you want to be reminded of later.
3. On iOS and iPadOS **swipe** from left to right on the message.
4. Tap on the **Remind Me** action. A popup will appear.
5. Select the **preferred reminder length**. If you select Remind Me Later another popup will appear where you can specify the exact date and time.

After you have set the reminder time, the message should be hidden from your mail list. Mail should notify you at the appropriate time. Next, let us look at what happens when Mail reminds you.

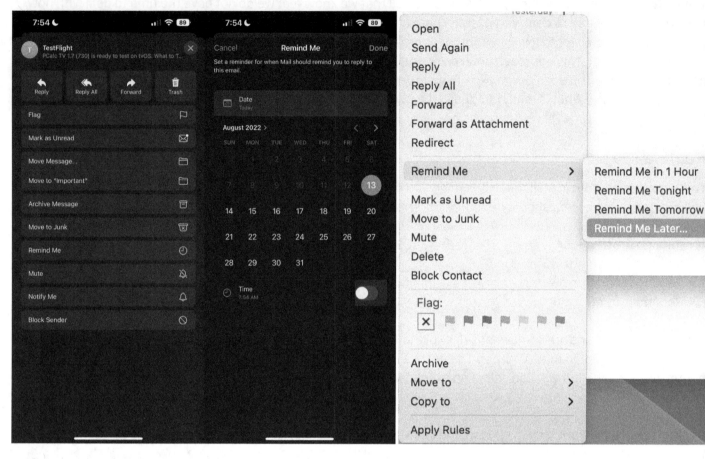

Menu Options for a message in
Mail on iOS

Calendar view for Being
Reminded

Remind Me Options on macOS Ventura

Being Reminded

As mentioned above, when you ask Mail to remind you, the email
message will reappear in your email list as if it was a brand new
email. It will still have the original date and time that you
received the email.

There is one thing to note about this feature. It will only work on
devices running iOS 16, iPadOS 16, or macOS Ventura. Any older
devices will not be able to be reminded. Emails will not be hidden
and will remain in the mailbox the same as under previous
versions of Mail.

Being able to schedule a reminder for an email is a great new
feature that will help people take action on some emails at a
later date. This is not the only change, let us look at another
called Undo Send.

Date and time for being reminded in mail on
macOS Ventura

Undo Send

When you are composing an email and you end up sending it, you may realize that you made a mistake and want to stop it from being sent. Often times this is not possible to do. Email is somewhat like a text message, once it is sent, it is sent. Many modern email apps have the ability to undo the sending of an email. Mail now joins that group.

The Undo Send option is enabled by default and cannot be disabled. When you send an email you will have 7 seconds to tap the **Undo Send** button, which will appear at the bottom of the Mail app screen. It may not be a long amount of time, but it should be sufficient given that the feature is intended for immediate recognition of errors in sending.

If you decide to not send the email and tap on the Undo Send button, the email message will not be sent and the mail message that you were going to send will reappear so you can edit it and then resend as necessary, or save as a draft, or even delete the email entirely. There is one other new feature for Mail, Scheduled send. Let us look at that now.

Schedule Send

There may be times when you want to compose an email and have it sent at a later time. You could put the mail into your drafts and then send it at the desired time, but if you are not available at the time you may not be able to send it. There is a solution for this scenario, the new Schedule Send feature.

Scheduled Send is available on iOS 16, iPadOS 16, and macOS Ventura. Similar to the Remind Me feature, you have four options. These options are:

- Send now
- Send 9:00pm Tonight
- Send 9:00pm Tomorrow
- Send Later...

Just like with Remind Me, the Send Later option will allow you to set the specific date and time for an email to be sent.

To schedule an email to be sent at a later time, perform the following steps:

1. **Compose your email** as you would normally including all of the email address that you want to send it to.
2. When you are ready to schedule the email to be sent on iOS or iPadOS **tap and hold on on the send button**. On macOS **click on the down arrow** next to the send button. On both platforms a popup will appear.
3. **Select the appropriate preset** or Send Later option. If you opt for the Send Later option you will need to select the appropriate time. Once you select the appropriate time the email will be scheduled to be sent.

The ability to send a message later from Mail is a welcome feature, but there are some things to be aware about regarding this.

Notes About Scheduled Send

When you schedule an email to be sent later, the email will be sent from that specific device. What this means is that if the device that you scheduled the email to be sent from does not have a connection to the internet, the email will not be sent. It will be sent as soon as soon as the device regains a connection to the internet.

Editing the Schedule for an Email

There may be instances when you realize that you have put in the incorrect date or time for the email that you want to send. Similarly, you may want to send an email sooner than one of the presets that you selected. It is possible to change these by performing the following steps:

1. Open **Mail**.
2. Scroll down to the **Send Later** mailbox.
3. **Locate** the message you want to change the scheduled time for.
4. **Tap** or click on the message.
5. **Tap** or click on the **Edit** link at the top of the message. A popup will appear.
6. **Select the new time** to send the email.
7. **Tap** or click on the **Done** button.

Once you have selected the new date and time, the email will be scheduled for that time. If you selected the current time your email will be sent out immediately. As with all of the other Mail features discussed thus far, this is a great new capability for Mail. There are a few other new features to cover about Mail.

Other Mail Features

Mail offers a few other features which only need brief mentions. These are Follow up, Missing Recipients, and Smart Search enhancements.

Follow Up

Follow Up is a new method of being able to follow up on a message. This is done by marking an email for follow up. When this is done, it will be moved to the top of your email box so you can follow up with it later.

Missing Recipients

When you are getting ready to send an email you may not always immediately fill in the recipients or attachments. Sometimes, you end up adding recipients but forget the attachments. Now, Mail will let you know if you are missing recipients or missing attachments. Mail will provide you with an alert to let you know that you might have forgotten something.

Smart Search Enhancements

When you do some searching in Mail, you may not always know how to spell someone's name or a word. Now Mail will provide some suggestions for correcting your mail search. Similar when you are searching your mail you will now also see Shared With You suggestions if they are relevant.

Closing Thoughts on Mail

Mail has long been an application that has not seen many changes. That now changes with iOS 16, iPadOS 16, and macOS Ventura. Mail now has the ability to delay sending an email with Scheduled Send, which is great if you want to send something later than the current moment.

When you are composing an email and forget a recipient or an attachment, you will now be notified so you can fix it. If you do send an email and realize you want to unsend an email, you can do so, but you only have 7 seconds to unsend the email. While this is not a long time, it is enough time to not send if you immediately realize something needed to be corrected.

In the case that you do not have time to deal with an email immediately you can have Mail remind you at a specified time or in a preset time in the future.

Dictionaries

One of the things that may need to occur during any communications would be that you would need to translate between English and another language. Apple's operating systems have a large number of existing dictionaries that you can use to translate between English and other languages. iOS 16, iPadOS 16, and macOS Ventura are adding an addition seven languages that can be used. These languages are:

- Bangla - English
- Czech - English
- Finnish - English
- Hungarian - English
- Kannada - English
- Malayalam - English
- Turkish - English

This is a small thing, but any addition to dictionaries that are available on Apple's operating systems are a great step forward.

Closing Thoughts on Collaboration

There are many new features that allow you to collaborate with others. FaceTime has added a few new options, including the ability to easily locate your installed apps that support SharePlay, so you can easily start a SharePlay session with others. Previously, if you wanted to use a different device while on a FaceTime call, you were out of luck, you would have to end a call and start a new one on second device. Now, with iOS 16, iPadOS 16, and macOS Ventura, you can easily move between devices by using a menu in the Menu Bar. When you are on a FaceTime call you can also enable Live Captions, which will transcribe what everyone is saying, and this will be done all on your device, so the information is never sent off to a server to be translated. FaceTime is not the only collaboration tool to see improvements.

Messages adds a few new welcome features, like Undo Send which will allow you to unsend a message for up to 15 minutes. Using Undo Send will not stop someone from having read it, and a note will be made in the chat transcript indicating that a message was unsent. Along with Undo Send, if you notice that you made a typographical mistake in a message, you will have up to 15 minutes to edit a message. If you edit a message, next to the Delivered or Read receipt, a note will be made to indicate that the message was edited. If someone has sent you a message and you want to get back to it later, you can now mark a thread as Unread, so you can easily notice that you need to get back to the thread. This will also add a badge to the icon so you will be able to see you need to check it without opening the app. The last new feature of Messages is the ability to recover deleted messages for up to 30 days. You can also permanently delete a message thread as well.

Notes also saw some updates. In particular, you can now create Smart Folders based on a myriad of metadata and not just tags. You can use fields like Date Created, Date Modified, Tags, if the Note is shared and with whom, as well as many other criteria. Now, you have the option to selectively make a note private, even more securely. You can either use your device's authentication, including passcode or biometrics, or you can create a separate password. If you use a separate password and you forget the password there is no way of unlocking the notes.

Apple is adding a whole new app called Freeform. Freeform is a way of being able to have a shared whiteboard that you can use for collaboration. Freeform supports a wide variety of media types, including PDFs, web links, images, drawing, text and much more. The edits that are made are done in real time so you can all easily contribute and discuss what is being shown.

Mail, the most ubiquitous communication app, has seen some significant upgrades including smart search suggestions, so you can get the spelling of something correct and even see items that have been shared with you. Mail also adds a new Scheduled Send feature, which will allow you to use a preset time of 9:00pm tonight, 9:00pm tomorrow, or Send Later, which allows you to specify an exact date and time for something to be sent. If you find yourself in a situation where you cannot tackle an email at the immediate moment, you can now have Mail remind you that there is an email that needs attention. This can be done using the Remind Me feature. Here you can be reminded in an hour, tonight, tomorrow, or you can specify your own date and time with the Remind Me Later option. When you send an email if you are missing any recipients or attachments you will be notified and should you realize that you made a mistake in an email that you just sent, you can use the Undo Send feature within 7 seconds to correct the email.

All of these additions and changes are welcome ones and should allow you to get more done when needed. Let us look at some changes around Let us next see what is new in Music, News, Maps, and Safari.

Music, Maps, and Safari

From time to time there are some apps that only see a few new features and when this occurs it does not always make sense to dedicate an entire chapter to these items. The reason for this is because sometimes the update are very minor. Throughout this chapter we will look at a bunch of small changes with Music, News, Maps, and Safari starting with Music.

Music

Music is an important part of many people's days. Sometimes people use music to relax, while others use it to get motivated, and yet others use as a background track for their day. Regardless of why someone listens to music it is quite likely that they might have some artists that they really enjoy and like to keep up with any new music that they release. In many cases super fans will know exactly when new music is released, but a single person can only keep up with so many artists. Even with this, sometimes artists still manage to surprise their fans with brand new music without any announcements.

To help with all of these the Music app in iOS 16, iPadOS 16, and macOS Ventura will now notify you when one of your favorite artists has something new. In order to receive notifications for an artist, perform the following steps:

1. Open the **Music** app.
2. Tap on the **Search** button in the lower right corner.
3. **Search** for an artist that you want to favorite.
4. Tap on the **Favorite** button in the upper right.

Artist not being set as a "Favorite" and then being set as "Favorited", in Apple Music on iOS and iPadOS

Artist not being set as a "Favorite" and then being set as "Favorited", in Apple Music on macOS Ventura

Once you do this, and the artist has something new, you should get a notification to let you know that there are new items. There is one item to note about this, you need to have an active Apple Music subscription to be able to add favorite artists. Let us now cover some changes to Maps.

Maps

When Apple Maps was introduced in 2012, it was not all that well received. It was not that the app itself was not functional, but the mapping itself was not what users expected. There were a number of issues, including display issues with roads, not enough detail when looking at a street view, and lack of details for some areas.

Apple quickly fixed some of these issues, while others took some additional time. Since then Apple has significantly improved the app including many features. One of the most requested features that has not been available, has been multiple stop routes.

When you are planning a trip to somewhere that you do not normally go, it is likely that you may want to make a few stops along the way. This is called multiple stop routing. Many web based mapping sites have had the ability to add multiple stops to a route, but Apple Maps has not. Starting with iOS 16, iPadOS 16, and macOS Ventura, this is now possible to do.

When you are building a route from one point to another point, you can add up to 15 stops to a route. As you add stops it will recalculate the route. While it is entirely possible to build a multiple stop route on an iPhone, it is sometimes easier on a Mac. If you are building a route on a Mac, and if you have finished, you are able to send your completed route to your iPhone, or share it via messages. The new multiple stop route is a long awaited addition to Maps, and one that many have wanted for a long time. Let us now look at some changes to Safari.

Safari

Safari is Apple's built-in web browser for iOS, iPadOS, and macOS. Safari is built using the open source WebKit engine and it provides a large number of features. Each release of Apple's operating system undoubtedly brings some new features to Safari, and given the open source nature of the WebKit engine, new features can be brought to Safari over the course of the year without needing a new system to support the new features. This year's additions include enhancements to Tab Groups, Translation enhancements, and syncing changes. Let u start with Tab Groups.

Tab Groups

In iOS 15, iPadOS 15, and macOS Monterey, Apple added a new feature called Tab Groups. Tab Groups are a way of being able to group tabs together into groups that make sense to you. Across all of this year's operating systems you can now share your Tab Groups with others. To share a Tab group you can use these steps:

macOS

1. Open **Safari**. The tab groups should appear on the left side.
2. **Hover** over the Tab Group that you want to share, a "**...**" should appear.
3. Click on the "**...**" button.
4. Tap on **Share Tab Group**. A share sheet should appear.

Share Tab Group on macOS

iPadOS

1. Open Safari
2. Tap on the button to expand the sidebar.
3. Tap and hold on the Tab Group you want to share. This will bring up the share menu.
4. Tap on the **Share** button.

Share Tab Group on iPadOS

1. Open **Safari**.
2. Tap on the tab view button.
3. Tap on the **Down Arrow**.
4. Select the **Tab Group** you want to share.
5. Tap on the **Share** button.

Share Tab Group on iOS

Here you can select who you want to share the group with. Once shared, everyone can add, remove, and view shared tabs with the group. Let us move to some Translation enhancements.

Translation

Safari has the ability to translate the current webpage that you are viewing from another language into your preferred language. As you might expect, Safari cannot translate between every language that webpages might be written in, but, there are a number that it can. Starting with iOS 16, iPadOS 16, and macOS Ventura you can translate between more languages. The new languages are:

- Dutch
- Indonesian
- Polish
- Thai
- Turkish
- Vietnamese

It is always a good thing to see additional translation languages within Safari because that means that more people will be able to obtain the information that they need. Next up is synching.

Syncing

Safari has long had the ability to sync things like bookmarks and passwords, and now Shared Tab Groups. Starting with Mac OS X 10.8 Mountain Lion and iOS 6, Apple introduced a new feature called iCloud Tabs. iCloud Tabs are a way of being able to access the tabs hat you have open on your other devices. This was an easy way of being able to reopen items without needing to use bookmarks. Now, there are a couple of other items that can be synchronized. These include extensions and website settings.

For extensions, if you enable an extension on one device and then subsequently install it on another device, it will automatically be enabled. Therefore, you no longer need to remember to enable newly installed extensions, if they are already enabled elsewhere.

Along with extension, all of your website settings should synchronize as well. This means that your preferences for notifications, reader mode settings, and whether to allow popup notifications for a website, will all synchronize across all of your devices. You no longer need to worry about setting up each device separately. This goes a long way to making it a lot faster and providing the same experience across all of your devices.

Closing Thoughts on Music, Maps, and Safari.

All of these changes with Music, Maps, and Safari are minor ones, but they are welcome ones. While you may not need all of these features on a daily basis, having them be available when you need them is always a good thing. There is another app that has seen some changes, that app is News, unlike Music, Maps, and Safari, the News app has seen some significant changes and they will need some time to cover, so let us look at these changes in the next chapter.

News

News is something that almost everyone encounters throughout their day. You might spend some time dedicated to looking at the news, or you might check the news sporadically, it is even possible that you just wait for push notifications to get the latest information. Regardless of how you get your news, the type of news that you consume can vary. This could be the latest national news, local news, sports news, tech news, or any other type of news. There is an app on Apple's platforms that is designed to help you keep up on the latest information, that app is the News app.

The News app has a variety of ways of being able to help you keep up on the news. You can use News to set notifications for various publications and alerts. With iOS 16, iPadOS 16, and macOS Ventura, there is now an additional option. You can set a channel as one of your favorites.

Favorites

When you set a channel as a favorite you will have quick access to it in the sidebar. Along with the sidebar your favorites will appear in the Today view as well. You can set a channel as your favorite on any of the supported platforms. To set a channel as your favorite, perform the following steps:

1. Open the **News** app.
2. **Locate the channel** that you want to add as a favorite.
3. On iOS 16 or iPadOS tap and hold on the channel. On macOS Ventura right mouse click on the Channel. A menu will appear.
4. Tap or Click on the **Add to Favorites** option.

By default the News app should have some of your favorites populated based on your previous reading habits. You can add additional favorites, or remove existing ones from your favorites. To remove a channel as a favorite, perform the following steps:

1. Open the **News** app.
2. **Locate the channel** that you want to remove as a favorite.
3. On iOS 16 or iPadOS tap and hold on the channel. On macOS Ventura right mouse click on the Channel. A menu will appear.
4. Tap or Click on the **Remove from Favorites** option.

Adding a specific channel as a favorite is not the only new feature. Next, let us look at another set of favorites that you can set, Local News.

Local News

It is important to be aware of what is going on in the nation, but it is equally, if not more, important to be aware of what is going on closer to you. In order to facilitate your ability to get local news, the Apple News app can allow you to do follow local news. Apple has begun adding coverage for certain cities. The list of cities that have local coverage includes:

- The Bay Area
- Charlotte
- Chicago
- Dallas-Fort Worth
- Houston
- Los Angelas
- Miami
- New York City
- Sacramento
- San Antonio
- San Diego
- San Francisco
- The Triangle (Raleigh, Durham, Chapel Hill in North Carolina)
- Toronto, Ontario, Canada
- Washington, D.C.

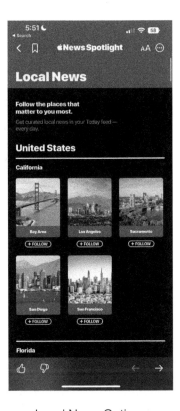

Local News Options

This is the initial list of cities and the list s likely to grow as time goes on. You can add local news by performing the following steps:

1. Open the **News** app.
2. Ta, or click on the **Today** tab.
3. Scroll down until you see the **Get Local Headlines Every Day** item. If it is not shown then perform a search for Local News.
4. Tap or click on the **Get Local Headlines Every Day** item. A popup will appear.
5. Tap or click on the **Cities and Areas** that you want to get headlines for. Each item should have a check mark next to it.
6. Tap or click on the **Done** button.

Once you add any cities you should start seeing in depth coverage from the local papers of that area. That is not the only only new item you can add to News. The next item is one that truly spans the globe. Let us now take a look at sports.

Sports Teams

Recently Apple has gotten into presenting sports with Apple TV. They have shown National Football League (NFL), games, Major League Baseball (MLB), games, and they have signed a deal with Major League Soccer (MLS), in the United States to be the exclusive streaming partner for all of the MLS games, starting in the fall of 2023. One other area where Apple is getting into Sports is within the News app.

You can now set your favorite teams in the News app. When you do this you will see news articles, highlights, schedules, and scores for your selected teams. To get started with adding your teams, use the following steps:

1. Open the **News** app.
2. Tap, or click, on the **Today** tab.
3. Scroll down until you see the **My Sports** section.
4. Tap or click on the **Get Started** button. A popup will appear.
5. Tap or click on the **Turn On** button to start adding teams. A Manage My Sports sheet will appear.

This screen has three sections, Following, Suggested, and All Sports. The first time you set up your favorite teams there will be nothing in the Following section. You can either search, using the provided search bar, add one of the suggested team, or browse all of the sports. You can add teams from a wide variety of different sports. The complete list of included sports is:

- National Football League (NFL)
- Major League Baseball (MLB)
- National Basketball Association (NBA)
- Women's National Basketball Association (WNBA)
- National Hockey League (NHL)
- College Football (U.S.)
- Men's College Basketball (U.S.)
- Women's College Basketball (U.S.)
- Soccer - Bundesliga, Champion's League, La Lia, League I, MLS, NWSL, Premier League, Series A, Women's Championship League, and Women's Super League
- Golf
- Tennis
- Mixed Martial Arts - UFC
- Motorsports - F1, Indy Car, NASCAR
- Boxing
- Pro Wrestling - AEW, WWE
- Road Cycling
- Fantasy Sports - Baseball, Basketball, Football, Hockey
- Sports Betting
- Horse Racing
- Cricket - International Cricket Council
- Rugby Union
- Running
- eSports
- Olympic Sports

You can navigate to any of the sports and possibly see subcategories. The sections that have subcategories are outlined above. The NFL, MLB, NBA, WNBA, NHL, College Football, Men's College Basketball, and Women's College Basketball all have their teams listed when you navigate into the section. You also have the option of being able to add an entire sport, if you want to get news related to that sport.

One sports experience for your Apple apps.

Follow your teams across Apple News, Apple TV, and other Apple apps.

The sports, leagues, teams, and athletes you are following will be associated with your Apple ID to sync across supported Apple apps, and used to personalize your experience and send you notifications. You can stop syncing anytime. See how your data is managed...

Not Now   Turn On

"My Sports" in News on macOS Ventura

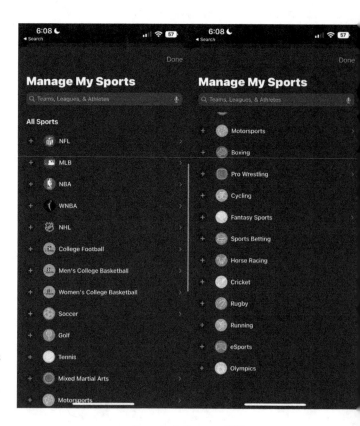

Sports listing on iOS

You can add as many teams from as many sports as you would like to follow. Once you have finished adding your teams, you can tap or click on the **Finished** button in the upper right corner. Once you have finished adding your teams, they should start appearing in the News app under a new section called My Sports.

You can then click on any of your teams and you will see information about the team, like current scores, standings, highlights, and more. Beyond this, you can also block teams. You will need to add them before being able to block them.

You are not limited to getting news just about the teams that you select. You can always see additional sports using the All Sports button in the menu area of the News app.

The addition of the teams is going to be helpful for a new feature that was previously covered. That feature is Live Activities.

Live Activities

Earlier in the book we covered the new Lock Screen on iOS. In the chapter we covered a new feature called Live Activities. Live Activities is a new framework that allows apps to provide near real time updates on things like deliveries, ride sharing arrivals, and sports scores. If there is a big game going on for one of your favorite teams, you might see live sports scores right on your Lock Screen.

Closing Thoughts on News

The News app got a big upgrade with the ability to manage favorite channels, the ability to add local news, and add favorite sports teams. When you add any of these items you will get local information from newspapers, scores, highlights, schedules and standings for your sports teams. All of these are great additions. The ability to personalize various aspects of apps is a plus, but one thing to always keep in mind is your privacy and security. Those are the topics of the next chapter.

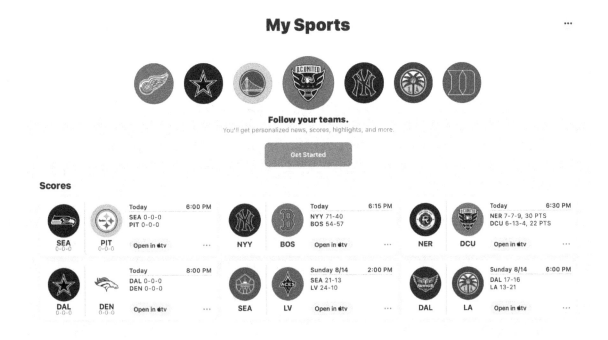

"My Sports" section in Today view in News on macOS Ventura

Privacy and Security

We all rely on our devices for all sorts of things. Some of the data is not intended to be private, but there is some data whose intention is to be private. In order to keep data as safe as possible, some changes are needed. This year Apple is introducing a set of changes that will not only keep your devices up to date, helping you see where you data is going, keeping your data private, and providing you with tools should you need help. Let us start with some changes to Streaming Improvements.

Media streaming improvements

There are times when you want to show someone something. This could be a movie, photo, or even just a quick video. You do have the option of showing it on your device, but that is not always convenient. In these situations you may want to stream to a device, but this can create security concerns. Under iOS 15, iPadOS 15, and macOS Monterey when you would start streaming to another device you would likely need to explicitly grant an app the ability to connect to all of your network devices, even if it only needed to connect to a single device. This could cause a problem because the app would then have access to investigate other items on your network. This changes with iOS 16, iPadOS 16, and macOS Ventura.

With the latest updates you will now have the ability to stream directly to a device that supports non AirPlay streaming, without needing to give the app Bluetooth or Local Network access. This will result in better security and it will make it easier for you to connect to a variety of devices.

Rapid Security Response

Unless a device is no longer supported, every device will need some sort of update. These updates can consist of security updates, bug fixes, or even new features. Typically, with Apple's devices, when there is an update it requires there are some steps that are performed: .

1. The update is downloaded.
2. The update is expanded and the update is prepared.
3. The update is installed.
4. The device is restarted.

If you have automatic downloads and installation of updates it is likely that these will happen overnight while you are sleeping. It is possible that the only way that you will know anything happened is because you have to enter in your device's passcode. There is also a notification indicating that it was updated, but the passcode entry will be required and likely noticed first.

There are some updates that may not require a full restart and could potentially be responding to security bugs that may cause problems. There are those aspects of these updates that might be useful to have as soon as possible. This may now be possible with a new feature called Rapid Security Response.

macOS has long had the ability to perform updates without a restart. However with iOS and iPadOS this was not possible. These updates without a restart have been expanded to iOS 16 and iPadOS 16. Along with this they have been renamed to "Rapid Security Response'

Rapid Security Response will be able to download, update, and install system configuration and security files. These are not considered standard updates and can be installed and downloaded separately. Some of these updates will not require a restart for the changes to become enabled, while others may not become active until you reboot your device.

By default these updates are enabled. On iOS and iPadOS you can change this by using the following steps:

1. Open the **Settings** app.
2. Tap on **Software Update.**
3. Tap on **Automatic Updates**.
4. Tap on the toggle button next to **Install System and Data Files** to turn this off.

On macOS you can use these steps:

1. Open System Settings.
2. Click on **General**.
3. Click on **Software Update**.
4. Click on the "I" information circle. This will bring up the Software Update settings.
5. Toggle **Install Security Responses and System files**.

It is recommended to leave this option enabled. Some of the types of data that may be included in the System and Data Files includes:

- Support for new top-level domains in Safari
- Updated Fonts
- Updated system voice dictation services
- System level support for digital camera RAW formats
- Updated definitions for SSL certificate types

These are just a few of the possibilities of what might be downloadable between major software updates. Therefore, it is recommended to keep this feature on for the best performance and to make sure your device stays secure. Let us look at another feature, an improvement to Pasted data notifications.

Pasteboard Improvements

One feature that many could not live without today is copy and paste. There was a time, between 2007 and 2009, when those who used an iPhone did not have the ability to copy and paste anything. Anybody using a device today has come to expect that it is a feature that is available. When a piece of data is copied on iOS or iPadOS this is copied to what Apple calls the Pasteboard.

Many users do not think about the types of data that they are copying and pasting. The type of data would not matter, it could be random text, an image, or some data from an app. However, it could have also been data like a phone number, a one-time code, or even a password for a website. Regardless of the type of data, for a long time apps had been accessing this without user's being notified.

In iOS 14 Apple decided to begin notifying users whenever their pasteboard was accessed by third-party apps. The reason for this was to keep users informed about what applications were accessing their copied data. This could be because the app was being nefarious and inspecting all copied data. It could just as easily be that apps were inspecting the data to see if they could use the data.

When the notifications were introduced, many users found these notifications annoying, particularly for apps that were accessing the pasteboard after every single keystroke. While it may have been annoying, it was accurately showing what apps had been accessing their data, without them previously knowing this. Many of these instances might have been innocent, but some apps might have been malicious with their intent. Either way, users were being notified of these actions, so they could now be aware.

In iOS 15 Apple introduced a change called Secure Paste, which would allow developers to receive data from other apps without actually knowing the contents of the pasteboard until it was explicitly pasted by the user. The pasting of data was either through a keyboard combination (Command-V) or by tapping on **paste** in the popup menu. The rationale for this was that an app could request the type of data, so the app could decide if it would be able to paste the data, without actually getting the contents of the data, at least until it was pasted. This was particularly necessary for drag and drop. If a developer implemented Secure Paste there was a significant benefit for users, the notifications that they were receiving whenever the Pasteboard was accessed would have been significantly reduced.

Now, iOS 16 and iPadOS 16 bring a slight improvement to this. Now, if a keyboard combination is used or if the user uses the paste action in the popup menu, a notification will not appear, regardless of whether secure paste is implemented. The reason for this is that the user is deliberately choosing to paste the data. Because this is a deliberate action, no notification is necessary. This is a minor change, but a very welcome one for many users.

While you might not think much about the security of the data that you are pasting, there is one area that you are more likely thinking about, and that item is passwords. There is an alternative to passwords, called PassKeys. Let us dive into that next.

Passkeys

There is one thing that everyone who uses an internet connected device has in common, they have to have an account for each website that they access. When you create an account for a website you will also likely have to have a password to go along with it. While there are some login processes that do not actually require a password, like logging in with a secure link, or using a login-service like **Sign in with Apple**, a vast majority of sites still have a username and password. The best practice that is recommended by security experts is to use a unique password for each and every website and account that you have.

There are ways of doing this. One is to use a password manager, which everyone should be doing now. Another is to use a password generation algorithm that you create that allows you to easily remember the password for a particular website. As much as everyone may try to use a unique password, it is possible that they might not always do so.

Passwords have been a mainstay of computers ever since the early mainframe days and even though they are somewhat convenient, they are not easy to fully secure. Adding a second-factor, like text message verification, a one-time password, or even a physical device that generates a one time key does help, but even these can be bypassed in some instances.

Instead, there is a new standard that will eventually obviate the need to traditional passwords. That standard is called FIDO2: Web Authentication (WebAuthn). Apple is calling their implementation of WebAuthn, Passkeys, so that name used going forward is Passkeys.

Passkeys uses a technology that you are fully aware of, even if you do not understand how it functions. It uses Public Key Cryptography in the form of a Private/Public Key Pair. This method is similar to the way that a web server is secured when using SSL, in that there is a private key that the server has, and a public certificate that your browser verifies.

With Passkeys, the entities which have each item are reversed. Instead, your device has the private key, while the server has your public key. Here is how the setup of Passkeys goes:

1. During account creation, your device generates a private/public key pair.
2. Your device stores the private key.
3. The public key is sent to the server to store.
4. The account creation is finished.

There is no problem with having the public key stored on the server, because the nature of a public key, is to be public, in that it can be given to anyone. Only those who have the private key, in this case your device, can prove that they have the proper private key to go with the corresponding public key. With Passkeys, a new public/private key pair is generated for each site where you use Passkeys.

After the key pair has been created, and you want to sign in, here is how the login flow will go:

1. Your device indicates they want to sign in.
2. The server you are trying to sign in on sends a challenge,
3. Your device signs the challenge with the private key. Only the private key can create a proper signature.
4. Your device sends the signature to the server.
5. The server uses the provided signature to verify the challenge by decrypting it with your public key.
6. If the decrypted challenge matches what was sent by the server, the server indicates that you are now signed in.

That is the way that Passkeys work. There are no passwords for either the client or server to remember, and there is no way for anybody to pretend to be you without the private key for that specific site.

The software strictly enforces that the website and the app that created it are the only ones that can use the private/public key pair. This means that nobody else can pretend to be you and sign in.

There are some downsides to Passkeys though. The biggest is that the public/private key pairs are stored on a physical device and the private keys never leave the device. That means that if you lose the device, you can not get back the private keys. Therefore, it would be imperative to purchase a second hardware key and have it stored in a secure place.

This may sound great, but it is not necessarily the right answer for everyone. Having a physical hardware item is not always convenient for everyone, so in order to accommodate everyone your Passkeys are stored in your iCloud Keychain.

Passkeys in iCloud Keychain

Passkeys in iCloud Keychain are just like other passwords. This means that they are end-to-end encrypted, backed up, and synchronize across all of your devices. The biggest benefit is that you can sign in with just a single tap. Passkeys works with iOS 16, iPadOS 16, and macOS Ventura, so you can use them on all of your devices.

You having access to your Passkeys is all well and good, but it is possible that you may share an account with someone, and Apple has accounted for this.

Sharing PassKeys

Passkeys are stored locally on your device and act very similarly to passwords, and there may need to be a way of providing access to accounts to other individuals. This possibility has been accounted for. You can share a passkey via AirDrop.

A Passkey can be shared by opening up Passwords, locating the Passkey from the list, tapping on the **share** icon in the upper right, and selecting the person or device you want to share your Passkey with. The passkey is sent using AirDrop. Once the Passkey is shared to the other person, it will be opened up in Passwords, and imported. At that point, the Passkey will be available for use.

When you share a Passkey in this manner it is the exact same as sharing a username and password, so that means that they have full access to your account, just as they would if it were a username and password being used to login.

Beyond sharing a passkey, there may be instances when you may need to use a Passkey on another device, where you cannot use AirDrop to transfer the Passkey. This is possible, so let us look at how that works.

Sign on using Other Devices

As of right now, there is no way to share Passkeys to other non Apple devices, but you are able to sign in on non Apple devices, as well as Apple devices that you do not own . The way that this is done is via a QR code. The example below will specify an iPhone, but this also works on iPads and Macs, and the process is the same. Here is the entire process:

1. The QR code is presented by the website from the device that you want to login on.
2. You scan the QR code with your iPhone.
3. A bluetooth advertisement is generated on your iPhone and this is sent back to the website with specific information, including a relay server to use and a shared key.
4. The device that you want to log in on and your iPhone connect to a relay server.
5. The device sends its authentication request to the relay server.
6. The relay server forwards the request to your iPhone.
7. Your iPhone sends its response back to the relay server.
8. The relay server forwards your response back to the client device.

The process seems complicated when you look at it, but the only step you need to perform is clicking on the Sign in on the nearby device and scanning the QR code. After that, everything else is handled for you. All of the information that is sent from your phone to the relay server is encrypted, therefore the relay server cannot see any of the data that is being passed.

Closing Thoughts on Passkeys

Passkeys are a technology that will eventually replace passwords. Passkeys are cryptographically secure, cannot be spoofed, and cannot be stolen, because it is a private/public key pair with the private key being stored on your device and the public key being stored on the server. With a private/public key pair, the public key is intended to be public and it can be freely provided.

Passkeys provide the ability for you to sign in on other devices using a QR code, which is done in a secure manner. If you need to share your Passkey this is possible to do via AirDrop, but you cannot share it with non-Apple devices. Your Passkeys are stored in iCloud Keychain, so they will automatically be available on all of your iOS 16, iPadOS 16, and macOS Ventura devices for you to use.

It will take a while before sites support Passkeys, but since it is an industry standard, it does have a shot of actually being brought to servers, but only time will tell on that.

We are almost done with Privacy and Security, there one other feature that we need to look at related to Security and that needs its own chapter .That feature is called Safety Check. So let us look at that next.

Safety Check

Safety Check is a new feature that will allow you to quickly review who has access to you information. Safety Check is composed to two separate features, **Manage Sharing & Access**, and **Emergency Reset**, let us look at both starting with Manage Sharing & Access.

Manage Sharing & Access

By their nature, us humans tend to need some sort of connection with others. Sometimes these connections are only temporary, while other connections may last for a lifetime. When these connections are more than fleeting, it is possible that you may end up sharing information with others or by providing them access to the information. As time progresses, it is entirely possible that you forgot that you provided access to certain items. These items may be things like photos, current location, notes, and almost anything else you can think of that is stored on your devices or in the cloud.

If it has been a while since you began sharing information you may not remember that you have shared the information. It can be somewhat cumbersome to go through each of the various apps and figure out what information is being shared and with whom. To help make it easier to do all this from a single place Apple has introduced a new iOS 16 feature called Manage Sharing & Access.

Manage Sharing & Access

In order to get to the Manage Sharing & Access you can perform the following steps:

1. Open the **Settings** app.
2. Scroll down to **Privacy & Security.**
3. Tap on **Privacy & Security** to open the privacy and security settings.
4. Scroll down to **Safety Check**.
5. Tap on **Safety Check** to open the Safety Check information screen.
6. Tap on **Manage Sharing & Access** to open up the Manage Sharing & Access start screen.

Once you have tapped on the start screen, you will need to authenticate with either Face ID, Touch ID, or with your iPhone's passcode. Once authenticated the Manage Sharing & Access information screen will be shown. This information screen will provide a brief overview of what types of information you can review. The types of information for review are:

1. Review People
2. Review Apps
3. Account Security

Safety Check Options

Once you tap on the **Continue** button. You will begin the process, starting with Reviewing People.

Reviewing People

On the Review People screen, you will have two ways of displaying information, either by person or by type of information. The People option will list each person that you are sharing data with. Below each name will be the types of information that you are sharing.

The Information tab will list the information by the type of information. Below each piece of information is how many individuals have access to that specific type of information. Here is an example of what it might show for Notes Sharing.

"4 people have access to 7 of your notes. You have access to 5 notes of 2 other people"

With either display type, you can select as many people, or pieces of information, as necessary. When you have finished your selection you can tap on **Review Sharing**, to go over each individual person or type of information.

If no one is selected you can also tap on the **Skip** button to continue allowing the same people to have access to the information. Alternatively, you can also tap on the **Select All & Stop Sharing** link to select everyone and stop sharing the information with them.

Reviewing an Individual

If you did select at least one individual a screen will be shown for each individual person. On this screen will be a list of information that you are sharing with them. Here you can tap on each individual item to indicate you want to remove their access. You can also Skip that person. The option Select All & Stop Sharing is also present. This will, as the name indicates, select everything and stop sharing. It should be noted that if you tap on this it will only apply to that individual.

Once you have reviewed the person, any additional individuals will be presented until everyone has been reviewed. After everyone that you selected has been reviewed, you will see a Step 1 Complete screen.

If you have opted to stop sharing with an individual, they will not be notified in anyway, but that does not mean that they will not notice that they no longer have access to the items that you stopped sharing with them. The next step is Review Apps, so let us look at that next.

Reviewing Apps

Reviewing Apps is similar to that of reviewing people. The information is also similarly shown as to Reviewing People. Instead of seeing individual people, you will see a list of apps. If you opt to review access organized by app you will see each individual app with its icon. Under the name of each app is the items that they have access. A couple of examples of what you might see are:

- CARROT: Location, Microphone, and 1 more
- discovery+ – Bluetooth
- Shazam: Microphone and Media Library

These are just a few examples of what you might see. Next to each app is an information icon. If you tap on this the complete list of items that the particular app has access to. Here you can tap on an item, or items, that the app should no longer have access to.

Of course, the list of apps and what permissions each has will be different for each iPhone. If you choose to organize the view by Information each access type will be shown with a list of apps directly underneath the name. A few examples of what you might see are:

- Location - CARROT, Dark Sky, and 4 more
- Microphone - CARROT, Shazam, and 1 more
- Camera - CARROT, Tweetbot, and 10 more

Each system service will have an Information icon next to it as well. If you tap on one of these you can see the full list of apps that have access to that particular system service. You can select one or more of the apps, and then remove access by tapping on the **Stop App Access** button, and the app's access to the indicated service, or services, will be removed.

Once you have reviewed all of the items that you need to, tap on the **Continue** button. This will bring you to the next step Account Security, so let us look at that next.

Safety Check - App access

Account Security

The Account Security section will allow you to remove devices from your account. The list of devices should be all of the devices that have access to your iCloud account. The types of devices could be iPhones, iPads, iPod touches, HomePods, Apple TVs, Macs, or even Smart TVs with the Apple TV app.

Next to each device is the Information button, which will show you some additional information about the device. The type of information should include:

- Model
- Operating System Version
- Serial Number
- Phone Number (Only on iPhones, iPad with Cellular, and Apple Watch with Cellular)
- IMEI (Only on iPhones, iPad with Cellular, and Apple Watch with Cellular)

Within the list, you can select any, or all, of the devices, to indicate that you wish to remove them from your account. It should be noted that you cannot remove the iPhone that you are using. You can also Skip removing devices by tapping on the **Skip** button at the bottom of the screen. After you have selected the device, or skipped, the next item is Update Apple ID Password.

Update Apple ID Password

Here you can have the option of updating the password for your Apple ID account. There are only two options, Update Password or Update Later in Settings. If you opt for the Update Password option, you will be presented with the Apple ID update password screen.

After you have updated your Apple ID password, or if you select the Update Later in Settings, you will proceed to the next step, Emergency Contacts.

Emergency Contacts

The Emergency Contact screen will allow you to manage who is listed as someone to contact in case of an emergency. When the screen appears, if you have any emergency contacts, they will be listed with a red "remove" icon. You can tap on any one of them to remove the person as an emergency contact.

Alternatively, you can add someone by tapping the **Add Emergency Contact** button. When you do this, a list of your contacts will appear. Only those with a phone number will be selectable. Locate the person you want to add as an emergency contact, and tap on their contact card. Once this loads, tap on the specific phone number to use as the emergency contact number. You can then also indicate the relationship you have with the person.

Once you have finished adding and removing emergency contacts, tap on the **Continue** button. The next screen to appear is the Update Device Passcode screen.

Update Device Passcode

The Update Device Passcode screen will allow you to update the device's passcode. The steps of this are:

1. Enter in your current passcode.

2. Enter a new passcode.
3. Confirm your new passcode.

During step 1, the enter a new passcode screen, you do have the option of changing the type of passcode used. This is done by tapping on the **Passcode Options** item below the passcode field. If you are using a numeric only passcode, it may be beneficial to change to an alphanumeric passcode. An alpha numeric passcode is harder to guess than a standard four or six digit passcode.

You also have the option of skipping the Update Device Passcode by tapping on the **Skip** button on the Enter in your current passcode screen. After you have updated your device's passcode, or skipped updating it, you will come to the completion screen. This screen will provide you with suggestions for additional items for you to secure. The list of items includes:

- Accounts & Passwords
- Social Media
- Other Devices
- Location Tracking
- Cellular Plan
- Family Sharing

This screen does not provide any links to other devices, but does provide a short explanation below each item. It would be good to note which ones of these you might want to look at and update the information accordingly.

Closing Thoughts on Manage Sharing & Access

It is a good idea to periodically use the Manage Sharing & Access feature to easily look over which individuals, apps, and devices have access to your data, your device's system services, and your iCloud account. Let us now look at the second item available in Safety Check, Emergency Reset.

Emergency Reset

It would be naive to think that everyone is good hearted. If you have been around for even a little while it is clear to see that this is not the case. There may be instances when you are in a domestic situation where your movements, actions, and other information might be monitored.

Today's modern technology can provide ways of being able to keep tabs on people. This may be via phone call, text message, or even social media. However, these are not the only ways. Some people will end up using tools for nefarious purposes. These tools may be ones that were meant for one purpose, but ended up being used for another. An example of this might be Apple's AirTags.

An AirTag is a physical device that utilizes Apple's Find My network to be able to locate items. AirTags are designed to allow you to track items, like bikes, bags, luggage, keys, wallets, and other items. AirTags were not intended to track individuals, yet some people have used them for such. Apple has provided mitigations for this and have also provided ways of notifying people if an unknown AirTag has been with them for an extended period of time.

If you are in a situation where you might be in danger from a person that has had access to your location information via sharing, you can use Emergency Reset to quickly revoke that access.

Emergency Reset is accessed on your iOS device by:

1. Opening **Settings**.
2. **Scroll** down to Privacy & Security.
3. Tap on **Privacy & Security**.
4. **Scroll** down to Safety Check.
5. Tap on **Safety Check**.
6. Tap on **Emergency Reset**.

Emergency Reset is a way of being able to immediately remove all access to a variety of items. This list includes:

- Access for people
- Access for apps
- Emergency Contacts

When you open the Emergency Reset screen you will be need to authenticate with either Face ID, Touch ID, or your iPhone passcode. After authentication, an information screen will appear to provide you with information with what will happen.

There are three steps to the process. These include:

1. Resetting Access to People & Apps
2. Reviewing Account Security
3. Emergency Contact Management

Resetting Access to People & Apps

When you tap on the **Continue** button, you will be brought to the Reset People & Apps screen. This screen will have a single button **Reset People & Apps**. If you tap on this a popup will appear. This popup will have a message that states:

"By continuing, all sharing and access will be reset. Anything you're currently sharing will no longer be shared, and apps will no longer have access to your information. If you don't want to reset all, you can manage sharing and access for specific people and apps."

The alert will have two options, Reset and Manage Sharing & Access. Tapping on **Reset** will remove access from anyone who you sharing with, as well as removing any app's access to your information. There are some other actions that are taken including:

1. Signing you out of iCloud on all other devices.
2. Restricting Messages and FaceTime to the device in your hand.

Note: It should be noted that there is no granularity with this step. It is an **all or nothing** step. Either you remove all sharing from everyone as well as remove system access to all apps, or you do not. There is no middle ground with this. Be sure you want to remove access before tapping on the **Reset** option.

If you do tap on **Reset**, the process of removing shared access from everyone as well as removing all system service access from apps will begin. This process may take a little bit of time. For instance, if you are sharing a lot of notes, each person's access to each note will need to be removed. The same applies to other shared items like Find My, Shared photo albums, or any other shared iCloud information.

When you perform this reset, each app that previously had access to Location, Photos, Camera, Bluetooth, Media & Apple Music, and Files and Folders will all be removed. This means that you will need to provide permissions again in order for any apps to be able to access this information.

After this has completed, a confirmation screen will appear   confirming that people and apps have had their access removed. The next step is Account Security.

Account Security

The Account Security screen is similar to that of the Manage Sharing & Access flow, in that you are shown a list of devices that are currently connected to your Apple ID. The types of devices could be iPhones, iPads, iPod touches, HomePods, Apple TVs, Macs, or even Smart TVs with the Apple TV app.

Next to each device is the Information button, which will show you some additional information about the device. The type of information should include:

- Model
- Operating System Version
- Serial Number
- Phone Number (Only on iPhones, iPad with Cellular, and Apple Watch with Cellular)
- IMEI (Only on iPhones, iPad with Cellular, and Apple Watch with Cellular)

Within the list, you can select any, or all, of the devices, to indicate that you wish to remove them from your account. It should be noted that you cannot remove the iPhone that you are using. You can also Skip removing devices by tapping on the **Skip** button at the bottom of the screen. After you have selected, or skipped the devices the next item is Trusted Numbers.

Trusted Numbers

The Trusted Numbers screen is where you can review who is allowed to receive verification codes on your behalf. These verification codes are for when you sign into an Apple Service. If you have two factor authentication enabled, a notification is sent directly to your devices. If you are not able to authenticate with a device, a text message notification could be sent to another cell phone. This is the Trusted Numbers list.

On this screen a list of existing phone numbers that you have trusted in the past will be shown. You have the ability to remove any number on the screen. You can also add a trusted phone number. If you need to add a trusted phone number here are the steps:

1. Tap on the **Add Trusted Phone Number** item.
2. Enter your **iPhone's passcode**.
3. Enter the **phone number** that you wish to add.

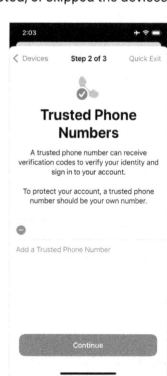

Trusted Phone Numbers in Safety Check

4. Select the type of **verification method**. The default is text message, but a phone call is also an option.
5. Tap on the **Send** button. A verification code will be sent to the new phone number. If you selected Phone Call, a phone call with the verification code will be made to the phone number.
6. When the message is sent, or a phone call is made, a popup will appear. **Enter** in the verification code provided. If verified, the phone number will be added as a trusted number.

After you have removed or added a trusted phone number tap on the **Continue** button to continue to the Update Apple ID Password page.

Update Apple ID Password

Here you can have the option of updating the password for your Apple ID account. There are only two options, Update Password or Update Later in Settings. If you opt for the Update Password option, you will be presented with the Apple ID update password screen.

After you have updated your Apple ID password, or if you select the Update Later in Settings, you will proceed to the next step, Emergency Contacts.

Emergency Contacts

The Emergency Contact screen will allow you to manage your Emergency Contacts. When the screen appears, if you have any emergency contacts, they will be listed with a Red Remove icon. You can tap on any one of them to remove the person as an emergency contact.

Alternatively, you can add someone using the Add Emergency Contact button. When you do this, a list of your contacts will appear. Only those with a phone number will be selectable. Locate the user you want to add as an emergency contact, and tap on their contact card. Once this loads, tap on the phone number to use as the emergency contact number. You can then also indicate the relationship you have with the person.

Once you have finished adding and removing emergency contacts tap on the **Continue** button, the Safety Check is now complete.

Safety Check Complete

When the Safety Check Complete screen is shown it will provide you with suggestions for additional items for you to secure. The list of items includes:

- Accounts & Passwords
- Social Media
- Other Devices
- Location Tracking
- Cellular Plan
- Family Sharing

This screen does not provide any links to other devices, but does provide a short explanation below each item. It would be good to note which ones of these you might want to look at and update the information accordingly.

Closing Thoughts on Safety Check

Safety Check is a new feature which has two parts that are similar, yet used in two distinctly different situations. The Manage Sharing & Access is the option to use to see who you are sharing information with and what devices have access to your Apple ID. It is a good idea to run this one periodically. This will provide you with an easy single place to be able to adjust permissions, including fine grain control over each step of the process. Even if you do not change anything, just having a single place to get an overall view is helpful.

The Emergency Reset option was developed with the intention of helping those who need to quickly revoke access to any information that they are sharing. Along with removing access to any of their shared information, all application permissions are reset on the device as well. This is an **all or nothing** reset. There are no fine grain options with this approach. It is everyone's hope that they never need to use this feature, but it does exist and can be used if needed.

Apple worked with a few nongovernmental organizations on the development of the features of Safety Check. The list of entities includes, the National Network to End Domestic Violence, the National Center for Victims of Crime, and the Women's Services Network. Next, let us look at some improvements with photos and video.

Photo and Video Improvements

We are quickly approaching the 200th anniversary of the world having photography, at least in terms of having evidence for such a picture. It is possible that there were pictures before then, but there is no evidence of such. The oldest surviving picture we have is called "**View from the Window at Le Gras**" and was captured by French inventor Nicéphore Niépce in either 1826 or 1827. As you might have guessed, technology has progressed leaps and bounds in the nearly 200 years since that first photo was taken.

Humanity has seen some milestones over those 200 years. Some of the milestones have included flash photography, color photography, handheld cameras, disposable cameras, instant photos, and even digital cameras. Prior to digital cameras being affordable, many people took their physical photos and scanned them to make them digital so they could either store them digitally or share them with others.

Digital cameras have made the process of taking photos significantly easier by allowing us to take multiple pictures and discarding the ones that do not make the cut. Digital Cameras made their debut almost 30 years ago, with the Apple Quick Take 100 and Kodak DC40. Prior to Digital cameras becoming feasible all photos were taken using film. Film was not super expensive to purchase nor was it that expensive to have developed, but there was a cost associated with it. Because of this cost, many limited the number of photos that they took to make sure that they got a good photo. Even with attempting to get a good photo, there were often blurry photos.

Throughout the 1990s and early 2000s Digital Cameras took off in popularity and became more commonplace and significantly easier to use. Beyond this, their quality became better. This ease of use combined with density of storage that can be fit into a small area has lead us to almost limitless possibilities.

If you look at the capabilities of the first-generation iPhone as compared to the iPhone 13 Pro Max, you would easily be able to tell that they were different devices from the outside, but they are still very similar in a broad sense. Both have a power button, volume buttons, power connection, and cameras. However, the processing abilities and capabilities of the iPhone 13 Pro Max are magnitudes better and faster than the original iPhone. In order to take those pictures on our devices, we need an app. Apple has one intuitively called Camera. The Camera app has seen some improvements with iOS 16 and iPadOS 16. Let us look at those changes.

Camera

The Camera app is the app that a majority of iOS users use to take pictures while using their iPhones. The Camera system on the iPhone is comprised of a couple of different things. The first is the physical hardware of the device. This has been improved on the physical devices every year since the original iPhone launch in 2007.

The second aspect to the Camera system on Apple's devices is the software. The software has seen significant improvements over the last 15 years. Over the past few years the Camera has gained the ability to take portrait images, Face ID, Photographic styles, and the ability to adjust the focus and exposure, just to name a few of the features that has been added to the system.

There are a couple of new additions for iOS 16 that might make your photos even better. These are changes for portrait photos and cinematic mode changes. Let us look at both, starting with Portrait Photos.

Portrait Photos

Portrait Photos are photos that allow the subject of the photo to be in focus while the background might have a blur applied to it. A Portrait photo is actually a photo that is comprised of a variety of layers and these layers are combined to create the portrait effect. Typically these photos have objects in the front in focus and the background is blurred. However, this is not always the way that you want a photo to appear. Sometimes there might be an object in the front of the photo that you would prefer to have blurred, because it is not the primary subject of the photo. Previously, this has not been possible to accomplish, at least not without some post-processing with third-party software.

Starting with iOS 16 and iPadOS 16 it will now be possible to have foreground blur in Portrait Photos. This is a good enhancement that will allow you to create even more realistic Portrait photos where the primary subject may be further back and not in the front of the photo. It is likely that this will be used in some creative and innovative ways. This feature is limited to only certain devices. This feature is currently available on the iPhone 13, iPhone 13 Pro, and iPhone 13 Pro Max. It is not available on any older models, nor is it possible to use on the iPhone 13 mini. Let us now look at Cinematic Mode.

Cinematic Mode

When you watch a movie you might notice some techniques that are not generally possible on smaller cameras. This is typically due to the fact that the larger cameras have more functionality available to them. It is entirely possible to create a movie using just a few iPhones. You might not expect the quality of the video to be up to par with the larger cameras. However, it can be just as good, if not better in some instances.

There is one technique that larger cameras have had for a long time that has only recently come to iPhones. That feature is called **Cinematic Mode**. Cinematic Mode is the technique of switching between people, or objects, within a frame with a very smooth transition from one person, or object, to another. When this is done the effect can add to overall professional look and touch.

With iOS 15, the ability to record Cinematic video came to the iPhone 13 mini, iPhone 13, iPhone 13 Pro, and iPhone 13 Pro Max. You could use other devices to edit the video, but only the iPhone 13 line is capable of recording the video.

The initial release of the technique was pretty good, but there were definitely some issues that people noticed. With iOS 16 there has been some improvement to Cinematic mode, specifically the depth of field effect is more accurate for profile angles, as well as around the edges of hair and glasses. This may sound small, but being able to provide accurate representation around hair and glasses only brings the iPhone closer to the level of the larger cameras.

Having a camera in our pockets, and with us at most points throughout the day, allows us to take photos no matter where we are. Take this and the significant increase in storage means that we can virtually take an unlimited number of photos. Having the ability to take a lot of pictures does not do any good if we do not have a way or being able to go through and organize all of the photos that we have taken. Apple has an app designed for that purpose. That app is named Photos.

Photos app

The history of the Photos app goes beyond its introduction in April of 2015 with an update to Mac OS X 10.10 Yosemite. In fact iPhoto was originally introduced in January of 2002, making it 20 years old now. Photos was a reimagining of how to manage photos and was a complete rewrite. While many complained about the limitations at the time of its introduction, the redesign and reworked Photos app has become the platform that Apple chose going forward.

Since 2015 Photos has gained a slew of features, including the ability to add photos as a favorite, additional Raw file support, and iCloud Photo Library. There are a couple of new features to Photos, Family Share Photo Albums, and Locking of certain photos. Let us look at both, starting with Family Shared Photo Albums.

Shared Photo Albums

Photos do not necessarily live in silos. While it is true that some photos are likely ones that we want to keep for ourselves, we often want to share photos with others. We can, of course, share photos on social media, but we do not often want to share all of our photos there. Apple does have a solution for sharing photos called Shared Albums.

Shared Albums are a way of being able to share individual photos with a single person or a small group of people. A Shared Album requires manually adding and removing photos. Shared Albums work well in many cases, but a shared album is not the same as having a shared library.

A shared photo library would be and act just like a standard library, except you would be able to share it with others. The group of people that you would most likely want to share a library with is your immediate family. When Apple introduced iOS 8 in 2014 they also introduced a new feature called iCloud Family Sharing.

iCloud Family Sharing allows you to create a family group of up to 6 people in iCloud. Once you have done this you can share things like iCloud storage, Apple One subscriptions, media purchases, and more. One thing that you couldn't do was have a shared library. Instead, what many have had to do is designate one person's photo library as the "family" photo library. This is the approach that most would take once imported, then they could be shared with others via an album or via some other means.

This approach would require everyone in the family to make sure that a number of the photos would be imported into the "family" photo library. It is almost certain that many photos have not been imported into these type of libraries, resulting in some photos never being shared when they could have been.

When Apple introduced Photos in 2015 and it did not include a Shared iCloud Family Album many figured that Apple had to limit features. At the time many thought that Apple would introduce a Shared Library within a few years. Unfortunately, for them, they did not. However, with iOS 16, iPadOS 16, and macOS Ventura, Apple is finally introducing an iCloud Shared Photo Library.

iCloud Shared Photo Library

An iCloud Shared Photo Library is very similar to that of a standard library, except it is separate library that is shared with family, along as they are part of the Shared Family group configured in iCloud.

Everyone in the iCloud Shared Photo Library has the same permissions. This means that they can all add photos, delete photos, favorite, delete, caption, or even apply filters and other edits. Once you are ready to add an iCloud Shared Photo Library you need to perform the setup, so let us look at how to do that.

Setting up an iCloud Shared Photo Library

The way that you setup an iCloud Shared Photo Library differs between iOS/iPadOS and macOS. Here is how to setup an iCloud Shared Photo Library on each platform:

macOS

To create an iCloud Shared Photo Library on macOS, use these steps:

1. Open **Photos**.
2. Click on the **Photos** menu item.
3. Click on **Settings** to bring up the settings for Photos.
4. Click on the **Shared Library** icon in the toolbar.
5. Click on **Start Setup** to begin the setup of the Shared Library. An Add Participants popup will appear.
6. On the **Add Participants** page, you can add participants or you can perform this later by tapping on Add Later. Once you have added any participants tap on the **Continue** button. The Move Photos page will appear.
7. On the **Move Photos** page you have a few options. All My Photos and Videos, Chose by People or Date, and Choose Manually. You can also click on the Move Photos Later option to decide on which photos to manage later. The Share from Camera will appear.
8. If you did not add any participants previously the Invite Participants screen will appear. Here you can add people to invite or you can copy the link to send via other means, like email.

If you do opt to copy the link, it will complete the setup of the shared Library.

iOS

To create an iCloud Shared Photo Library on iOS, use these steps:

1. Open **Settings**.
2. Scroll down **Photos**.
3. Locate **Shared Library**.
4. Tap on **Shared Library** a sheet will appear.
5. Tap on **Start Setup**. The Add Participant screen will appear.
6. On the **Add Participants** page, you can add participants or you can perform this later by tapping on "Add Later". Once you have added any participants, tap on the **Continue** button. The Move Photos page will appear.
7. On the **Move Photos** page, you have a few options. All My Photos and Videos, Chose by People or Date, and Choose Manually. You can also tap on the Move Photos Later option to decide on which photos to manage later. The Share from Camera will appear.
8. On the **Share from Camera** screen, you can either Share Automatically or Share Manually. You can adjust this later.

Those are all of the steps needed to create an iCloud Share Photos Library. There is a bit more information to cover, which we will do in a bit. But first there are a few things to mention regarding the Shared iCloud Photo Library.

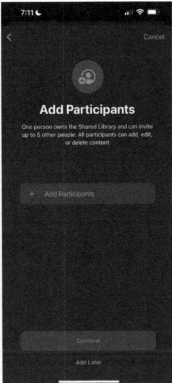

| Setup Shared Library | Shared Library - Get Started | Add Participants to Shared Library | Shared Library Camera Sharing Options |

The first thing is that the person who creates the Shared Library will be the one whose iCloud storage will be used for the library. The second thing to keep in mind is that only up to 5 additional people can be invited. These individuals do not need to be part of an iCloud Shared Family. The next thing to note is that you can only participate in one Shared Library at a time. The fourth item to keep in mind is that you have to be using the system's photo library and that library must have iCloud enabled for you, or a participant, to be added to a Shared Library.

Joining a Shared Library

If you are sent an invitation to a Shared Library you will need to act on that invitation in order to join. The steps to join on iOS, iPadOS, and macOS are similar. Let us look at both.

On iOS and iPadOS

1. Tap on the Shared Library **invitation** that was sent to you. A Shared Invitation popup will appear.
2. The person who is asking you to share will be shown on the screen. Tap on **Get Started** to begin joining the Shared Library. The Move Photos to Shared Library screen will appear.
3. On the Move Photos to Shared Library you have a few options. All My Photos and Videos, Chose by People or Date, and Choose Manually. You can also tap on the Move Photos Later option to decide on which photos to manage later. The Ready to Join screen will appear.
4. On the Ready to Join screen tap on **Join Shared Library**. This will join you to the Shared Library. The Share from Camera will appear.

5. On the **Share from Camera** screen, you can either Share Automatically or Share Manually. You can adjust this later in settings. When you select the appropriate option the Your Shared Library is Ready screen will appear.
6. The Your Shared Library is Ready screen is an informational one, tap the **Done** button to finish the setup.

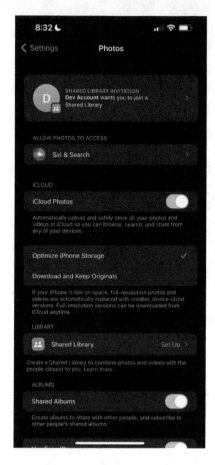

Shared Library invitation in Photo Settings

Shared Invitation detailed information

On macOS.

1. Click on the Shared Library **invitation** that was sent to you. A Shared Invitation popup will appear.
2. The person who is asking you to share will be shown on the screen. Click on **Get Started** to begin joining the Shared Library. The Move Photos to Shared Library screen will appear.
3. On the Move Photos to Shared Library you have a few options. All My Photos and Videos, Chose by People or Date, and Choose Manually. You can also click on the Move Photos Later option to decide on which photos to manage later. The Ready to Join screen will appear.
4. On the Ready to Join screen tap on **Join Shared Library**. This will join you to the Shared Library.

At this point you have joined the Shared Library and if you opted to have any of your photos moved, they will be moved from your personal library to the Shared Library. It cannot b emphasized enough, but this step is **MOVING** the photos, not copying them, but actually removing them from your personal Photo Library and moving them to the Shared Photo Library.

Switching Library Views

Once you have joined a Shared Library, the default view is to show everything from both your Personal Photos Library and the Shared Library that you joined. You can easily switch between both. On iOS this is done by tapping on the "**...**" Button in the upper right corner and then tapping on the appropriate library. On macOS, this dropdown is shown in the menu bar. So you can click on the dropdown and then select the appropriate library.

Shared Library Photo Options

There are a number of options that you can set for a Shared Library. These options can all be accessed on iOS and iPad OS by going to

1. Open **Settings**.
2. **Scroll down** to Photos.
3. **Tap** on Photos
4. Tap on **Shared Library**

On macOS use these steps;

1. Open **Photos**.
2. Click on the **Photos** menu item
3. Click on **Settings** to bring up the Photos settings.

Once you have joined a Shared Photo Library you will then be able to add photos. As mentioned earlier there are two different sharing options. These are Share Automatically, or Share Manually.

The Share Automatically option will automatically add any photos that you take to the Shared Library when your phone detects that you are sharing with other participants.

Meanwhile, the Share Manually option allows you to control which photos are added to the Shared Library.

There is another option called "Share When At Home", that is enabled by default. If you enable this in the Photo Settings on your iPhone or iPad, all of the photos and videos that you take while at Home will be sent to the Shared Library, whether there are other participants there or not.

There is one last option called "Delete Notifications". When this is enabled any photos or videos that you have added are deleted by someone, other than yourself, you will receive a notification.

Adding to a Shared Library

As mentioned above there are two ways of sharing, either Automatically or Manually. When done automatically the photos will be added to the Shared Library as needed. For manually, you have the option of adding them yourself.

In the Camera

Regardless of which option you have enabled in the Photos Settings, you can manually decide whether or not to add a photo to the Shared Library. This is done by enabling or disabling the Shared Library icon. This is in the upper left corner and is a picture of two people together.

In Photos

If you are in Photos you can also manually move items to and from the Shared Library. To do this perform these steps:

1. Open **Photos**.
2. **Locate the photo** you want to move.
3. **Tap and hold** or right-mouse click on the photo.
4. Click on **Move to Personal Library** or **Move to Shared Library,** depending on the photo's current location.

Once you have selected the appropriate option, the photo will be moved. Not everyone can move photos. Only the person who uploaded a photo or video can move it between the Shared Library and their own Personal Library. This makes sense because the person who took the photo or video is the actual owner of the file. Next, let us look at how to leave a Shared Library.

Leaving a Shared Library

The owner of the Shared Library does not necessarily need to be the one to manage participants, they can voluntarily leave a Shared Library. You can leave a Shared Library by using the following steps:

On iOS and iPadOS

1. Open **Settings**.
2. Scroll down to **Photos**.
3. Locate **Shared Library**.
4. Tap on **Shared Library** the Shared Library settings will appear.
5. Tap on **Leave Shared Library** a sheet will appear.
6. On the Leave Shared Library popup select either **Keep Everything** to keep a copy of everything or **Keep Only What I Contributed** to keep just what you contributed.
7. Tap on the **Leave Shared Library** button. Another popup will appear.
8. Tap on **Leave Shared Library** to confirm that you want to leave the Shared Library.

Let us now look at how to do this on macOS.

On macOS

1. Open **Photos**.
2. Click on the **Photos** menu item.
3. Click on **Settings**.
4. Click on **Shared Library** the Leave Shared Library popup will appear.
5. On the Leave Shared Library popup, select either **Keep Everything** to keep a copy of everything or **Keep Only What I Contributed** to keep just what you contributed.
6. Click on the **Leave Shared Library** button. Another popup will appear.
7. Click on **Leave Shared Library** to confirm that you want to leave the Shared Library.

One you have confirmed that you want to leave the Shared Library, depending on your selection of Keep Everything or Keep Only What I Contributed, that data will be copied into your personal iCloud Photo Library. The amount of time that this takes will depend on the amount of data for the selection. You will need to wait until this process is finished before you can join or create, another Shared iCloud Photo Library. Next, let us look at how the Shared Library owner can manage participants.

Participant Management

If you have created a Shared Photo Library with your immediate family it may be possible that you might want to add or remove someone from the shared library. The reasons for this could be anything from the start of a relationship to the ending of one, to someone wanting to go and create their own Shared Library. Let us look at how to add and remove participants.

Adding Participants

You can add a participant by using the following steps:

On iOS and iPadOS

1. Open **Settings**.
2. Scroll down **Photos**.
3. Locate **Shared Library**
4. Tap on **Shared Library** the Shared Library settings will appear.
5. Tap on the **Add Participants** item at the bottom of the participants list.
6. Enter a name, email address, or phone number of the person you want to invite to the Shared Library.
7. Tap on the **Add** button.

Shared Library Invitation within Photos on macOS

At this point an iMessage to the individual will be shown. You can add a comment and then send the invitation.

On macOS

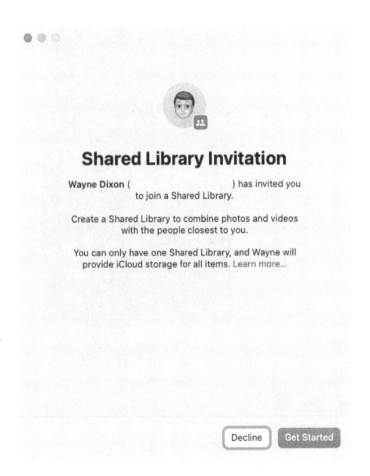

1. Open **Photos**.
2. Click on the **Photos** menu item.
3. Click on **Settings** to open the Photos Settings.
4. Click on **Shared Library** the Shared Library info will be shown.
5. Click on the **Add Participant** button. A popup will appear.
6. Enter a name, email address, or phone number of the person you want to invite to the Shared Library.
7. Click on the **Add** button. The participant will be added and a popup with the invitation will be populated.

You can send the message to the participant or you can just send them a link via email or by other means. Let us move onto removing participants.

Shared Library invitation on macOS

Removing Participants

There may be times when you want to remove a participant from a Shared Library. You can do that by following these steps:

On iOS and iPadOS

1. Open **Settings**.
2. Scroll down **Photos**.
3. Locate **Shared Library.**
4. Tap on **Shared Library** the Shared Library settings will appear.
5. Tap on the **Participant** that you want to remove.
6. Tap on the **Remove [Name of Person] from Shared Library**. A popup will appear.
7. Tap on the **Remove [Name of Person]** to confirm you want to remove them.

At this point an iMessage to the individual will be shown. You can add a comment and then send the invitation.

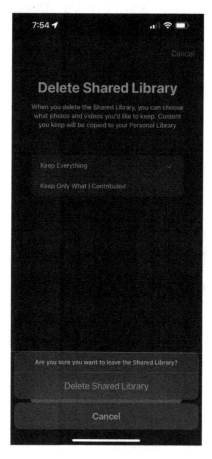

Delete Shared Library
Confirmation on iOS

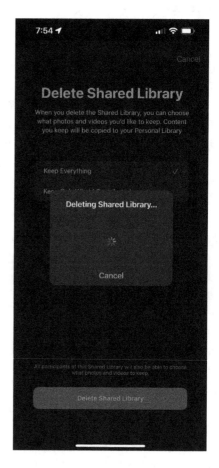

Deleting Shared Library Popup
on iOS

On macOS

1. Open **Photos**.
2. Click on the **Photos** menu item.
3. Click on **Settings**.

4. Click on **Shared Library** the Shared Library popup will appear.
5. **Locate the participant** that you want to remove.
6. **Hover** over the participant.
7. Click on the "**...**" button that appears.
8. Click on **Remove** a popup will appear.
9. Click on **Remove [Name of Person]** to confirm you want to remove them.

Once you have confirmed that you want to remove a participant, on either iOS or macOS, all of the Shared Library items will be copied over to their personal libraries and they will be removed from the library.

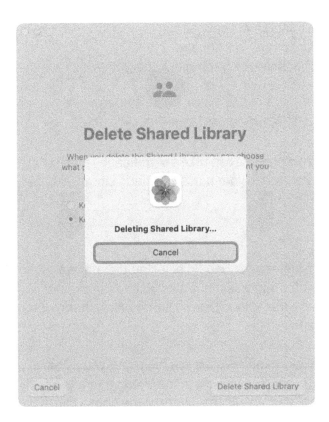

Shared Photo Library being deleted on macOS

Shared Photo Library being deleted on macOS

Deleting a Shared Library

There may come a time when you want to delete a shared library. The reason as to why can vary. To delete a Shared Library perform the following steps:

On iOS and iPadOS

1. Open **Settings**.
2. Scroll down to **Photos**.
3. Locate **Shared Library**.
4. Tap on **Shared Library** to open the Shared Library Settings.
5. Tap on **Delete Library** a popup will appear.
6. On the **Delete Library** popup you will have two options, either Keep Everything or Keep Only What I Contributed. Either option will move the subset of items into your own Photos Library.

7. Tap on the **Delete Shared Library** button a popup will appear.
8. Tap on the **Delete Library** option to confirm you want to delete the Shared Library.

On macOS

The process for deleting a shared library on macOS is similar to that of iOS and iPadOS. To delete a Shared Library perform the following steps:

1. Open **Photos**.
2. Click on the **Photos** menu item.
3. Click on **Settings**.
4. Click on **Shared Library** in the menu bar. The Shared Library screen will appear.
5. Click on the **Delete Library** button. The Delete Shared Library popup will appear.
6. On the **Delete Library** popup you will have two options, either Keep Everything or Keep Only What I Contributed. Either option will move the subset of items into your own Photos Library.
7. Click on the **Delete Library** button a popup will appear.
8. Click on the **Delete Library** option to confirm you want to delete the Shared Library.

There is one thing bear in mind when deleting a Shared Library. This process can take a significantly long time. It appears as though any changes that might not have been synchronized to your personal iCloud Library may be delaying the final deletion of a Shared Library.

Closing Thoughts on iCloud Shared Library

If someone were to say that Apple FINALLY added a Shared Photo Library, they would be using that phrase appropriately. It has been nearly 8 years since the redesigned Photos app was made available to the general public and in all of that time there has not been the ability to have a true iCloud Shared Library. Now there is finally that ability.

The ability to not only manually add photos, but have it automatically handled is a great feature. If you do have Shared Automatically enabled, photos and videos you take while other participants in the Shared Library are around will be added for you. Even if something is automatically added you, as the owner of the photo, can move the photo to your personal library. Others can share it and even delete it, but they cannot move it to their library.

You can also manually move items from your library to the Shared Library and you can even opt to add Photos or Videos in the Camera app. Therefore, if you want to share a photo to the Shared Library it can be done quickly and easily and you are in control of when it gets shared and when it does not.

Everyone who is part of the library can add, delete, edit, or tag images and videos. It is good to see Apple adding the ability to have a Shared Library. In order to use the Shared Library you have to be using the default Photos Library and you have to have iCloud Photos enabled for that library, otherwise the system will not work.There is another item to cover related to Photos, and that is Hidden and Deleted photos.

Hidden and Deleted Photos

The way that we organize our photos varies from person to person. In the organization of our libraries we may decide that we may want to remove some photos from our library. There are two ways of removing photos from one's library. One way is to hide them. Hiding a photo removes it from the main list of photos, but it remains in the actual library, and it is just hidden from view. Another way to remove a photo is to delete it. When you delete a photo it goes into a Deleted folder to allow you to recover them for up to 30 days.

The reasons as to why we might want to hide, or delete, a photo can vary. You may choose to hide a photo because it might be from a time in your life that you may not want to be reminded of, but you cannot bring yourself to actually delete the photo. The photo could be a photo of a loved one, which is currently too painful to see, but you may hope to return them to your main photo album at a later time.

You may choose to delete a photo because it contains personal sensitive information, such a social security number, and you needed to capture it for a time. A common type of photo that we may want to either hide to keep for later, or to delete because we only wanted it temporarily may be, shall we say, a bit more risqué in nature.

Regardless of why you want to hide, or delete a photo, the fact that you want to remove it from your main photo library should infer some sort of privacy. But that has not been the case, until now.

Starting with iOS 16, iPadOS 16, and macOS Ventura both hidden and deleted photo albums will require either biometric or passcode authentication in order to view. This is enabled automatically for you. For those devices that do not have Biometric authentication, you will need to enter in your password in order to unlock these albums. You can disable this requirement if you so choose.

Disable Requiring Biometrics or Password.

By default, iOS 16, iPadOS 16, and macOS Ventura will require you to either use Biometrics or a passcode to unlock the Hidden and Recently Deleted albums within Photos. However, you may not want this behavior. If you do not want this behavior you can disable it by using the following steps:

On iOS and iPadOS

1. Open the **Settings** app.
2. Scroll down to **Photos**. Alternatively you can also search for Photos.
3. Tap on **Photos** to bring up the settings.
4. **Locate** the option Use Face ID or Use Touch ID.
5. Tap on the **toggle** next to Use Face ID or Use Touch ID.

On macOS

1. Open **Photos**.
2. Click on the **Photos** menu item.
3. Click on **Settings**.
4. At the bottom of the screen locate the **Privacy** setting.
5. **Uncheck the checkbox** next to Use Password.

Once you have disabled the toggle or unchecked the checkbox, you will no longer need to use biometrics or a password to view the Hidden or Recently Deleted albums.

Overall, this is a great addition for privacy when it comes to photos, some of which might be sensitive in nature.There is another new feature, extracting objects from images.

Extracting Subjects from Images

Apple has been making a concerted effort to use machine learning to identify more and more objects in photos. For instance, one of the new features of iOS 16 and iPadOS 16 is door detection when using magnifier for those who may need to know where doorways are because they may have an visual impairment .

In iOS 15 Apple introduced a new feature of being able to identify various items like species of dogs, types of trees, and types of flowers. All of this object detection has resulted in a new feature, the ability to extract objects, and people, from photos.

There are a couple of different ways of extracting subjects of photos. The first is from within Photos. To extract a subject from a photo perform the following steps:

1. Open **Photos**.
2. **Locate** the photo with the subject you want to extract.
3. **Tap and hold** on the photo. The subject should be highlighted and extracted.
4. Continue **holding and drag** the extracted subject to the destination, like messages, or a note.

This approach can be a bit difficult to do when on an iPhone. On an iPad or a Mac, this process should be pretty easy to accomplish. However, it may be easier to extract the subject while looking at a photo on the internet.

Extract Subject using Copy   Extract Subject using Tap and Hold

When you are browsing the web you are likely to come across a photo of someone, or something while browsing the web you can more easily extract the subject. To do this perform the following steps:

1. **Locate** the photo in which you want to extract the subject from.
2. **Tap and hold** or right mouse click, on the image.
3. Tap or click on **Copy Subject**.

It is just that simple. After the subject is copied, you can paste it where you need to. This might be in preview, an email, in messages, or any other place where you can put an image. When you are tapping and holding on an image, it is possible that even though you can easily identify a subject, the algorithms may not be able to do so. Therefore, not all photos will be able to extract a subject. Beyond this, there are a few other things to keep in mind when trying to use this feature.

The first is to keep in mind it has to be an image file for the Copy Subject action to show within Safari. If it is not an image, say it is a picture that is the background of an image, it may not detect the subject properly, and you will not see the Copy Subject option.

The second item to be aware of is that the extraction of the subject may not be 100% precise. In some cases it works really well, in others certain subjects may either be fuzzy around the edges, or in the case of a couple of tests that were performed for this book, the subject is missing parts. One test that was performed was a picture of a dog. A vast majority of the dog was detected without a problem, except the dog's tail was not extracted. To be fair, in one of the photos the tail was entirely obscured because the dog was lying in the grass.

The third thing to bear in mind is that this is not limited to just people and dogs. In one test Photos on iOS was able to extract a part of a building. In another test, an Apple Watch on its side was detected as the subject.

The last thing to keep in mind is that subject extraction cannot complete the subject. What this means is that it will only be able to extract what it can find, so if there is only the upper half of a person in the photo, only the upper half will be extracted. This should go without saying, but it is a good thing to keep in mind anyway.

The ability to copy subjects will work in a number of places. Some of these include Safari, Preview, Photos, Quick look, and Screenshots, amongst others. Unfortunately, the Copy Subject option is not available on all devices.

Device Limitations

The ability to extract a subject from a photo is not available on all devices. Here is a list of the devices that can support the feature:

- iPhones with an A12 Bionic or newer, meaning iPhone XR or newer.
- iPads with A12 Bionic or newer, meaning iPad Pro 12.9-inch 3rd generation or newer, iPad Pro 11-inch, iPad Air 3rd generation or newer, iPad 8th generation or newer, and iPad mini 5th generation or newer
- All Macs that support macOS Ventura.

The list of supported devices is most of those that can run iOS 16 or iPadOS 16. There are actually fewer devices that cannot support it, as compared to those that can.

Closing Thoughts on Extracting Subjects

The ability to copy a subject from a photo is an interesting one. At the moment it may not seem as though there is a use case for having the ability to extract a subject out of a photo. Even though this may be the case now, that may not always be the case. It is likely that someone will come up with an interesting approach in the not too distant future.

On the topic of subjects, let us talk about another feature Visual Lookup.

Visual Lookup

Last year with iOS 15 and iPadOS 15 Apple introduced a new feature called Visual Lookup. Visual Lookup would allow you to take a photo and identify a variety of different types of items. For instance, Photos could identify:

- Dog breeds
- Tree types
- Landmarks
- Animals
- Books
- Plants
- Art

If Photos was able to identify an image from one of the above categories, you would be able to get some additional information related to the subject that was identified. This feature works quite well and can allow you to do some additional research with the suggestions. With iOS 16, iPadOS 16, and macOS there are three additional categories of items that might be able to identified. These new categories are:

- Birds
- Insects
- Statues

It should be no surprise that there are new categories available. Last year's release was just the start and it would not be a stretch to think that there may be other categories coming in the future.

Visual Lookup Requirements

Visual Lookup requires an A12 Bionic or newer and is only available in a limited number of languages and regions. Specifically Visual Lookup is available in English (Australia, Canada, India, Singapore, UK, U.S.), French (France), German (Germany), Italian (Italy), Japanese (Japan), and Spanish (Mexico, Spain, U.S.).

There is a feature that is tangentially related to extracting subject. That feature is Live Text, let us look at changes around that next.

Live Text

Live Text is a feature that allows you to identify and extract text from a photo. One of the best parts of Live Text is that the text does not always need to be 100% clear in order for the algorithms to be able to identify the text. Beyond this, the text does not need to be completely centered either. May of the demonstrations that Apple has given with the feature have shown it working with text that is askew, and yet it is still able to identify the text.

There has been one area where this feature has not been able to be used has been in videos. In order to be able to copy the text out of a video, you would have to pause the video and then take a screen shot. Once you have taken the screenshot, it is an image, and you could easily copy and paste the text without any issues. Starting with iOS 16, iPadOS 16, and macOS Ventura, that all changes, because Live Text should now work with videos. In order to make this work perform the following steps:

1. **Locate the video** that has text that you want to copy.
2. **Play the video** until the point where the text is shown.
3. **Pause** the video.
4. **Tap and hold** on the video to be able to copy the text out of the video.

That is all that it takes to be able to copy text from a video. Yes, it does need to be paused, but this is a lot easier than having to take a screenshot of the video and then copying the text from the screenshots.

Closing Thoughts on the Photo and Video Improvement

Photos and Video are significant part of our lives. Each has its own place within our modern society. There have been some improvements with the way that we can manage Photos with the new iCloud Shared Photo Library. With iCloud Shared Photo Library, you can now have a separate shared photo library with those in your Shared Family group. This means that you can all contribute photos and videos either manually or automatically. With an iCloud Shared Photo Library, all users have the same capabilities. This means that everyone can add, favorite, organize, or even delete photos within the library.

If you have some photos that you would rather not be shown you might opt to hide them. Previously there would be no security on the hidden or deleted albums, but now with iOS 16, iPadOS 16, and macOS Ventura. This is enabled by default, but you can disable it if you so choose.

The ability to copy text directly from a paused video is a very welcome one. Previously you would have to take a screenshot of the video, but that is no longer the case. Now, as soon as you pause the video you can begin selecting the text, and subsequently copying it and using it as you would have previously.

The most interesting new feature is the Copy Subject feature which will identify and copy the primary subject of a photo. This could be a photo within your photo album or it could be a photo on the web, a screenshot, or many other places. Once the subject has been copied you can then paste it in Messages, within a note, or within another app and continue to use it as needed. This feature is not perfect as some parts may be missing or the edges may not be super crisp. Many may not find this feature to be super useful at the moment but, it is likely that someone will come up with an innovative use for this feature in the not too distant future.

All of these are great additions to Photos and Videos and it would not be a stretch to think that the Copy Subject feature is only a start.

Files and iCloud

The types of devices, as well as the way that people use them, has evolved significantly over the last two decades. For as much as they changed in the last decade, it is nothing compared to the last 75 years. Computers have gone from room sized mainframes to devices that can power a smart watch. The types of interfaces have change just as much. What started as punch card systems, progressed into command line terminals, to graphical user interfaces that required a mouse and keyboard, to todays interfaces where you can simply touch on and navigate through the system. In some instances, you do not even need to touch an interface because you can simply ask a digital assistant to handle a variety of tasks. As much as we might all like to be able to control everything with our voices, we are not that at that point yet. Instead, we still need to interact with our devices.

Whenever we use our devices we inevitably create data. Sometimes this data is local only to our devices, like temporary caches that can easily be removed as needed, while other items are things that we want accessible from everywhere. For a vast majority of the history of computers data was only available on the device we created it on, or if we were prudent, also existed on some sort of backup media. These items could be moved using media, like floppy disks (kids ask your parents), CDs, zip drives, thumb drives, tape drives, or even an external hard drive. For a long time this was all that we had for options, physical media. The reliability of physical media has improved, but physical media does have its limits in terms of storage and usability.

It was not until about 20 years ago when broadband internet service became commonplace that this reliance on physical media changed. Once broadband internet service was something that more people could get, options for being able to save our data to the internet became viable. Today, saving our data somewhere "in the could" is the default. Only saving data to our local device is not something that we do as often anymore.

One place where you can save data that is fully integrated into all of Apple's products, is iCloud. iCloud is Apple's cloud data service that has its origins as far back as 2002. Today iCloud is used as a syncing platform, password storage, photo storage, notes storage and synchronization, and of course as a file storage mechanism. Most of the time data is accessed through apps, like Pages, Keynote, Numbers, Notes, or any number of third-party apps. There are those times when it might make sense to access the data on iCloud to find a specific file and upload it elsewhere or send it to someone. If you are on a Mac, you can simply use Finder to locate the files and do what you need with them. You can also access the iCloud web interface to get access to a file, but this is not ideal on an iPhone. There is an app that allows you to browse all of your files in iCloud, that app is aptly named Files.

Files

The Files app was introduced in 2017 with the introduction of iOS 11. The Files app allows you to browse all of your files in one place. This could be locally downloaded files on your iPhone or iPad, or it could be in iCloud. It is also possible that you could use another service, like Microsoft One Drive or Dropbox. You could even use Files to connect to a Mac, Windows computer, or even a Linux server and access data located on those devices.

In the last five years of its existence, Files has seen some improvements, including the ability to copy, delete, moving files, and even adding tags. However, one thing that you could not do is view a file's extension. This is now possible.

Showing File Extensions

One of the most basic functions of any file management tool is the ability to see almost every aspect of a file. You may not be able to view the contents of the file, but you should be able to do basic things like viewing the file's extension. The extension of a file generally indicates the type of file. The extension of a file can be misleading, but often it is correct. A file's extension is also used by apps to allow them to filter out files that they are not capable of handling.

The Files app has not been capable of showing you the extension for a file, but starting with iOS 16 and iPadOS 16 you can enable this. To enable showing of all file extensions perform the following steps:

1. Open the **Files** app.
2. Tap the **Box Icon** in the toolbar.
3. Tap on **View Options**.
4. Tap on **Show All Extensions**.

Once you have tapped on Show All Extensions, the extension will be shown for all files. If a file does not have an extension, there will not be one. Beyond showing extensions, you may want to change the extension of a file. This is now possible as well, so let us look at that.

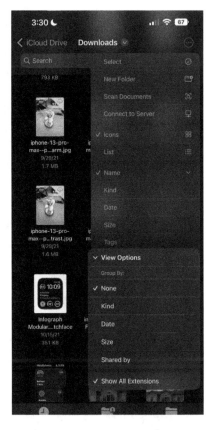

View Options in Files on iOS and iPadOS

Changing a File's Extension

Files has long had some limitations. The chief amongst them is the fact that a file's extension was not viewable. Because you could not view the extension of a file, you could not change it if you needed to. You now have the ability to change a file's extension. In order to do this perform the following steps:

1. Open the **Files** app.
2. **Navigate** to the location where the file whose extension you want to change is located.
3. **Tap and hold** on the file you want to rename. This will bring up a menu.
4. Tap on the **Rename** option. The name of the file will be selected.
5. Move the **cursor** to the end of the file extension.
6. **Change** the file's extension to the desired extension.
7. Tap on the **Done** button. A popup will appear that says Change file extension from.
8. Tap on the **Use .jpg** where jpg is the file extension you entered.

Once you have renamed the file, it will be uploaded to iCloud with the new extension. As is the case with any files, changing the extension of a file may make the file unusable by some applications, but this can be very useful if you know the extension is incorrect.

Rename Photo on iOS and iPadOS

Creating Folder with Selected Items

As much as we might all try we cannot always be as fastidious about how we organize our files. Most of the time when you create a file you might put it in the proper place. However, if you are in a hurry you may just put it in one place temporarily. If you are using the Synchronize Desktop & Documents option in iCloud, this might be in the root of Documents, or even in the Downloads folder. Regardless of where the file is actually are located, it is likely that after a while you may need to do some cleanup.

When you are doing cleanup on a Mac, it is simple enough to move things. The overall process on iOS and iPadOS is similar to that on macOS, but it does have its own distinct steps. When you are organizing things, you may realize that you have a single file that needs to go into a folder that you will fill with more files later. This would have to be two steps, first you would create the folder and then you could move the file. Now, with iOS 16 and iPadOS 16 you can now do all of this in one step with a new option New Folder with Item, that works on a single item. To do this perform the following steps:

1. Open **Files**.
2. **Locate** the file that you want to create a new folder with.
3. **Tap and hold** on the item. A context menu will appear.
4. Tap on **New Folder with Item**. The new folder with the item will be created.
5. **Rename** the folder as needed.

Once you have followed the steps above, you will have a new folder with the one item in it. You can move other items into the folder or do what you need to with it. This is a nice feature, you no longer need to accomplish this in two steps since it is combined into a single step. This is not the only new thing. There is some additional information in the Get Info pane, let us look at that now.

Multiple File Options on iOS and iPadOS

Get Info

There are many things that the Mac has been capable of doing that iOS and iPadOS have not, particularly when it comes to files and folders. One of those tasks has been getting the size of a particular folder. With iOS 16 and iPadOS 16 this is now possible. One of the actions that you can perform on a folder is to Get Info. When you do this there is an addition piece of information shown, Folder Size.The Folder Size info will only work for folders in iCloud, you cannot get the Folder Size when you are connected to other servers, even if it is another Mac.

Under iOS 15 and iPadOS 15 you could get the size of a file, but not the folder, so the addition of being able to get the size of a folder is a nice addition. Maybe at some point in the future you will be able to get the size of a folder when you are connected to a server and not just with iCloud.

Earlier when you were creating a new folder with the item, you may have noticed a bunch of new actions. Let us look at those next.

Additional Menu Actions

Within the Files app you can perform a number of actions on a file. These include:

- Getting Info
- Renaming a file
- Compressing
- Duplicating
- Quick Look
- Modifying Tags
- Copy
- Move
- Share
- Delete

Within Files you might have some photos. With an image you can perform some additional actions. These are called "Quick Actions'" and are in their own menu item when you tap and hold on a file. The available Quick Actions are:

- Markup
- Rotate Left
- Rotate Right
- Create PDF
- Convert Image
- Remove Background

The first four of the items above were available in iOS 15 and iPadOS 15, but the last two, Convert Image and Remove Background are new.

Convert Image

Often you might find yourself needing an image in a different format. You might need a JPG instead of a PNG, because PNG files can be rather large. If you need to convert an image you can now do so, right within Files. You can convert a JPG, PNG, or HEIF file into any of the three formats. Tapping on the **Convert Image** item will allow you to select the format and then select the intended image size. The options are Small, Medium, Large, and Original. Once you tap on the intended size the image will be converted.

Menu Actions on iOS and iPadOS

Similarly, if you are viewing an image within the Files app you can tap on the new dropdown arrow and then tap on **Export** and it will perform the same action of allowing you to select the format and the size.

Remove Background

The new Remove Background option uses a new detection mechanism in iOS 16 and iPadOS 16 that can separate out the primary subject from the rest of the photo. When you do this a new file is created within the same folder.

Most of the files that you browse with Files are stored in iCloud. That has seen a couple of changes as well. Let us look at those next.

iCloud

When iCloud was introduced in 2011, it had a rocky start, to say the least. However, Apple quickly smoothed out some of the rough spots and today iCloud is used to power a significant portion of all of Apple's services. Last year iCloud+ added a couple of new features. One of these was iCloud Private Relay, which keeps your browsing private from websites. Another feature was the ability to use custom domains with your @icloud.com email address. This feature is called Custom Email Domains, and there have been some enhancements.

Custom Email Domains

As just mentioned, a custom email domain is a way of being able to use your @icloud.com email address as the actual email address to receive emails for a domain that you control. This was a great addition, however there were a couple of limitations. The first limitation is that you could only have up to three email addresses associated with a particular domain. While this worked for many, it was quite limiting and was not always enough email addresses. Beyond this, there was no catch all address, meaning that if someone sent an email to an address you did not specify, it would not go through. This latter item has changed.

Catch All Email Address

You can now create a Catch All address so that any email that does not match one of your explicitly set email addresses will be sent to your iCloud email address. This can be done right from within iOS 16, iPadOS 16, or macOS Ventura. This can also be done via the iCloud website. To enable the catch all address via the iCloud website perform the following steps:

1. Go to **iCloud.com**.
2. **Login** with your Apple ID that has the custom domain on it.
3. In the upper right corner **click on your name** to bring up a dropdown.
4. Click on **Account Settings**. This will bring up the account settings screen.
5. Under **Custom Email Domain**, click on the Manage button. A popup will appear.
6. **Click on the domain** that you want to enable the catch all address for.
7. Once this screen loads click on the **Turn on Allow All** button.

Once you have enabled this on the domain any emails that are sent to an email address that is not specified in your list of emails will still be sent to your iCloud email address. This is a good feature for those who might need more than three email addresses allowed for a single domain, and do not mind having them all go to their iCloud email address.

In order to use the Custom Email Domain feature, you would to have already purchased the domain that you wanted to use. This is now possible to do right from settings or through the web interface.

Buying an Email Domain

The process of buying a domain can be somewhat daunting to those who have not done it before. Even if you have purchased a domain, then making the necessary changes to the domain records can be challenging. Apple has simplified this process a bit. You can now buy a domain through the web interface or through iCloud within settings.

Buying a domain on iCloud.com

If you want to add a custom email domain, you will need a domain. You can buy one right through the iCloud.com website. These purchases are made through CloudFlare, but the entire process is integrated. In order to do this perform the following steps:

1. Go to **iCloud.com**.
2. **Login** with your Apple ID that has the custom domain on it.
3. In the upper right corner **click on your name** to bring up a dropdown.
4. Click on **Account Settings**. This will bring up the account settings screen.
5. Under **Custom Email Domain** click on the Manage button. A popup will appear.
6. Click on **Buy a new domain**. You will be brought to the Search for a Domain page.
7. **Enter** in the domain name that you want to use for your custom email.
8. Click on the **Search** button. A search will be done to see if the domain is available.
9. If the selected domain is not available, a list of alternatives will be displayed, along with the prices.
10. Select your desired domain and click on the **Continue** button.
11. You will be **redirected to CloudFlare** to complete your purchase.
12. Once you have **completed the purchase** your domain will be added to the domains that you manage.

Having the entire process of purchasing a custom domain to having it automatically configured and enabled will go a long way to having more people enable custom email domains. The fact that everything is configured for you makes it so much easier and it is easy enough for anybody to be able to do.

Family Checklist

There is one last item to discuss regarding iCloud. iCloud allows you to share a number of things, including purchases, subscriptions, and it also allows a parent to approve purchases. There may be a number of things that you might not realize that you can configure for a family. For instance, you may not be aware of that you can setup emergency contacts, add a recovery contact, or even share your location. These are just a few of the possible things that you may not have configured. Now within the Family Settings of iCloud you can see what options you can configure all from one place. This feature is called Family Checklist. To access the Family Checklist perform the following steps:

1. Open the **Settings** app.
2. Tap on **Family** which is directly underneath your Apple ID at the top.
3. Locate the **Family Checklist** option.
4. Tap on **Family Checklist**.

Once this is opened, the list of tasks that you can perform should be listed. As

Family Checklist Items on iOS

mentioned above, this could be a variety of things like Adding your Family to Medical ID or adding a Recovery Contact. To perform any of the suggestions, simply tap on the link below each item and it will walk you through how to perform the checklist item.

Closing Thoughts on Files and iCloud

Files are something that we all have to deal with. iPhone OS was originally designed to hide away the management of files from the user. However, this did not last for too long. The Files app has added a couple of new features related to File extensions.

You can now show all file extensions all the time as well as change a file's extension. When you change the extension for a file you will be prompted with a confirmation that you want to change it. This has long been a feature that many have asked for and now it is here with iOS 16 and iPadOS 16.

iCloud is where you store all of your files. iCloud+ offers the ability to use a domain you own and use iCloud to host the email by forwarding it to your iCloud email address. This process has been streamlined by allowing you to search for a domain, complete the purchase with CloudFlare, and then get redirected back to your iCloud account with the custom domain all setup and configured for your email. This should make things significantly quicker and easier for everyone involved.

Accessibility Improvements

When Apple builds its devices and operating systems it is with the intent to be as inclusive as possible. What this means is that it should be usable by everyone, regardless of capabilities. Apple's software is designed with this in mind, and the vast majority of users will not need to modify the default settings of iOS, but for those that do there is a whole category of settings that can help people adjust their devices to fit their usage. That group is called Accessibility Settings.

Within the Accessibility Settings you can find options like Voice Over, Voice Control, Sound Recognition, Guided Access, and much more. One of the options available is the Magnifier, there has been an enhancement with the Magnifier.

Magnifier

There are those that might have some difficulty seeing things and they could use some help identifying objects. This is where the magnifier can be helpful. With iOS 16 and iPadOS 16, the Magnifier can describe images, detect people, and detect doorways. This Detection Mode is a specific mode within Magnifier. To enable these modes follow these steps:

1. Open the **Magnifier** app.
2. Tap on the **Settings** button.
3. Under Other Controls locate **Detection Mode**.
4. Tap on the "**+**" button next to Detection Mode to add Detection mode to the controls.
5. Tap the **Done** button to close settings.
6. Tap on the **Detection Mode** button.

Once you do this Detection Mode will be started. On the left hand side there are three icons, two people, a door, and a speech bubble. These three icons enable People Detection, Door Detection, and Image Descriptions, respectively. You can enable or disable any, or all, of these options. When you enable them, the Magnifier app will begin detecting the items enabled. The items as they are detected will be displayed in text on the screen as you move across items.

This improvement to magnifier should help anybody who needs assistance identifying things, to be able to get that assistance within the Magnifier app. That is not the only new addition to provide help, there is another item specifically related to gaming, called Buddy Controller.

Buddy Controller

There are those who may have some difficulties getting past a particularly tricky part of a game. It is possible that someone could hand off a controller to someone to get past that part of the game, but there are some controllers that are optimized for certain configurations and these are not always easy for everyone to learn. Instead of passing off a controller, it would be helpful for a second controller to be able to connect and be used to help. That is exactly what Buddy Controller does.

Buddy Controller allows a caregiver or friend to connect a second controller to a game and assist someone with getting past a particularly difficult part of a game. Buddy Controller will help more people have positive experiences when gaming on iOS, iPadOS, and macOS.

Hang Up with Siri

When you are on a phone call and it ends you may want to hang up the call, but it is not always easy for someone to do. You can now enable an option to ask Siri to hang up a call. To enable this setting perform these steps:

1. Open **Settings**.
2. Scroll down to **Siri & Search**.
3. Tap on **Siri & Search** to open Siri's settings.
4. Locate the option **Siri Call Hangup**.
5. Tap on **Siri Call Hangup**.
6. Tap on the **toggle** next to Siri Call Hangup to enable the option.

When you enable this, you can ask Siri to end a call by saying "Hey Siri, hang up". When you do this while on a call others on the call will hear you speak this, so they will know you are hanging up. This works for both Phone calls as well as FaceTime calls. All of the processing is handled on your device, so the request is not send to any server. In order to use this you will need a device with an A12 Bionic processor or newer. This is also available using certain languages. The supported languages are:

- Cantonese (Hong Kong)
- English (Australia, Canada, India, United Kingdom, and United States)
- French (France)
- German (Germany)
- Japanese (Japan)
- Mandarin Chinese (China mainland, Taiwan)
- Spanish (Mexico, Spain, and United States)

While it may not be used by many, for those that do use the option to hang up a phone call using Siri, it should be a welcome feature.

Dictation

When you are writing a message or text there may be times that you need be able to add an emoji to a message or text. In order to do this you would need to stop dictation, and then manually add the emoji after the fact. Now, with iOS 16, iPadOS 16, and macOS Ventura you can automatically add emoji as your dictate. This means that you do not need to do this manually, as dictation can now support adding emoji. Dictating in emoji is supported in only some languages. These languages are:

- Cantonese (Hong Kong)
- English (Australia, Canada, India, United Kingdom, and United States)
- French (France)
- German (Germany)
- Japanese (Japan)
- Mandarin Chinese (China mainland, Taiwan)

- Spanish (Mexico, Spain, and United States)

In order to use this you need to have a Mac running an M1 or M2 processor, or an iPhone or iPad that has an A12 Bionic processor, or newer. Along with emoji, punctuation will automatically be included as you perform dictation.

Being able to dictate emoji is not the only change with regards to dictation. You can now seamlessly move between typing, dictation, Quick Type suggestions, and even Scribble (iPad only). The same requirements apply to this as using dictation with emoji. There are some addition languages supported though. These additional languages are:

- Arabic (Saudia Arabia)
- Italian (Italy)
- Korean (South Korea)
- Russian (Russia)
- Turkish (Turkey)

Having the ability to seamlessly move between dictating, typing, and using Scribble makes the entire experience a lot better. This along with being able to dictate emojis will make things a lot simpler for anyone who uses dictation.

Live Captions

In the Communication and Collaboration chapter we discussed the new option within FaceTime called Live Captions. Live Captions is not only available with FaceTime, but can be enabled for the entire system.

1. Open the **Settings** app.
2. **Scroll** down to Accessibility.
3. Tap on **Accessibility** to open Accessibility settings.
4. Scroll down to **Live Captions**.
5. Tap on **Live Captions** to open the Live Captions.
6. Tap on the **toggle** next to Live Captions to enable the feature.

When you enable Live Captions there will be an overlay that will provide controls for Live Captions. These controls allow you to minimize the overlay, pause Live Captions, enable the microphone, or expand the Live Captions transcript.

There is another option for Live Captions, and that is the appearance. There are three customizations you can make, Text Size, Text Color, and Background Color.

The text size options are the same as the standard system text sizes but, the text size setting for Live Captions is independent of the system setting.

For the Text Color and Text Background, you can set any color that you want using the system color picker. If you have set a Text Color and Text Background color, you can also reset the colors back to their defaults. Just so you are aware, when you reset the colors, there is no confirmation and the colors are reset instantly.

As is the case with the FaceTime Live Captions, the Live Captions is in beta, meaning it will not be perfect. Furthermore, Live Captions will take some additional battery power to process the Live Captions. This is because it is done entirely on the device.

Live Captions is available in English in Canada and the United States and requires an iPhone11 or later, or an iPad with an A12 Bionic or later. To run it on a Mac, the Mac needs to have Apple Silicon. These are the same requirements as Live Captions on FaceTime, which makes sense, it would be quite strange to actually have the requirements differ between the two.

Closing Thoughts on Accessibility

The additions that have been made to the Accessibility features should allow even more people to be included in the Apple ecosystem. The Magnifier app adds detection for doors, people, and the ability to describe items. This should help a lot of people who might have visual impairments.

For those with motor control impairments, there is the new Buddy Controller option that will allow a caregiver or friend to assist someone with a game when needed.

Dictation has seen some additions with the ability to dictate emojis, and use punctuation automatically. The ability to move between all of the various input types, keyboard, voice, Quick Type, and Scribble should create a smooth experience for everyone.

Other iOS and iPad Features

The original iPhone was announced in January of 2007 and became available on June 29th of the same year. The iPhone was joined by the iPod touch, which was the "iPhone without the phone" in September of 2007. The operating system for both of these was called iPhoneOS. iPhoneOS was the only mobile operating system that Apple had for a while. Three short years later the iPad would be introduced and would become available on April 3rd, 2010.

When the iPad was first introduced it had its own operating system, iPhoneOS 3.2. Which was a special build of the iPhone software built specifically for the iPad.

April is only a few months before the traditional time of Apple's World Wide Developer Conference where the company usually introduces the new operating systems at these conferences. WWDC 2010 was no different. At the conference Apple introduced version 4.0 of its iPhoneOS, except that because it was used on more than just the iPhone, but also on the iPad, the name would be shortened from iPhoneOS to iOS.

Both the iPad and iPhone would continue to use the same name until just three years ago when Apple introduced a separate operating system for the iPad. That operating system is aptly named iPadOS.

Even though the iPhone and iPad have their own operating systems they still share a significant amount of the same code and even the same interface items. Because of this many of the things that you can do on the iPhone you can also do on the iPad. Due to this fact, it made sense to cover some changes that are coming to either of the platforms within this chapter of the book.

Let us look at one change that is coming to both, the ability to manage Wireless networkings right from Settings.

Wi-Fi Network Management in Settings

A significant number of the settings that you have on your device are synchronized across all of your devices. This can include passwords, website history, and other information. The mechanism used for synchronizing data is iCloud Keychain. One piece of information that is stored in iCloud Keychain, and is visible and manageable on the Mac is which wireless networks you have connected to or have configured.

Settings within iOS and iPadOS allows you to set most of the settings for the system, as well as some settings for apps. Within Settings you can connect or disconnect to a wireless network. What you have not been able to do is see the wireless networks within iCloud Keychain. With iOS 16 and iPadOS 16 this changes because you can now see and manage your wireless networks right from within Settings. In order to view and manage your wireless networks, perform the following steps:

1. Open the **Settings** app.
2. Tap on **Wi-Fi**. This will bring up the Wi-Fi Network information screen.
3. Tap on the **Edit** button in the upper right corner. This will bring up the Wi-Fi Management screen.
4. **Authenticate** with Face ID, Touch ID, or by device passcode.

On the Wi-Fi Management screen you will see two groups of items, Managed Networked and Known Networks. The Managed Networks are networks that are managed for you. This can be from your cellular carrier or it can be due to a device being managed as part of a school or business. You cannot delete any of the Managed Networks. You can view the information by tapping on the "**i**" button next to each network.

Under the Known Networks section you will see each of the networks that are in your iCloud Keychain in alphabetical order. Here you can tap on the "**-**"button to delete the network, or you can tap on the "**i**" icon to see its details. You can also adjust any of the settings by tapping on the "**i**" and modifying them as needed.

Once you have finished removing any of the networks that you want to remove tap on the **Done** button. If you have deleted any networks you will see a popup with the title Remove Wi-Fi networks?. The note on the popup states: "Your devices using iCloud Keychain will no longer join these Wi-Fi networks." Tap on **Remove** to confirm you want to save your changes. Your changes will be synchronized to other devices using iCloud Keychain.

Wi-Fi Network Passwords

When you setup a wireless network it is a good idea to use a secure password so someone cannot easily guess it and connect to your network. There may be times when you either need to share your Wi-Fi password with someone or you need to connect a new device to your network. It is possible that you remember the password, but in the event that you do not, you may need to find out what it is. This is now possible to do right from within Settings on iOS and iPadOS. To get the password of any network perform the following steps:

Delete Wi-Fi Network in Settings

Confirmation of Removing Wi-Fi Networks

1. Open the **Settings** app.
2. Tap on **Wi-Fi**. This will bring up the Wi-Fi Network information screen.
3. Tap on the "**i**" button for your currently connected network to being up the additional details screen.
4. Tap on the **Password** field.
5. **Authenticate** with Face ID, Touch ID, or with your device's passcode. Once authenticated the password will be shown.

You can then copy the password or you can enter in your Wi-Fi password on the device you are trying to set up. If you are editing your list of known networks the process is the same, Tap on the "**i**" icon to show the details, and then tap on the password field. But you do not need to authenticate because you already authenticated when you entered into the Edit Networks screen.

The ability to manage your wireless networks has been on macOS since the beginning, but now having the ability to manage your wireless networks on iOS and iPadOS is a great addition that has been a long time coming. Managing Wi-Fi networks is not the only change for the operating systems, let us turn to the Stocks app.

Stocks App

Everybody wants to be able to retire someday. In order to be able to retire you need to make sure you have enough money set aside to do so. Some are able to do this by saving their entire lives, while others may use investments to supplement their savings. If you have any investments, whether for retirement or for other reasons, you may want to be able to quickly glance at some stocks. There are a few new additions to Stocks. These changes are Custom Watchlists, additional widget options, and Earnings dates.

Custom Watchlists

You may have a variety of stock symbols that you want to keep track of. The stocks symbols may be grouped by sector, by possible investments, or any other grouping that suits your needs. Previously you only had one list of stock symbols. Now you can create as many different watchlists as you need. To add a watch list perform the following steps:

1. Open **Stocks.**
2. Underneath the Stocks app tap on **My Symbols**. A popup menu will appear.
3. Tap on **New Watchlist**. A popup will appear.
4. Enter in a **name** for the watchlist.
5. Tap on the **Save** button to save the list. The watchlist will be saved and the search box will be selected.
6. Enter in the **symbol** or company name for the stock you want to search for. You can use AAPL as an example.
7. In the list of symbols matching your list Tap on the "**+**" symbol next to the stock that you want to add.
8. Tap on the **Done** button when finished adding symbols.

You can now easily switch between watch lists by tapping on the Watchlist dropdown below the search bar. You may start out naming the watchlist one thing but end up realizing you need to change it. So, let us look at how to do that next.

Managing a Watchlist

In the event that you need to rename a watchlist, you can do so. This is done by following these steps:

1. Open **Stocks**.
2. Tap on the **Watchlist dropdown** directly below the search bar.
3. Tap on **Manage Watchlists**. A sheet will appear from the bottom of the screen.
4. **Locate** the watchlist you want to modify.
5. Tap on the **Pencil** next to the name of the watchlist you want to rename. A popup will appear.
6. Type in the **new name** of the watchlist.
7. Tap on **Save** to save the changes.

Add New Watchlist in Stocks app

Beyond changing a watchlist, you may want to remove a watchlist entirely. This can also be done by using these steps:

1. Open **Stocks**.
2. Tap on the **Watchlist dropdown** directly below the search bar.
3. Tap on **Manage Watchlists**. A sheet will appear from the bottom of the screen.
4. **Locate** the watchlist you want to modify.
5. Tap on the red "**-**" button next to the name of the watchlist to be deleted. A button will slide in on the right.
6. Tap on the **red trash can** button. A confirmation dialog will appear.
7. Tap on the **Delete** button to confirm you want to delete the watchlist. The watchlist will be deleted.

You can add as many stocks and watchlists as you need. Being able to add a list of stocks to watch to a custom list is a nice addition, as well as being able to manage them. This ability is useful when it comes to the widgets for the Stocks app. Let us look at those next.

Stocks Widgets

As is the case with many of the builtin Apple apps, the Stocks app has its own set of widgets that you can add to the home screen of either the iPhone or the iPad. There are a variety of different widgets to choose from on iOS 15 and iPadOS 15. There are four different widgets:

1. Watchlist small
2. Watchlist medium
3. Watchlist large

4. Symbol small

The symbol widget will allow you to configure single stock ticket symbol for the widget. The Watchlist widgets do not allow for customization. The smallest watchlist widget shows you the first three symbols you have in your list. The information shown on this is the symbol, the company name, the current stock price and its daily change.

The medium widget shows the same as the smallest widget, but also has a graph between the symbol and name, and the current price and the daily change.

The largest widget is the same as the medium widget, except that it shows the first six items instead of only three.

The type of widgets remain the same on iOS 16 and iPadOS 16 as the previous versions. The big change is that now these widgets can be configured to show one of your custom watchlists.

Customizing a Stocks Widget

To choose a custom watchlist for any of the three Watchlist widgets from the Stocks app perform the following steps:

1. Locate one of the **Stocks widgets** on your home screen.
2. **Tap and hold** on the widget you wish to modify. A popup menu will appear.
3. Tap the **Edit Widget** menu item. The widget will enter its configuration mode.
4. Tap on the dropdown in the **Watchlist** configuration item.
5. **Select** the appropriate watchlist.
6. Optionally enable the **Show Watchlist Name** toggle.

This will allow you to show your custom watchlist and its name. There is one last configuration item titled Show More Details. Enabling this option will as indicated show addition details.

Show More Details

When you enable the Show More Details option, there will be more stocks shown in each widget, except for the smallest one. There are still only three stock symbols shown. For the Medium widget, you will have four symbols instead of three previously. For the Large widget the number of stocks show goes from six to twelve, so doubling the number shown previously.

The number of stocks shown is not the only change, the actual information changes as well. With More Details enabled you will see the following information:

- Stock Symbol
- Current Price
- Percentage change
- Price change

The symbol and current price are on the left and the percentage of change and the price change will appear on the right. As is the case with all stocks, green will indicate that he price has risen while red means that is has gone down.

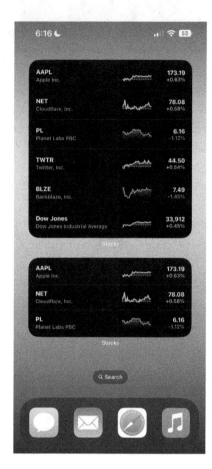

Standard View on Stocks
Widgets

More Details on Stocks Widgets

Closing Thoughts on Stocks

You would think that once you have created an app that tracks Stocks you would be done, but nothing stays the same forever particularly when it relates to the stock market. With Stocks on iOS 16 and iPadOS 16 you can now create as many custom watchlists lists as you would like. Once you do this you can then take those custom watchlists and configure widgets on your home screen to show those custom watchlists.

iOS Specific Features

While iOS and iPadOS might share a lot of code and features, there are some things that are still designed just for the iPhone. The reasons why something might be tailored just for the iPhone can be due to the form factor and use cases. One example where this is absolutely the case is when it comes to the Wallet app.

Wallet

The Wallet app is designed to be used on the iPhone. There are some features that do appear on the iPad, like the ability to see your balance, change the default settings like shipping address, email, and phone number for a card. A vast majority of the actions that you perform with the Wallet app are on the iPhone. There is a new feature that is specifically designed for the iPhone. That feature is the ability to add orders to the Wallet app.

Orders

It is quite possible that when you order something on your iPhone that you will use Apple Pay with a card in your Apple Wallet to pay for the product. The process of using Apple Pay is fairly straightforward. You press the Apple Pay button, a confirmation appears on your iPhone or Apple Watch, or you can use Touch ID on your Mac, and once you confirm the purchase you will likely receive an email. At that point you must do all of the tracking via the merchant's website. What would be better would be the ability to track your order directly from the Wallet app.

Starting with iOS 16 this is exactly what you can do. When you make a purchase with Apple Pay you might be able to add it to the Wallet app. When you do this, you will be able to see the merchant, order date, item ordered, a picture, and estimated arrival time. Orders will be broken into two different sections, current orders and completed orders.

For this feature to work there will need to be support from merchants. Apple is partnering with Shopify, one of the biggest commerce platform vendors to make this happen.

In the Wallet app on the iPhone there is a dedicated orders button right at the top of the screen. When you tap on this you will see your order summary at the top and completed orders at the bottom. You will be able to tap on any of the orders and view additional details.

The ability to view orders where you used Apple Pay will be a great addition and will make it easier for people to keep track of their orders. When you purchase something you may want to be able to pay for an item over time, this is also possible with the Apple Pay Later service.

Apple Pay Later

There are those times that you might need to purchase something but funds might be a bit tight. In these instances it might be helpful to be able to spread those payments out. With the **Apple Pay Later** service this might be possible.

Apple Pay Later is a service for U.S. customers provided by Apple that will spread the payments for an item into four separate payments over six weeks. The first payment, which is 25% of the total, would be paid when you complete the order, with the remaining three payments being due every two weeks.

There are some possible limitations to this. First, this will not be available to everyone. Second, this is limited to Apple Pay transactions on the Mastercard Network. For Visa or American Express cards, this will not be possible. Third, Apple will not charge a fee, but if a debit card is used the card issuer may charge a fee for insufficient funds.

If you need the ability to pay every two weeks instead of all at once, this could be a good option for you, provided it is available to you. There is a one last set of changes for Wallet to discuss, and this one is about IDs and Keys.

IDs and Keys

An iPhone is one of those devices that can hold a significant amount of personal information and can also provide us with a lot of convenience. The Apple Wallet can store a lot of our information, like credit cards, transit cards, and loyalty cards. With the introduction of iOS 13 Apple added another item, Car Key. Car Key is a way of being able to have a digital car key that you can share with others and then revoke access when it is no longer needed. Car Key is being added to more cars, but that will take time for it to roll out.

Last year with iOS 15 Apple another key that could be stored in the Wallet app. A Room Key. This option would allow a hotel, motel, or other entity to provide a room key to someone via iMessage. Therefore, instead of needing to provide a physical key, there would be a digital key. This way, someone may be able to go straight from the airport to their hotel without necessarily needing to check in, or at minimum, it could make the checkin process that much faster.

Also last year Apple introduced another new item that could be added to the Wallet, an ID card. A State ID card would be a great item to have so you could prove who you are without needing your physical ID in certain situations. This would need support from each state, because they are the ones who are verifying the identity. At launch there were only a handful of states who were looking into this.

The ID portion has been expanded with iOS 16 to where apps can request access to a digital ID card. When this happens only the necessary information will be shared. For instance, if an app only needs to know if someone is over 18, then the iPhone will provide that information, but not the user's exact age, because the app does not need to know the information. Users will be able to provide consent before the information is shared and they will need to confirm with biometrics or their devices passcode.

Closing Thoughts on Wallet

The Apple Wallet app is getting new features as time goes on. With iOS 16 some of these new features include the ability to add orders to the Wallet app, so you can easily track the status of your order, provided you used Apple Pay to order the item. If you need to spread out payments for something, you may have the ability to do so with the new Apple Pay Later Service. With this you can pay for your order in four installments over six weeks, with the first payment being upon completion of the order. This will not be available in all states, nor to everyone, but if you do need it and it is available it will be a good option to have. Lastly, if your state supports a digital ID card through Apple Wallet, apps may be able to request verification of information from the digital ID. When this happens only the necessary information will be show. All of these are great additions and should make things a bit smoother.

Headphone Changes

Many people use headphones while they are connected to their iPhone or iPad. While hey are using them they may need to adjust things, like enabling or disabling noise cancellation, or enabling or disabling Spatial Audio. You can perform some of these from within Control Center, but you cannot perform everything there. In order to access the settings for your headphones you normally have to use these steps:

1. Open the **Settings** app.
2. Tap on **Bluetooth**.
3. **Locate the headphones** you want to change settings on.
4. Tap on the **info circle** next to the headphones you want to change settings on.

Once you have tapped on the Info Circle you can see and change all of the settings for your headphones. These steps are not too onerous to complete, but it can be difficult to find that information sometimes. Now with iOS 16 and iPadOS 16 you can use these steps:

1. Open the **Settings** app.
2. **Tap on the Headphones** that are shown right below your iCloud information.

This is a minor change, but one that will make it quicker to access the settings for your headphones. There are a couple things to note. First, only the connected headphones will have a shortcut shown. Secondly, only while the headphones are connected with the shortcut be shown. This is a nice addition but there is also another change, specifically related to Spatial Audio, let us look at that next.

Personalized Spatial Audio

In May of 2021 Apple announced that the some tracks on Apple Music would be getting a new feature called Spatial Audio. Spatial Audio is a technique of recording music that makes the audio that you are listening to seem as though it is coming from all around you. Spatial Audio makes audio sound as though it is all around you, not just from the left and right, as it would with stereo headphones.

Spatial Audio tracks

Now with iOS 16 and iPadOS 16 there is a new option called Personalized Spatial Audio. Personalized Spatial Audio will allow you to scan your left and right ears, using the true depth camera to create a personalized audio profile exactly for your ears. When you do this a custom Spatial Audio profile will be created just for your ears, which will make the experience significantly better.

There are a couple of requirements for this feature. The first thing is that you need a pair of AirPods (3rd generation), AirPods Pro, or AirPods Max in order to use this feature. There may be some Beats headphones that will support this as well. The second thing is that you need to have a device with Face ID. This is needed to be able to personalize the scanning of your ears. This means that the iPhone 8 and iPhone 8 Plus do not support Personalized Spatial Audio.

To begin the setup of Personalized Spatial Audio perform these steps:

1. Open the **Settings** app.
2. **Tap** on your 3rd generation AirPods, AirPods Pro, or AirPods Max.
3. **Scroll** down to Personalized Spatial Audio
4. Tap on **Personalized Spatial Audio**. This will bring up an information screen.
5. Tap on **Personalized Spatial Audio** to begin setup. A detailed information screen will appear.
6. **Remove** the AirPods from your ears.
7. Tap on the **Continue** button. The Front View Capture screen will appear.
8. Tap on the **Start Front View Capture** button.
9. **Scan the front** of your face, following the instructions.
10. Tap **Continue** to start the Right ear capture.
11. Capture your **right ear** using the True Depth camera.
12. Once completed tap the **Continue** button to begin the scanning of your left ear.
13. Scan the **left ear** similar to how you scanned your right ear.
14. Tap the **Done** button to complete the personalization.

Once you have finished scanning your personalized Head Tracking profile will be synchronized to all of your Apple devices. When you enable Spatial Audio your personalized audio profile will be used automatically.

The addition of a Personalized Spatial Audio profile should make Dolby Atmos audio a better experience for everyone.

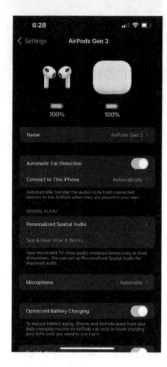

Spatial Audio - Setup in
Settings

Personalized Spatial
Audio - Start Screen

Personalized Spatial
Audio - Front View

Personalized Spatial
Audio - Right Ear

Personalized Spatial
Audio - Left Ear

Personalized Spatial
Audio - Complete

That concludes all of the changes that are available on both iOS and iPadOS. Let us look at some others feature that are iPad only.

iPadOS Specific Changes

What some might not know is that the iPhone was not actually the first device Apple worked on to use a multi-touch interface, it was in fact the iPad. Apple ended up temporarily shelving the project because they could not get the necessary technology to work on such a large screen. Instead, they ended up creating the iPhone, and the rest is as they say, history.

As mentioned earlier iPadOS was introduced as its own operating system in 2019 alongside iOS 13 and watchOS 6. While the first version of iPadOS did not have too many distinctive iPad features, that has since changed, including this year's release of iOS 16 with the new feature Stage Manager which is only available on iPads running an M1 processor. Stage Manager is not the only new feature for the iPads, there are also a few others. These relate to the Display and using external devices.

Display Resolutions

In 2012 Apple made a huge change to the iPad line with the 3rd generation iPad. That change was adding a higher-resolution display that they called a Retina Display. This change effectively doubled the screen resolution from 1024x768 to 2048x1536, all with the same physical screen size. This resulted in sharper text and a better looking screen.

In 2014, Apple introduced a huge shift. This time for the iPhone. That change was two different screen sizes a 4.7-inch and 5.5-inch screen. On the larger 5.5-inch screen you had an option of using a Zoomed display or the Standard display. This was not a hardware feature, but instead it was all in software, and supported by the hardware. When you used the Zoomed display, icons would be larger as would text. This was different than the dynamic text size because it would be physically larger.

Now some iPads have this option available to them. There are three display modes, Zoomed, Standard, and More Space. To set the Display Zoom level perform these steps:

1. Open the **Settings** app.
2. Scroll down to **Display & Brightness**.
3. Tap on **Display & Brightness** to open the settings.
4. Tap on the **Display Zoom** option. A popup will appear.
5. Tap on the **Display Zoom level** you want to use, Zoomed, Standard, or More Space.
6. Tap on the **Set** button. A confirmation dialog will appear.
7. Tap on the **Use** button.

Once you tap on the **Use** button, the display will reset and the new Display Zoom level will be used. The ability to change the screen resolution is only available on the 5th generation iPad Air or newer, the 5th generation 12.9-inch iPad Pro or newer, and the 3rd generation 11-inch iPad Pro or newer. All of these devices have an M1 processor.

Even though it is limited to a few iPads, it is a good feature to have going forward because it will likely be supported on future iPads. There is another new feature that some users will be able to utilize and that feature is Reference Mode. So let us look at that next.

M1 iPad Display More Space Setting   M1 iPad Display Zoomed Setting

Reference Mode

When you are working with certain media like photos and videos, you may want to make sure that the color that you are seeing on the screen is indeed the actual color being displayed. This is called Reference Mode. If you have used a Mac that natively supports Reference Modes or a Mac with an Apple Studio Display or Pro Display XDR, it is possible that you have used a reference mode on the display. Reference mode on iPadOS is slightly different.

In order to use Reference Mode on iPadOS, you will need a 12.9-inch iPad Pro with Liquid Retina Display, which is the 5th generation 12.9-inch Pro. To enable Reference Mode on the iPad Pro, use the following steps:

1. Open the **Settings** app.
2. Scroll down to **Display & Brightness**.
3. Tap on **Display & Brightness** to open the settings.
4. Scroll down to **Reference Mode**
5. Tap on the **toggle** next to Reference Mode to enable the option.

When you enable Reference Mode a few things will happen. First, True Tone will be turned off. This is because True Tone uses the current light to adjust the temperature to make it look more natural. The second thing is that brightness will be disabled. The reason that this is turned off is because the brightness can affect the color and therefore the reference color would not be true. The last thing that occurs is that Night Shift is disabled. Night Shift will automatically adjust the colors of the display. It is obvious why this is disabled.

When you toggle Reference Mode off all of your previous settings will be returned, meaning your true tone, brightness, and Night Mode will all be set to their previous levels. The is a small touch, but it ultimately makes Reference Mode that much easier during the times that you need to use it.

There is one thing to keep in mind about using Reference Mode and that is that your battery life may be affected when you use Reference Mode. This is because options like True Tone, automatic brightness, and Night Shift can help increase battery life.

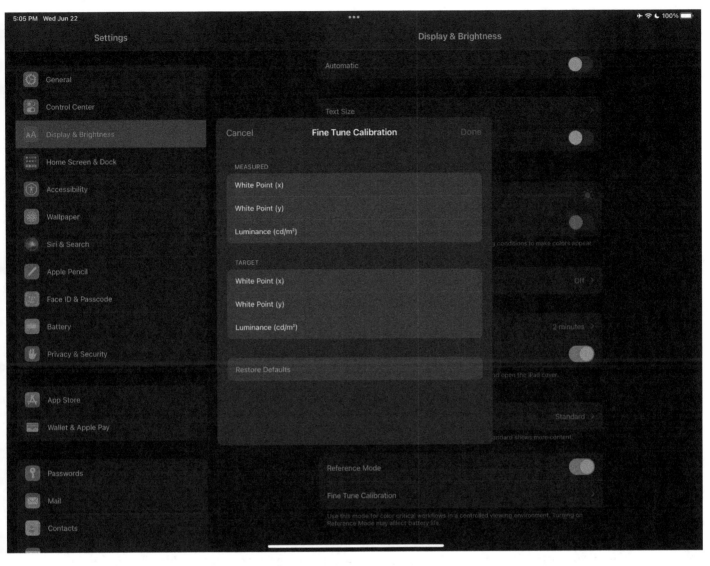

Reference Mode on iPadOS 16

Secondary Reference Mode on iPad using Sidecar

Beginning with iPadOS 13 and macOS Catalina Apple introduced a new feature called Sidecar. Sidecar allows you to use your iPad as a second display for your Mac. When you do this you are able to use your iPad as a secondary display. This means that you can move applications or just windows of applications to the iPad. You can also use the Apple Pencil with the iPad when in Sidecar mode. This includes using the Apple Pencil for navigating application windows, controls, and anything else.

With iPadOS 16 and macOS Ventura, this behavior is expanded. If you have an iPad Pro that can use Reference Mode and you have an Apple Silicon Mac you can use the iPad Pro as a secondary Reference Monitor for your Mac. This means that you can move things to the iPad and still use it in Reference Mode so you can get the right color using your iPad. This is particular useful if you need to use the Apple Pencil on the item that you are looking at because the Apple Pencil with the iPad Pro can be very precise.

Closing Thoughts on Reference Mode.

Adding Reference Mode to the iPad Pro makes it even more of a productivity device than it already was. Reference Mode will allow you to be able to make sure that the videos and image that you are working on have the proper color applied to them. You will even be able to use Reference Mode on the iPad when used in Sidecar, as long as the Mac that you are using is a Mac with Apple Silicon. Let us now look at another new feature coming to the iPad, DriverKit.

DriverKit

All iPads have a way of being able to connect to devices. The types of devices can vary. The device could be an external monitor, external thumb drive, or another device. Many devices just work when you plug them ins but there may be some devices that need software to work with the connected devices. This type of software is called a driver.

A driver is a custom piece of software that allows an app to talk to a device. If any device could just load any software, this could become a security issue on the device. Instead of allowing just any software to run, Apple has developed DriverKit.

DriverKit is a safe way for developers to create drivers that connect a device to a device. Previously, DriverKit was only available on macOS, now with iPadOS 16, the same drivers can be used on an iPad. This means that as long as as a developer creates an app that will allow an external device to work on the iPad, they can easily bring their drivers to the iPad. This should allow some new experiences and interactions to occur, but it may take time for developers to bring these apps and drivers to the iPad. Next, let us look at some interface changes coming to apps on iPadOS 16.

Interface Changes

When the iPad was initially introduced in January of 2010, Apple positioned the iPad between the iPhone and the Mac. It was true in 2010, managed to be less so through 2019, but today, the iPad truly is between the iPhone and the Mac. iOS and iPadOS share a lot of the same code and have multi-touch in common. At the same time, the iPad shares some commonalities with macOS, like Stage Manager, Desktop Safari, keyboard navigation, and support for pointing devices like trackpads.

iPadOS 16 extends the commonality between the iPad and the Mac with new features like customizable toolbars, consistent search field placement, and multiple context actions. Let us briefly look at each of these, starting with Customizable Toolbars.

Customizable Toolbars

The screen of the iPad provides more space to be able to use apps. With these apps you can usually add more buttons on the screen. One feature of many macOS apps is the ability to customize toolbar buttons. This is now possible with some apps on iPadOS 16. When the ability to customize a toolbar is implemented, you will be able to add or remove buttons from a toolbar and your changes would be saved between application launches. To see an example of what this might look like, let us use Notes. To customize the toolbar within Notes, use the following steps:

1. Open **Notes**.
2. Tap on the "**...**" button.
3. Tap on **Customize Toolbar**. A toolbar editor will appear.

Once the Customize Toolbar popup shows you can perform a couple of tasks. You can move buttons from the toolbar into the button drawer. The second thing you can do is rearrange the button icons. You can do this by tapping on a button and moving it to where you would like it to be. Once you are finished, tap on the **Done** button and your edits will be saved. If you want to reset everything back to the way it was, you can use the Reset button and everything will go back to the default.

There is one thing to note about apps with customizable toolbars. Application developer's will need to add support for this within their apps. It is not a feature that is just automatically enabled. Let us turn to another new enhancement Search Improvements.

Search Improvements

When you do a search within an iPadOS app on the iPad, you may have had a hard time figuring out where to perform the search, and where the subsequent results would show. This all changes in iPadOS 16. Now when you search the placement of the search bar, as well as the location where results show up, should be consistent between apps. Along with this, when you do a find and replace in Apple's apps, this is also now consistent and in the same location. These are minor changes, but consistency is always a good thing to have.

Scribble Improvements

When the first iPad Pro was introduced in the fall of 2015 it included a new input item, the Apple Pencil. The Apple Pencil can be used for both navigation on the iPad as well as input. Starting with iPadOS 14 the Apple Pencil was able to use a new feature called Scribble. Scribble converts your handwriting with the Apple Pencil into actual text.

When the text is translated it is not sent to the cloud or any other service. Instead, all of the transcription happens on your device, so the text you enter stays private. Starting with iPadOS 16, Scribble gets a bit more support, Emojis. Now you can use Scribble to add emojis to your text.

When you are writing, iPadOS 16 will also straighten out your text.

Closing Thoughts on iOS and iPadOS Changes

iOS and iPadOS both get new features each year and this year's releases of iOS 16 and iPadOS 16 are no exemptions. One of the most welcome changes is the addition of being able to manage Wi-Fi networks right on your iPhone or iPad is a very welcome and long overdue addition, particularly since iCloud Keychain stores the information already. You are able to remove wireless networks, view passwords for your networks, including managed networks by carriers, schools, and companies.

The Stocks app has gotten a big upgrade with the ability to create custom watchlists so you can group different stocks together for whichever purpose you need. These watchlists work great with the Stocks widgets because you can now configure the various Stocks widgets with your newly created custom watchlists so you can keep an eye on various stocks throughout the day. There is a new more details option which will provide more symbols and more data for each all within the same size widgets.

The iPad has gained a lot of new features, like DriverKit support, which allows companies to enable customers to connect devices to the iPad directly and use them within apps. While this may take a while for companies to create, if they have created DriverKit extensions for macOS, most of the handwork is done.

The 5th generation 12.9-inch iPad Pro with Liquid Retina display now also has support for Reference Mode. Reference Mode allows you to make sure that your video or image project that you are working on has the proper color calibration. If you are using an Apple Silicon Mac you can also use Reference Mode while the iPad is connected using Sidecar mode. This arrangement works well if you need to check colors but your primary monitor does not support reference mode.

Sometimes you need more space on your iPad and with the new More Space Display Zoom setting. You can always use the default, which is what you have come to expect in iPadOS 15, or if you need larger icons there is also the Zoomed mode. These levels are independent of the text size options. Now that we have covered iOS and iPadOS, let us turn to changes in macOS.

macOS Changes

It is arguable whether Stage Manager as discussed earlier, is the biggest change on macOS or not. It is not clear which group of macOS users will use Stage Manager more, non-power users or power users. It is possible that it will find usage amongst a variety of users. Even if Stage Manager is the biggest change, there is one that is more notable, a big change to System Preferences. It is no longer called System Preferences, it is now called System Settings. So let us look at that change.

System Settings

System Preferences did not change that much from its first introduction with Mac OS X 10.0 Cheetah, introduced in 2001, up through macOS Monterey. Of course there were changes. Most of the changes during that time were new icons, an occasional new preference pane, and new settings were added over time as well.

As just mentioned System Preferences has now been renamed to System Settings. This change makes sense in that it brings macOS inline with the naming conventions of iOS, iPadOS, and watchOS. On all of those platforms the system wide place to make adjustments is just called Settings. The reason that it has been renamed to System Settings stems from the fact that each individual app can have its own set of Settings, so to differentiate between an app's Settings and the macOS Settings, the term System Settings is used. Under macOS Monterey, and earlier versions of macOS, each app had its own Preferences, and the macOS system wide ones were called System Preferences. The naming scheme has remained the same, just with a different name to bring it all inline with the other operating systems.

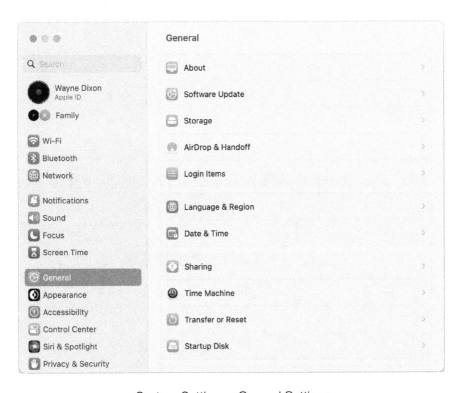

System Settings - General Settings

One of the thing that you might notice if you were to really look at each of the old System Preference panes is that there is no consistency between the layout of the old preferences panes. This all changes in System Settings. System Settings is built entirely on SwiftUI and has two implications. In case you are not aware SwiftUI is Apple's own cross-platform framework for building apps. The first implication is that if a Setting is available on all of Apple's platforms, like Wi-Fi, the preference only needs to be developed once and it can work on all platforms. The second implication is that all of the Settings will have a similar look. Depending on your own personal preferences this could either be a good thing or a bad thing.

Organization

The System Settings has a very similar look to those in iOS and watchOS, but it resembles the iPadOS arrangement more. The Settings app on iPadOS is a split view, with a column on the left that has the various settings and the actual settings on the right. The System Settings app on macOS is laid out in a very similar manner.

The System Settings app has the list of various groups of settings on the left. When you click on one of them you will see the individual settings on the right. As you might expect when a major app is being rewritten it is also the perfect time to rethink the overall organization. And that is exactly what Apple has done.

System Settings is broken down into nine overall sections. One thing to note is that these are not official designations, but ones that I have come up with in order to be able to talk about the various Settings in a much easier manner. These sections are:

1. Accounts
2. Connectivity
3. Notifications and Focus
4. General
5. Display
6. Device Security
7. Internet Security
8. Connected Devices
9. Third-Party Settings

System Settings - Appearance Settings

System Settings - Network Settings

This arrangement of System Settings on macOS is similar to the arrangement on iPadOS, but still customized for the Mac. The reason that macOS needs its own customizations is because macOS can have different interaction types, as compared to iOS or iPadOS. This is due to certain implicit expectations for the Mac. The Mac has a keyboard, mouse, and trackpad based interaction, whereas iPadOS has a touch first interaction, with the option of keyboard, mouse, and trackpad.

An example of a distinct interaction within System Settings on macOS Ventura occurs, when you click on Wi-Fi settings. When the Wi-Fi settings load you will see the Wi-Fi network that you are currently connected to, as well as any detected nearby networks. You would see the same thing on iPadOS. The difference between the two lies in the fact that as you move over various Wi-Fi network names on macOS you will see a connect button appear as you hover over a row. This type of interaction is possible due to a trackpad or mouse being expected. When you click on the connect button, you will get a popup asking for the Wi-Fi password, if one is required.

With a redesigned app, it may not be easy to find what you are looking for just by clicking. For these instances you can use the search, so let us look at that.

System Settings Search

With the System Settings app being reconfigured you may not always be able to easily find what you are looking for. For this you can use the improved search function. At the top of the left column is a search box. Here you can search for any preference or word that you might be related to the specific System Setting you are looking for.

For instance, if you search for wifi, you will get all of the results related to Wi-Fi. The possible System Setting panes that might apply, at least for this search include, Network, Sharing, and of course Wi-Fi.

Another example is if you search for password. As you might expect one result is the Login Settings pane, as well as the Password Settings pane. What you might not have thought of, or expected, is to get the Extension Settings pane.

The search within the new System Settings pane is a bit more robust and granular than the previous System Preferences search. You should be able to use it to find the exact setting that you are looking for.

Layout

All of Apple's own System Settings panes all fit within the default size of app, which is actually slightly wider than the older System Preferences pane was. Even though it is a bit wider, there is actually less space for each set of preferences because of the left side bar with the individual System Settings panes. One area where has been some improvement is that there is the ability to adjust the height of the entire System Settings app, so you can have more Settings shown on the screen at once.

As you navigate through System Settings you will undoubtedly find some preference panes that still have their own unique look buried deep in various preferences. While it is not always the case, it seems like it was just the first level of settings that were rewritten and many of the other deeper System Settings panes remain the same as they were before.

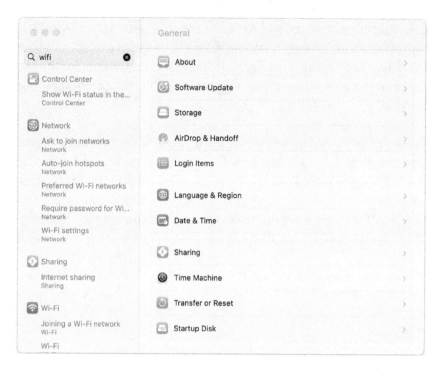

System Settings - Search Results

You can view all of the top System Settings by using the View menu bar item. This was also possible in the macOS Montgomery System Preferences, except now there are no icons showing in the menu, just the name.

There is one last thing to cover with the System Settings, and that is older Preference Panes.

Older Preference Panes

The new System Settings app still supports the older Preference Pane. All of Apple's own panes have been rewritten, however it will take third-party developer's a while to update their Settings panes. When these are loaded, they will look and feel the exact same as before, that is unless the third-party has already done the work to reconfigure their own Settings panes. These will take up the same amount of space as they did before, so the width of the System Settings app may expand depending on the third-party System Settings panes installed. When these do load, the left sidebar is still visible.

Closing Thoughts on System Settings

The System Preferences app has not only been renamed, but has been completely redesigned. The new System Settings app now closely mimics the Settings app on iPadOS with a two column split view. On the left are the various Settings groups and on the right are the individual settings that you can configure.

Even though the System Settings app has been built with Apple's SwiftUI technology, it still feels like it is part of macOS. This is done through the various distinct interactions that are possible only on macOS like hovering over a Wf-Fi network and being able to connect to it.

Let us look at an app that is not new to Apple's platforms, but is new to macOS, the Clock app.

Clock app

macOS has always had a place in the Menu Bar for the date and time and this is still present in macOS Ventura. This clock can still be customized through System Settings. But there is now also a dedicated app just for the Clock. The Clock app on macOS Ventura is the same one that appears on iPadOS and iOS. There are four different tabs:

- World Clock
- Alarm
- Stopwatch
- Timer

Let us look at each of these in turn, starting with World Clock.

World Clock

There is a strong possibility that you may want to know the current time in other parts of the world. Keeping track of time differences within your own country is likely something you can easily do without much forethought. That is unless there are specific territories that still change their clocks twice per year, and even within those territories there are some places that do not do change their clocks at all. With all of this uncertainty it can all become quite muddled.

If there are places that you are interested in, whether it be because you have friends or family living there, or just because you are interested in that location, you may want to know the current time. This has been possible, to some extent previously with the Clock widget, but widgets are limited to the Notification Center, which is not always shown on macOS, and it is not likely that people access the Notification Center just for widgets consistently throughout the day.

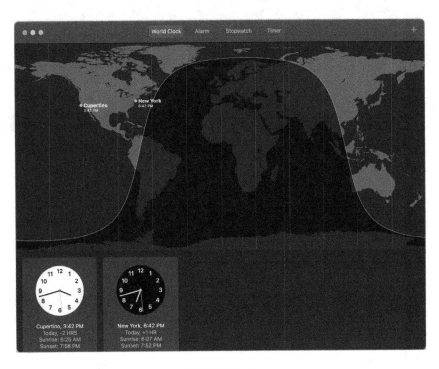

World Clock

Just like on iPadOS, the Clock app on macOS will have two sections, a map of the cities and their time, and the list of cities with their current time below.

Adding a City

Now with the Clock app you can enter in a variety of cities. This is done by opening the Clock app and then tapping on the "**+**"button in the upper right corner. When you do this, you will be shown a list of cities and their country. You can scroll through the list or you can use the search bar at at the top of the screen.

If you perform a search the list of cities will be filtered to match the text that was entered in your search. You can add a city by clicking on it. Once you add the city, it will be appended to the existing list of cities.

There is one key difference between the World Clock on macOS, as compared to iOS and iPadOS. That difference is that on macOS you can drag and drop the cities in any order that you would like, without needing to enter into Edit Mode.

Add a City in World Clock

Alarm

There may be occasions when you need to set an alarm. This has been possible on iOS, iPadOS, and you could even set an alarm on a HomePod, but you could not set an alarm on macOS. On macOS the only option you had for some semblance of an alarm has been to use the Reminders app, but that is not exactly the same.

The reason why you may need an alarm can vary. It could be something like making sure you are aware of a meeting, or a phone call, or just about for any reason. You can now set an alarm on macOS using the Clock app. To set an alarm perform the following steps:

1. **Open** the Clock app.
2. Click on the **Alarm** tab at the top of the screen.
3. Tap the "**+**" button in the upper right to add an alarm. A popup will appear.
4. Enter in the specific **time** that you would like the alarm to trigger.
5. Select whether this should be **AM or PM**.
6. Optionally select the days that you would like the alarm to repeat.
7. Optionally set a label for the alarm. The default is Alarm.
8. **Select a sound** for the alarm. You can use one of the more modern sounds, or one of the classic sounds.
9. By default the **Snooze** options is enabled. You can disable it if you do not need an option to snooze.
10. Click the **Save** button to save the new alarm.

There may seem like a lot of steps, but the process is one that can be accomplished very quickly. You can modify any alarm by simply double clicking on it, and then modifying the alarm options as needed.

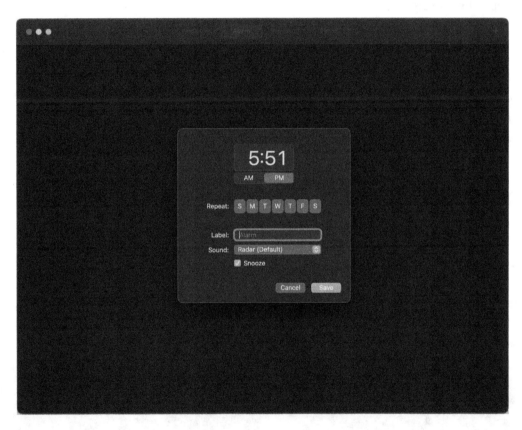

If you need to delete an alarm you can do so in the same area as modifying an alarm. There is one thing to note about deleting, there is no confirmation, so once you click on **Delete**, the alarm will be deleted. Alternatively, you can hover over any of the Alarms that you have set and you can click on the "**X**" in the upper left corner to delete the alarm. You do not have to manually create alarms, you can also use Siri. Let us look at that now.

Using Siri for Alarms

Now with macOS Ventura you can set an alarm using Siri as well. To do this, activate Siri and say "Set an alarm for 9:15", and an alarm will be created. If you already have an alarm for that specific time, Siri will enable that alarm, another one will not be created.

You can ask Siri to create an alarm for a specific day using something like "Set an alarm for 9:15 on Tuesday". If an alarm that meets this criteria is already set, then it will be enabled, otherwise a new alarm will be created. Siri is smart enough to take the current time into account.

Say for instance it is currently 9:30AM. If you ask Siri to "Set an alarm for 9:15", Siri will create an alarm for 9:15PM. However, if you say "Set an alarm for 9:15 tomorrow", Siri will presume you mean 9:15AM, and set an alarm accordingly.

When you create, or enable, an alarm using Siri a popup will appear to provide confirmation that the alarm has been created or enabled. On this notification, you do have the ability to disable the alarm right there, by tapping on the toggle to disable it. When Siri creates a new alarm, the default name of Alarm will be used. Furthermore, the default Radar sound will be used, and snooze will be enabled for the alarm.

The next area to look at is the stopwatch.

Stopwatch

From time to time you may need to time something. This could be a presentation, download time, or just about any other reason. When you need to time something, you would likely use a stopwatch. While it is possible that you might have a physical stopwatch, it is unlikely. In case you do not have a physical stopwatch, you can use the Clock app for your stopwatch.

When you open the Clock app and tap on the Stopwatch tab, you will see a giant 00:00:00 with a list of recorded splits. At the bottom of the window is a Start button and a Lap button. To start a timer click on the **Start** button. Once you do this the timer will begin.

You can click on the **Stop** button to stop the timer. Alternatively, if you need to keep track of multiple times, you can use the **Lap** button. Each new lap will be recorded in the list below the timer.

There two displays for the timer, the default is the digital timer. But if you prefer an analog timer, you can switch this by going to the View menu and then click on View Analog Stopwatch. The analog stopwatch will show as long as you do not use the Lap button. If you do, then it will switch to the Digital Stopwatch.

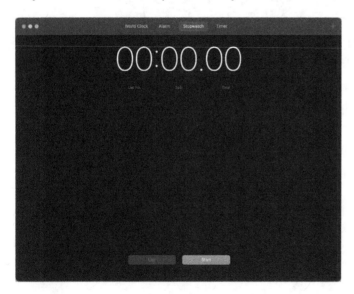

Stopwatch

Stopwatch with multiple laps

Let us look at the last item, the Timer.

Timer

There are occasions when you want to be able to set a timer for something, so that you are alerted to something. This could be something like checking on something cooking, checking to see if someone is available, to time a presentation when given a limited length of time, or just about any other possible reason. Much like setting an alarm, you have had the ability to set a timer on an iPhone, iPad, or a HomePod, but not on macOS. That now changes with the Clock app.

You can set a timer by opening the Clock app and going to the Timer tab. Once the tab is open you will see a box with a default timer of 15 minutes configured. Below this you will see an option for a tone to play when the timer is done. There are also two buttons, Done and Start.

To set a timer simply change the length of the timer to your desired amount. It is in the format of Hours:Minutes:Seconds. Once you have set the time, click on the **Start** button to start the timer.

Timer in the Clock app on macOS Ventura

Timer running in the Clock app

After the timer starts it will be replaced with a circle with a countdown clock in the middle. The circle around the time will move as the timer counts down. You can change the sound that will be played at any point. You can also pause the timer by clicking on the **Pause** button, which replaced the start button. If you need to stop a timer, click on the **Done** button.

Just like with an alarm, you do not need to manually set a timer. You can use Siri to create a timer. To enable Siri say something like "Set a timer for 5 minutes", or whatever length you need for the timer.

Limitations

There is a limitation to timers on macOS Ventura. You can only have one timer going at a time. This means that if you need multiple timers, you will need to use another device, like an iPhone, iPad, or HomePod. It should be noted that the HomePod can support multiple active timers, while iOS and iPadOS can only have a single timer going.

Closing Thoughts on Clock

The addition of the Clock app is nice to have. I am not sure how often people will use the functions of the Clock app on a day to day basis, but having continuity between iOS, iPadOS, and macOS is a definite plus. With the Clock app you can see a number of various cities and their current times using the World Clock tab.

If you need to set an alarm for any reason, you can do so using the Alarm tab. Alternatively, you can also ask Siri to set an alarm, which is entirely new to macOS Ventura.

In the event that you find yourself needing to time the length of something, the Stopwatch tab can help you with that, including the ability to show an analog Stopwatch, if you prefer.

If you have a preset time in mind, and you need to countdown from that time, the Timer can help you with that. While you can only have a single timer at a time, it is better than not having a timer at all. Plus, you can always ask Siri to set a timer for you.

Let us look at another new feature coming to an existing feature of macOS, Continuity Camera.

Continuity Camera

Most Macs come with a camera, and for the two models that do not, the Mac mini and Mac Studio, you could possibly add a camera when you purchase an Apple Studio Display. The Studio Display is not an inexpensive purchase however. It is possible that you already have a high quality camera, and that is the one in your iPhone.

If you needed to insert a picture into a document, note, or other supported application, you could do so with a feature called Continuity Camera. On an iPhone, or iPad, and you could use one of these functions:

- Take Photo
- Scan Documents
- Add Sketch

Each of these would perform the appropriate item within your iPhone or iPad. What would be nice is if you could use an iPhone as your webcam in apps like FaceTime, Zoom, or any other video app. Now you can do just that with the enhanced Continuity Camera. In some instances, you will just be able to do just that without needing to take any steps.

Supported Devices

There are a variety of features within the enhanced Continuity Camera. The ability to use a particular function depends on your device. Below is the breakdown of the feature and the minimum device needed to be able to use the particular feature.:

- Continuity Camera - iPhone XR or newer
- Portrait Mode - iPhone XR or newer
- iPhone as Microphone - iPhone XR or newer
- Center Stage - iPhone 11 or newer
- Desk View - iPhone 11 or newer
- Studio Light - iPhone 12 or newer

Continuity Camera is the base functionality of being able to use an iPhone as a video camera when connected to a Mac running macOS Ventura. This is supported on all iPhones that can use Continuity Camera.

Portrait Mode is Apple's technology that allows a person, or object, to be the focal portion of the screen, while simultaneously allowing the background to be blurred using a bokeh effect, or blurred background. This is supported on all iPhones that can use Continuity Camera.

iPhone as Microphone is where you use your iPhone as the microphone while you are using the app. This is supported on all iPhones that can use Continuity Camera.

Center Stage is a technology that allows an iPhone to track a person, or people, within the view of the camera an automatically adjust the angle of the camera to keep the subjects in focus. When enabled, the tracking occurs automatically without any intervention or action needed by the subjects. There is a limited range for this feature, since there is a limited viewing angle for the iPhone camera. This feature requires an iPhone 11 or newer.

Studio Light is a filter that can be applied to make a person's face a bit brighter, all while maintaining a clean picture. This feature requires an iPhone 12 or newer.

Enabling Features

When you open FaceTime on macOS Ventura, you will have the option of connecting your iPhone camera to your Mac. This can be done by opening FaceTime, or another app that supports Continuity Camera. After the app is open, you can use Control center to enable or disable the features.

There may be instances where you need to connect the camera manually. This is possible to do within the app that you are using. In the case of FaceTime you can connect to your iPhone by going to Video -> [Name of your iPhone]. Once your iPhone is connected, the features will be available to be enabled in Control Center.

 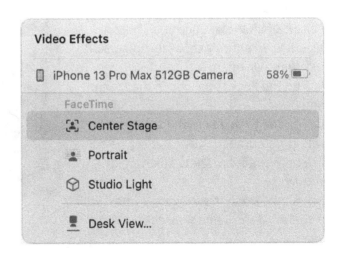

Video Effects in Control Center on macOS Ventura

Once you click on Control Center you will see an item called Video Effects. Click on this and you will see your iPhone and the available features for your device. You can enable any of them by simply clicking on them. Only the features that the connected device can support should be shown. This means that if you have an iPhone 11 you should not see Studio Light.

There is one last feature to discuss, Desk View, and that a new feature that requires a bit of discussion.

DeskView

DeskView is a new application that will allow you to use your iPhone's camera to show your physical desktop. The use cases for this are limitless, but a few examples might be working with students to perform an activity where you can physical show them what needs to be done. Another example might be working with someone where you need to show anything on your physical desktop.

The way that Desk View works is by utilizing the ultra wide camera lens in conjunction with your other camera lenses. While the ultra wide focuses on your desk, the wide lens can be used to keep focus on you, so that you can see both the desk and the person at the same time. In order for this to work properly, you may need a stand of sorts to be able to hold the iPhone in place while using Continuity Camera. There should be a variety of stands available from accessory manufacturers to be able to hold your iPhone in the proper position.

Let us look at how to enable Desk View, using FaceTime as our app of choice. To enable Desk View use the following steps:

1. Open **FaceTime**.
2. **Start a FaceTime call** with the person whom you want to use Desk View with.
3. Once in the FaceTime call, click on the **Video** menu.
4. Click on **your iPhone** to connect your phone and use it the camera for FaceTime.
5. Click on **Control Center** in the Menu Bar.
6. Click on the **Video Effects**.
7. Click on **Desk View**. Once you click on DeskView an entirely separate app called Desk View will open.
8. Click on the **FaceTime** icon in the Menu Bar.
9. Click on the **Share Screen** button in the lower right corner.
10. Click on **Window** to share a particular window.
11. Click on the **Desk View** window, and it will be shared at the same time as your other camera.

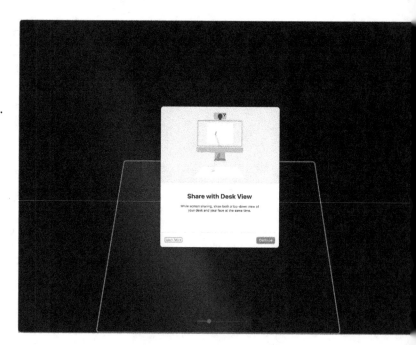

Desk View when connected to FaceTime

While these steps are for FaceTime, they will be similar for other video conference apps, like Zoom, Microsoft Teams, and any other app.

Closing Thoughts on Continuity Camera

Continuity Camera is a great enhancement to the already existing ability to use your iPhone camera to take pictures and import them into a document or note.

Continuity Camera requires an iPhone XR or newer phone. All supported models will allow for Portrait Mode and iPhone as a microphone. You will need an iPhone 11 or newer for Desk View and Center Stage. In order to use the Studio Light feature you will need an iPhone 12 or newer.

The addition of Desk View will make it easier for many to share their screen without needing an expensive or complicated set of cameras. Next, let us look at some changes on watchOS.

watchOS Changes

The Apple Watch is the smallest device that Apple produces that has its own dedicated operating system. Because of its size it has a limited surface area and your primary interactions on the device occur by touching the screen. However, there are still two physical controls, the side button and the digital crown. The Digital Crown is a great way of being able to quickly move through content, like a list of items. The Digital Crown has a few other uses, like being the mechanism used to take an Electrocardiogram, or ECG. There has been a change with one interaction used with the Digital Crown.

Digital Crown

There are a few modes on the Apple Watch that will ignore touch inputs or at least make sure that the actions are deliberately done. The two that come to mind are Sleep Mode and Swimming/Water Mode. When you are in one of these modes you would need to explicitly exit them. The way that you can exit them is by spinning the Digital Crown until the screen was unlocked.

This interaction changes with watchOS 9. Now, instead of turning the digital crown, you simply press and hold on the digital crown until the device unlocks. This is a small change in the grand scheme of things, but it is a big change for those who may have muscle memory for using the digital crown to disable Sleep Mode or Swimming/Water Mode. However, this is a significant advance for including those who may not have the dexterity or capability of being able to spin the Digital Crown to unlock the Apple Watch. This is not the only change for those who may have issues with being able to manipulate the Apple Watch. Let us look at a new feature called Mirroring.

Hold to unlock on watchOS 9

Mirroring an Apple Watch

As mentioned in the previous section there are those who may have some mobility impairments. When someone has mobility impairments it may be difficult for them to interact with the Apple Watch. For these individuals it can be frustrating to say the least. With watchOS 9 and iOS 16 these users will be able to mirror their Apple Watch right onto their iPhones. This will be done using the existing AirPlay technologies.

To enable AirPlay Mirroring for the Apple Watch perform these steps:

1. Open the **Settings** app on your iPhone.
2. Scroll down to **Accessibility**.
3. Tap on **Accessibility** to open the Accessibility settings.
4. Scroll down to the **Physical and Motor** section.
5. Tap on **Apple Watch Mirroring**.
6. Tap on the **Toggle** to enable Apple Watch Mirroring.

| Not Mirroring | Connecting | Connecting and Mirroring |

Once you have enabled this option, the screen of your Apple Watch will be shown right on your iPhone. It might take a couple of seconds while the connection is made, but once it is established the display of the Apple Watch will take up the screen. Depending on your device, the view might be larger than the actual Apple Watch screen, which will make it easier to see.

Once opened you can control your Apple Watch as you would if you were doing so on the Watch itself. You can tap on the location where the Digital Crown and side button are in the view and it will perform the same actions.

This feature does require watchOS 9 and iOS 16, and it is only supported on the Apple Watch Series 6 and newer. If you have devices that meet these criteria, it will be a great addition for users who need it. Let us turn to Watch Faces.

Watch Faces

The Apple Watch is likely one of the most personal devices that one can use. The reason for this is because many wear the Apple Watch for a majority of the day and the night, and only charge when the battery is low or intermittently throughout the day. There are many ways of customizing the Apple Watch including which apps are installed, which complications are shown, and of course which Watch Faces are configured. The term complication comes from the physical watch world where any additional feature of a watch would make producing a watch a bit more difficult, or in a word, complicated. The Apple Watch has 47 different watch faces. Of these 47 there are four new ones to discuss, and a big change to some other faces. Let us begin with the new watch faces, which include:

1. Metropolitan
2. Astronomy
3. Lunar
4. Playtime

Let us look at each of these in turn, starting with the Metropolitan watch face.

Metropolitan

The Metropolitan watch face is one that allows you to choose the font on the numerals. There are a few different customization options including the color, numeral style, dial style, and complications.

You can choose from four different numeral styles. **Style I** has a number shown on each hour. **Style II** only has numbers shown on the even hours. **Style III** has numerals on 3, 6, 9, and 12. **Style IV** only has numerals showing on 6 and 12.

After you have selected a style for the numerals, you can then select the style of Dial. There are five different options. **Dial I** has a light background with the complications being shown in your selected color. **Dial II** is your selected color on the background with a white dial. The complications on this watch face are white. **Dial III** has your selected color as the background, and a shade of your selected color as the dial. Just like Dial II, the complications are in white. **Dial IV** has your selected color as the background and a dark dial, while the complications are a dark color with the accompany text in white. **Dial V** has no background and just a dark dial color, with the complications in your selected color.

There are four complication areas that you can specify. These are the four corners around the dial and are all the corner complications.

Metropolitan Dial V

Metropolitan Dial II in Color

There is also a multicolor variant for the dials. **Multicolor Dial I** has a muted multicolored background and a gray dial, with complications being in white. **Multicolor Dial II** is the same as Multicolor Dial I, but has brighter colors. The complications are also white. **Multicolor Dial III** inverts the dial and background color as Multicolor Dial I, meaning the background is white and the dial color is the muted multicolor. The complications on this face are white. **Multicolor Dial IV** is the brighter multicolor dial. **Multicolor Dial V** is just a multicolored dial with no background, and the complications are in white.

The Metropolitan watch face is a nice alternative to existing watch faces.

Astronomy

The Astronomy watch face is somewhat similar to the Astronomy & Weather Lock Screen, but also different. The Astronomy watch face has four different things you can customize. These items are Font, View, Style, and Complications.

Fonts

There are three different fonts to choose from Classic, Modern, and Rounded. The **Classic** font has an old-time feel to it and is rounded. The **Modern** font is a thinner font, but has more modern sensibilities. The **Rounded** font is actually more of a square font and feels like one that would be used in space.

Views

There are four different views Earth, Moon, Solar System, and Random. The **Earth** option will show you the Earth, for your current location with an accurate sun position and even cloud cover. You can even use the digital crown on the Apple Watch to look at the different positions of the Sun. You can travel either forward or backward as far as you would like to go.

The **Moon** view will show the Moon and similar to the Earth view, you can use the digital crown to move backward and forward. When you do this you will see the date in the upper left and the phase of the Moon shown and the number of days in the past or future at the bottom of the screen.

Moon Astronomy Watch Face

Earth Astronomy Watch Face

The **Solar System** view will show you the Solar system as though you were looking at it from above. Once again the digital crown can be used to see the position of planets for a specific day. The specific day will be in the upper left corner and the difference in time will be shown at the bottom left.

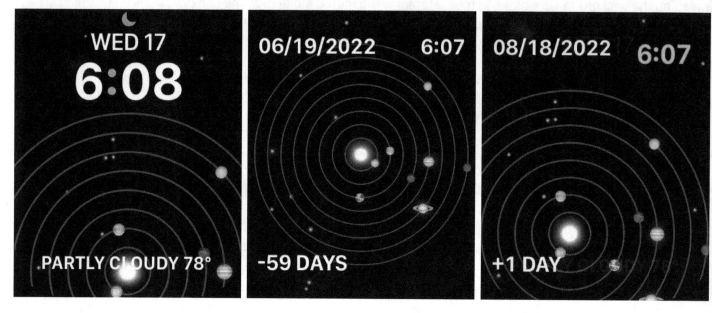

Solar System Astronomy Watch Face   Solar System - Traveling Backward   Solar System - Traveling forward

There are two Styles that you can select, either Full or Random. For the **Full** view you will see the whole Earth, Moon, or Solar System. For **Random** you will see a random part of the selected view. For the Earth view you will see a random place, but your current location will still be within the random section somewhere.

Complications

There are two complication areas that you can specify for any of these items. These are at the top of the screen above the time and at the bottom of the screen. Both of these are line complications.

The Astronomy watch faces are good ones for those who want to want to have an astronomical related watch face. The interactivity is great touch and adds a bit of flair to them.

Lunar

The Lunar watch face is used to provide you information about the Lunar calendar. There four things to customize. These items are Color, Calendar, Time, and Complications.

You can select any color that you would like for the indicator for the seconds. You can choose a color to match your watch band or from one of the color items and then fine tune it with the slider.

The Calendar has three choices, Chinese, Hebrew, and Islamic calendars. The dates and text will change to the specific Lunar calendar that you choose.

The Time option allows you to choose either an Analog or a Digital time. The analog option will have a standard analog seconds hands. For the Digital time the seconds will move around the digital time in the color you choose.

Chinese

Hebrew

Islamic

There are four complication locations that go around the outside corners. You can configure them using whichever complications you need that will fit in those corners.

Playtime

The Playtime watch face is a watch face that was designed in collaboration with Chicago based artist Joi Fulton. From their website, jofulton.com,

"Their works consist of bright punchy colors, and simple friend shaped buddies. She takes a lot of her inspiration from her time when she was a teacher assistant at a daycare and an after school art teacher for kindergartners."

The Playtime watch face definitely fits this description. There are only two options for the Playtime watch face, the Color and whether the Background is on or off. The Playtime watch face shows only the time, but it does this in a way that has some playful characters. These characters are balloon-like and ones that you might see in a children's animated show.

You can select from nine colors for the background. The available options are Black, Red, Orange, Tangerine, Yellow, Green, Blue, Purple, and Pink.

Playtime in Black

Playtime in Orange

Playtime in Green

Playtime in Purple

When the Background option is set to on there will be some objects in the background. When the background is off, these items are not in the background.

It is good to see Apple expanding the Apple Watch face options to include artists who can bring a different take to an Apple Watch face.

That covers all of the new watch faces, but from time to time there are changes that occur that some people might not necessarily like, or that some might enjoy. watchOS 9 has a couple of these changes. One of the changes is a removed watch face and another is some additions to an existing watch face. let us look at some changes to other watch faces, like Modular.

Modular Watch Faces

When the Apple Watch was announced back in 2014, and subsequently released in April of 2015, it included a variety of watch faces, there were ten of them with the release of watchOS 1. In watchOS 8, the original ten were still included. However, in watchOS 9 that is no longer the case because the original Modular watch face has been removed.

The original Modular watch face was designed for the original 38mm and 42mm Apple Watches. This watch face was the epitome of a digital watch because you could have up to five different complications. Four of these would be small complications that were along the upper left, lower left, middle bottom, and lower right. The largest complication was the one in the middle of the Apple Watch face.

Starting with watchOS 9 this version of the Modular watch face is no longer available. The reason for this is because the last remaining 38mm and 42mm Apple Watches, the Series 3, are not supported in watchOS 9, therefore the watch face has been removed. We will come back to this watch face in a bit, let us now turn to a variant of the Modular watch face called Infograph Modular.

Infograph Modular

In 2019 Apple unveiled a new Apple Watch, the Series 4. This watch would be different in a couple of ways. The largest among them was that it came in two new larger screen sizes, a 40mm and a 44 mm. This may not sound like a lot, and in terms of absolute size, it is only 2mm, or about 0.08 inches, but in actuality this is a 4.8% increase In space and on screens that small it is a lot of space.

In order to be able to utilize that amount of space Apple introduced a new watch face, the Infograph Modular watch face. The complications on this watch face were larger and more suited for the screen size. With the Infograph Modular watch face you could have a total of six complications, which is one more than standard original Modular watch face.

With watchOS 9 the Infograph Modular watch face is being renamed to just Modular. What does this mean for the Original Modular watch face? It means that if you have the original Modular watch face configured, it will be upgraded to the new Modular watch face. Your complications should remain, but you will now be able to take advantage of the newer

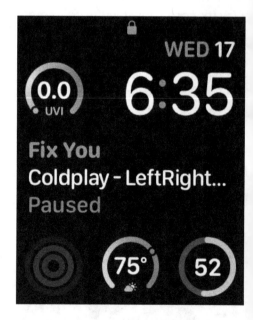

Modular in Multicolor

complications that the Infograph Modular watch face offered. Now, this is not the only change with new Modular watch face, so let us look at those next.

Adding Color to Modular

With the change to the new Modular watch face, watchOS 9 also adds the ability to customize the background color of the watch face. You can choose from one of 18 standard colors. If you select one of these colors, a slider will appear and you can then pick the exact shade of that color that you would like to use. You can also choose from one of the colors that match your Apple Watch Band from any of the pre-defined colors. These styles go back to the original release in 2015 and are organized by season and watch band colors released at that time.

If you choose to enable the background color, the color that you choose will be shown on the background. There will also be a complementary color shown on each of the complications. Now, you may think that having a bright background on all the time would get distracting and might use up battery power, and you would be correct. When the watch face becomes inactive, the background color is removed and the color that you chose will be used as the color of the complications.

Modular with a Green background

Modular with a Multicolor background

There is also a Multicolor option. This will provide a rainbow of colors in a gradient across the entire watch face. These colors options do not apply solely to the Modular watch face, but you can make the same selection on the Modular Duo and X-Large watch faces as well. These will both behave the same way when the watch becomes idle. Now let us turn to one last watch face that has seen an improvement, the Portrait watch face.

Portrait Watch Face

With the release of watchOS 8 in 2021 Apple added a new watch face called **Portraits**. The Portraits watch face allows you to use photos that were taken as Portrait Mode photos on your iPhone and use them as a watch face on your Apple Watch. This has been a pretty popular feature, but there is one thing that could make it even better, the ability to use your pets and guess what watchOS 9 now supports adding?

That is correct, you can now use pictures of your cats and dogs in the Portraits watch face. In order to configure a Portraits watch face, you have to add it using the Face Gallery within the Watch app on your iPhone. You can add photos of your pets as you would any other Portrait photo. When you add a portrait photo of your pet, the iPhone will detect your pet as the subject of the photo and you can then apply a color to the background, or leave the natural color. You can also apply a color, or pair of colors, to the entire photo.

This is a great addition for those who like having portrait photos on their Apple Watch, they can now add photos of the pets, just as they would other portrait photos that they have taken.

Closing Thoughts on Watch Face Changes

The Apple Watch is a fashion item as much as it is a functional item. This means that sometimes fashions come and go and the Series 3 Apple Watch is definitely now seen as out of fashion, and beyond this, watchOS 9 does not support the model. The Apple Watch adds a slew of new watch faces and updates to others.

The new Playtime watch face is a collaboration with a Chicago based artist that adds some playfulness to a watch face. The redesigned Astronomy watch faces will allow you to choose between the Earth, the Moon, and the Solar System adding a bit of pizazz and interactivity to the Apple Watch. The Modular watch face will allow you to choose a background color that will be shown while the Apple Watch is active, but not while it is inactive.

There is one other change to discuss, this one related to notifications.

Notifications

The Apple Watch is a fantastic platform for being able to quickly act on notifications and keep up to date on information. In most cases it is likely that you are only using your Apple Watch for short amounts of time. There may be those instances when you are actually using it for a longer time. One thing that can be quite irksome is what happens when you are actively using your Apple Watch and a notification comes in. With watchOS 8 when this happens it takes over the entire screen and interrupts what you are doing. This behavior changes in watchOS 9.

Now, if you are actively using your Apple Watch instead of being a full screen notification the notification will just be a banner at the top of the screen, similar to how many notifications occur on the iPhone. If you are not using your Apple Watch and a notification comes in, it will still be full screen as before. When a banner notification does come in you can tap on it and then interact with as you normally would, or you can swipe it up the screen to dismiss into the Notification Center. This is a small, but welcome change to notifications.

Closing Thoughts on watchOS

For those who may have some difficultly in manipulating the Digital Crown on the Apple Watch there are two changes. The first is that for instances when you need to unlock the device, because it is Water-locked, or you are in a Sleep Focus, instead of needing to spin the digital crown you can simply press and hold on the Digital Crown to unlock the device.

The second enhancement is that you can now mirror your Apple Watch display to your iPhone. When you do this the Digital Crown and side button will continue to work as expected, you will get haptic feedback, and the actual size will be a large view.

On the topic of the Earth let us look at another set of changes with something that we all experience, Weather.

Weather

It is commonly stated that humans all share 99 percent of the same DNA and it is the remaining 1 percent that makes us individuals, at least on a physical level. No two people have the exact same experiences, so those are entirely our own. Similarly, we all share a number of experiences. No matter where you live on the planet you will, at some point, experience some sort of weather. This can be a blizzard in the middle of winter, a light rain in spring, an extensive heat wave in the summer, or that first cool morning in the fall. In order to prepare for these types of events you will likely want to have the ability to see not only the weather for today, but also the likelihood of the weather in the next few days. One way of being able to do this is through a weather app.

There are only a handful of apps that have been on the iPhone since its introduction in 2007. Some of these include Phone, Notes, Maps, and Weather. When Apple added the Weather app to the iPhone it has used a variety of different sources depending on your location. Some of the sources used have included:

- Australian Government Bureau of Meteorology
- BreezoMeter
- Deutscher Wetterdienst
- Environment and Climate Change Canada
- EUMETNET - MeteoAlarm (European Union)
- European Centre for Medium-Range Weather Forecasts (ECMWF)
- India Meteorological Department
- Instituto Nacional de Meteorologia (Brazil)
- Japan Meteorological Agency
- National Weather Service/National Oceanic and Atmospheric Administration (NOAA)
- QWeather
- Servicio Meteorológico Nacional (Mexico)
- Thai Meteorological Department
- The Met Office (UK)
- The Weather Channel

One aspect to all weather services is that by their very nature they require your exact location, or something very close to it. While most apps may not do so, it is possible for these weather apps to take your location data, then correlate your location with other third-party identifiers and data, and thereby they can gain an extensive look into a variety of different aspects of who you are. If they did not correlate the data themselves, your data could have easily been sold to a data broker, because location is a very good data point to have. Clearly this is not good for privacy.

For a while Apple did not do much with the Weather app for its devices. This left an opportunity for third-party developer's to come along and make various alternative weather apps. Weather apps all require a few pieces of information, namely a location, the more precise the better experience for the end user.

One of the more popular, and privacy abiding, apps was Dark Sky. Dark Sky consisted of two parts, the Dark Sky app and the Dark Sky Application Programming Interface (API) that developers could use. In March of 2020 it was announced that Dark Sky was being acquired by Apple. After finalizing the acquisition Apple shutdown the Android App on August 1st, 2020. The iOS app is scheduled to stop functioning on December 31st, 2022. The reason that the Dark Sky app will stop working is because they have moved all of the functionality into their own native Weather app.

The Dark Sky API has been rebuilt into a new API from Apple called WeatherKit. You can read all about WeatherKit in the developer section of this book. The old Dark Sky API will remain active until March of 2023, at which point it will stop working.

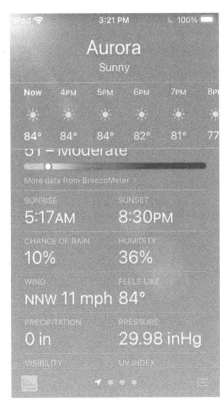

| Weather on iPhone OS 1 to iOS 4 | Weather on iOS 12 | Weather on iOS 14 |

With the release of iOS 15 Apple rewrote the entire iOS Weather app using SwiftUI. The redesigned iOS Weather app provided all of the data that was previous available, but it did so in a manner that was more appealing. Each piece of information was presented in its own container. Some of these containers provided a way to scroll to see more information, while other information was self contained. A second way that Apple made the information more appealing was by adding additional color, indicators, as well as additional text.

One thing that Apple did not do was have an iPad app. On iPadOS 15 and macOS Monterey there is a widget for Weather that will allow you to see the weather. This was convenient on the iPad, because you could place the Weather widget directly on the the iPad home screen, so you could quickly see the weather. However, when you would tap on the Weather widget it would take you to the source for the weather, which was okay, but not ideal. In the United States this was the Weather Channel, but could be another source. All of this changes in iOS 16, iPadOS 16, and macOS Ventura because there are now apps on all of these platforms. Let us look at the Weather app on the iPad.

Weather on iPad

There is now a native Weather app from Apple on both iPadOS 16 and macOS Ventura. The Weather app on all of Apple's platforms is now the exact same app, it is just the presentation that is different on each platform. On the left-side is the List of Cities, The rest of the data is presented on the right side. There are a number of different pieces of data provided. The data within the detail view includes:

- Current Temperature
- Hourly Forecast
- 10 Day Forecast
- Weather Map
- Air Quality
- UV Index
- Sunrise/Sunset
- Wind
- 24-Hour Precipitation Forecast
- Feels like Temperature
- Humidity
- Visibility
- Air Pressure

All of these were present on iOS 15, but there is one thing to note. All of the items below, except for the Current Temperature, are now interactive, including on iOS 16. Therefore, all of the information below applies to all three platforms.

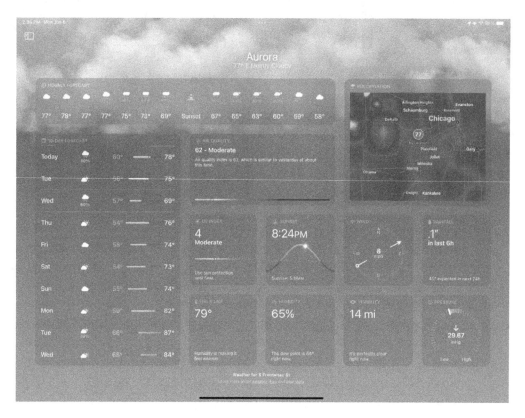

Weather on iPadOS

Item Detail View

There are actually two different types of layouts for each of the detail views. There is the 10-day detail view layout and the Informational view.

The 10-Day Detail View

The 10-Day Detail view is comprised of 4 sections. These sections are:

- 10 Day Bar
- View specific information and selection dropdown.
- Graph with specific view information
- Summary

10-Day Bar

The 10-Day Bar has the upcoming 10 days along the top. The days are just a single letter with the full date below the 10 day bar.

View Specific Information

The View Specific information is the individual piece of data for that specific view. For some examples, the Temperature will show the current temperature, an icon representing the conditions, the high and low of the day. Meanwhile, Humidity shows the humidity percentage and dew point, and Visibility shows the current visibility and a brief description of conditions.

The selection dropdown will allow you to change the information that is shown. The items that all share the 10-day view are:

- Temperature
- UV Index
- Wind
- Precipitation
- Feels Like
- Humidity
- Visibility
- Pressure

Graph

The graph's information will depend on the information being shown. For Temperature, the graph shows a line graph of the various temperatures for the selected day. There is an indicator for the High temperature and another for the Low temperature. There is also a dividing line at the current time, so you can easily differentiate between what has already happened and what is going to happen.

The Humidity graph would show a similar line graph, but instead of the temperature it would be the humidity There are no indicators for high or low, just the line graph.

The Precipitation graph does not show a line chart, but instead it shows a bar chart with the possible precipitation along the y-axis and the hours along the x-axis.

Summary

The summary will, as the name indicates, present a summary of what is being shown in the graph above. For Temperature, it will have a concise forecast. The Humidity details will provide an average humidity for the day, as well as the range for dew point.

Some items will have additional information that is relevant to the item. These sections with additional information include:

- UV Index
- Wind
- Feels Like
- Humidity
- Visibility
- Pressure

Next, let us look at each of these individually, starting with the List of Cities.

List of Cities

On the iPad and macOS there is the option for a sidebar. The sidebar has a list of all of the locations that you have configured on iOS. Each city has a graphical background showing the current conditions. In the upper left corner is the name of the location, right below this is the current time. Below these are a brief description of the current conditions. A few example of current conditions that you might see are:

- Sunny
- Mostly Sunny
- Clear
- Cloudy

To the right, and the largest piece of information is the current temperature. Below the current temperature is the forecasted high temperature and low temperature.You can tap on any of the cities and it will show the information for the selected city on the right hand side.

Weather Detail

On the right hand side is the detailed view of your selected city. The background of the entire view should reflect the current conditions for the city. Therefore, if it is sunny, the sun should be shown. Similarly, if it is cloudy, then there should be clouds. Beyond this, if it is early in the morning, the background may appear as though the sun is just rising, without an actual sun. Similarly, during early evening the background may appear as though there is a sunset in the background.

List of City with their weather detailed

Forecast

At the top of the detail view is the name of the city, the current temperature, the current conditions, and the high and low.

Hourly Forecast

The Hourly Forecast section shows the forecast for the never 24 hours. Each hour has the hour at the top, with an icon representing the forecast, and the temperature for the hour at the bottom.

10 Day Forecast

The 10-Day Forecast presents the potential forecast for the next 10 days. Each day has its own line. Each line has four pieces of information. From left to right it is a shortened form of the day, an icon representing the conditions for the day, the low temperature, and the high temperature. Between the low and high is a slider with a variety of colors. The colors will vary depending on the temperature. Lower temperatures are blue, while higher temperatures will be red.

Air Quality

The AirQuality item will provide you with four pieces of information. The current Air Quality index number, the general description of the quality, a detailed description, and an indicator at the bottom. The description might say something like:

> "Air quality index is 45, which is similar to yesterday at about this time."

Of course, the actual description will likely be different than that. The scale for Air Quality depends on the locality and what one area may consider "Good", may not be adequate for another area.

The detail screen for the Air Quality Index has a map with the selected city in the center. The background of the map is a color representing the Air quality in the surrounding area. Below the map is the same information as with the item on the main screen, albeit with the scale and for which locality.

Below the detailed information is some additional information regarding Health Information about the Air Quality index and possible Primary Pollutants for the current Air Quality Index.

There are two things to note. Firstly, Air Quality Index may only be available in United States. Secondly, the Air Quality Index information is provided by Breezometer in the United States, and QWeather for China,

Weather Map

The Weather Map will show a very wide view of the country centered on your location. The Map View has three buttons. These buttons are My Location, City List, and Map Type.

The **My Location** button will center on your current location.

The **City List** button will show all of the cities that you have entered into the Weather app. When you click on this button a popup will open and you can select one of the cities. When you do this, that location will be shown on the map.

The **Map Type** button will allow you to select between three different views, Temperature, Precipitation, and Air Quality. When you tap on one of these views, the map will switch to that view. For locations that do not have a source for Air Quality, this information will be blank.

Precipitation Weather Map   Temperature Weather Map

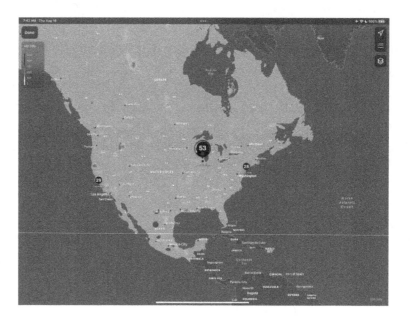

UV Index Weather Map

UV Index

The **UV Index** item will show the current Ultra Violet Index in the upper left corner. Directly below this is the intensity, of Low, Medium, High, or Very High, depending on the index level.

The graph for UV Index is a line graph that shows the hours along the x-axis and the UV index along the y-axis. Along the top is the UV index for the hour. The line for the graph will be a different color based upon the UV Index for that hour.

Sunrise/Sunset

The Sunrise/Sunset item shows the current time that the sun with either set or rise, depending on the current state of the sun. The bottom of this item shows the next sunset or sunrise, again depending on the current state of the Sun. Between these two is a line that shows the current location of the sun, in relation to sunrise and sunset.

The detail screen for Sunrise/Sunset does not show a graph. Instead, there is a graphic at the top that shows the progression of the sun throughout the day. The hours of 12AM, 6AM, 12PM, and 6PM are shown at the bottom of the graphic.

The second area shows a table that includes this information:

- First Light
- Sunrise
- Sunset
- Last Light
- Total Daylight

The last section is another table. This table shows the Sunrise and Sunset Average. Each month is shown in the table with the average sunrise and sunset time fore each month. Directly below the header is either the day with the longest daylight, along with the length of daylight.

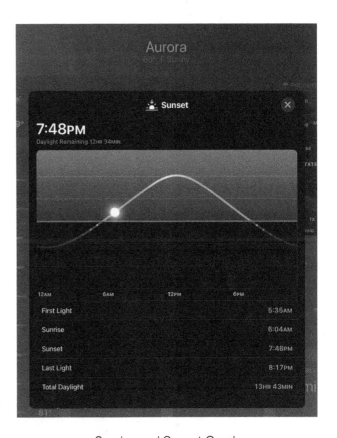

Sunrise and Sunset Graph

Wind

The **Wind** item has a compass with the arrow pointing in the current direction that the wind is blowing. In the middle of the compass is the strength of the wind.

The graph for Wind has two line graphs. The prominent lower line is the actual wind speeds and the higher and less prominent line indicates the gusts. Along the x-axis are the hours in the day. The y-axis shows the wind speed. Along the top of the graph are the directions of the wind.

Overall, the Wind graph can give you a pretty good idea of what the wind will do, all by quickly glancing at the graph.

24-Hour Precipitation Forecast

The **24 Hour Precipitation Forecast** item will show you how much precipitation has been received in the last 24 hours as well as the expected precipitation in the next 24 hours.

The graph for the 24 Hour Precipitation shows the hours along the x-axis, and shows the amount of precipitation along the y-axis, and shows the conditions along the top of the graph.

Feels Like Temperature

The **Feels Like Temperature** item will indicate what it feels like outside. At the bottom of this item is a brief description of what might be causing the difference in Feels Like temperature as compared to the current temperature.

If the two are the same, it will say something like "Similar to the actual temperature". If the Feels Like temperature is warmer than the actual temperature, it might say something like "Humidity is making it feel warmer". If the Feels Like temperature is lower, it might say "Wind is making it feel cooler".

The graph shows a line graph. The graph shows the hours along the x-axis and the Feels Like temperature along the y-axis. The conditions are across the top, and there are High and Low, Feels Like temperature indicators along the line graph.

Humidity

The **Humidity** item shows the current humidity percentage at the top. Along the bottom is a short sentence with the current dew point.

The graph is a line graph. The graph shows the hours along the x-axis, with the percentage of humidity along the y-axis. Along the top is the approximate percentage for the hour.

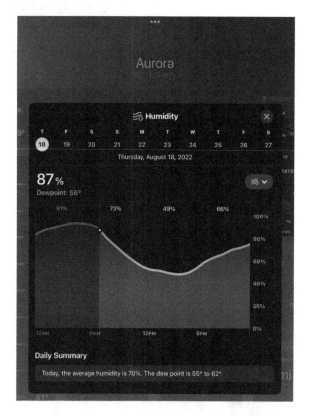

Humidity Chart within Weather on iPadOS

Visibility

The **Visibility** item shows the current visibility at the top. Along the bottom is a short sentence with the current conditions that are affecting the visibility, if at all.

The graph is a line graph. The graph shows the hours along the x-axis, with the visibility along the y-axis. Along the top is the average visibility for the hour.

Barometric Pressure

The **Barometric Pressure** item shows a radial dial with the current barometric pressure. Barometric pressure is measured using inches of mercury, abbreviated as "inHg". The current pressure is shown along the dial and the pressure is also shown in decimal in the center of the radial dial. Directly above the pressure in decimal is an indicator of which direction the pressure is headed. If the pressure is dropping, a down arrow will be shown. If it is trying the same, an equals sign will be shown. If the pressure is headed up, then an up arrow will be shown.

The graph is very similar to that of other graphs. Along the x-axis are the hours with the pressure along the y-axis. Along the top is an indicator as to whether the pressure went down, stayed the same, or rose during that hour.

Closing Thoughts on Weather

The Weather app saw a big redesign using SwiftUI in iOS 15. That design has been expanded to support more screen sizes. The Weather app is now also available on iPadOS 16 and macOS Ventura, and it is a fantastic addition. You can now quickly view information right within the app, including things like current temperature, air quality index, ultra violet index, and even wind speed, amongst additional items.

Each of the items can be opened to see even more detailed information, including graphs, charts, and tables, depending on the item you tapped.

On iPadOS and macOS if you tap on a widget it will no longer open a weather website, instead it will open up the native Weather app. This is a much better experience for everyone regardless of the platform being used.

Beyond just being able to see the information, including details about each of the items, the source of the information has changed to Apple's own WeatherKit, which used to be Dark Sky, which Apple acquired in 2020. No longer will you need to worry about your data being sent off to a third-party and possibly being correlated with other third-party data to perform tracking.

While looking at the Weather for your current location, you may check out the Air quality index to make sure that it is safe to do things outside. One of those outside activities might be some sort of physical fitness, which is the topic of the next chapter.

Health and Fitness

Apple has been putting effort into a variety of different areas. One area that they have been focusing on since 2015 is Health and Fitness. The reason that Apple is focusing on this is due to the Apple Watch. When the Apple Watch was introduced the intention was to be a small iPhone. However, it quickly turned out that users did not want to use apps in that way on their Apple Watches. Instead, focusing on health and fitness, as well as notifications, is what users wanted to do. With this feedback Apple doubled down on all three of these things.

Each release of watchOS brings new features and enhancements to Apple's wrist computer. With watchOS 8, Apple introduced a new Meditation app, and with watchOS 9, they have added another app. The term **health** is a broad term. It can encompass physical fitness, but it also also encompass overall wellbeing. We will tackle improvement to both Health and Fitness. Let us start with something health related, Medications.

Medications

As long as humans have been around, we have ailed in one way or another. Modern science has allowed many of the things that people dealt with a century ago to become a thing of the past. One area where modern medicine has helped is when it comes to alleviating symptoms that we may be experiencing. The way that this is usually done is by taking some sort of medication, usually in pill form. As much as we may try to avoid it, it's inevitable that at some point that you will need to take some form of medication. This may be for a short-time, or it might be for a lot longer.

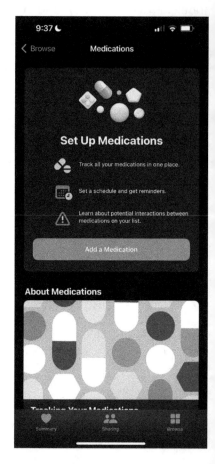

If you take any medication it is quite likely that you will forget to take it at some point. There have been many techniques to help us remember. This could be through daily pill boxes where you put all of the medication that you need to take into a designated box for the day. You may even have two different boxes, one for the pills you take in the morning and one for the pills you take in the evening. If you take a pill every day, it is quite possible that you will remember, however if you need to take a pill say once or twice a week, it is entirely possible that you might forget. What would be good is if our devices could remind us to take our pills. Starting with iOS 16, this is exactly what you can do.

Medications

Within the Health app on your iPhone you now have the ability to enter in the medications that you take. To enter in a medicine that you take in to the Health app use the following steps:

1. Open the **Health** app.
2. Tap on the **Browse** tab.
3. Scroll down to **Medications**.
4. Tap on **Medications**. You will be brought to the Setup Medications screen.
5. On the Setup Medications screen tap on **Add Medication**. This will bring up the Add Medication screen.

Setup Medications in Health app

On this screen there are two items. The first is a search box where you can perform a search for the medicine that you take. The second is a button to use your camera to scan the medications that you take. Let us look at each in turn.

Searching

For our walkthrough let us use ibuprofen as an example. As you type, the word ibuprofen results will update to match your current search term. You can scroll through the list to see if you can find an exact match. If you find your medicine, tap on it. There is a second option for detecting medication. The other option is to use your camera to identify the medicine.

Search for Medication

Using Camera for Searching

The way that you use your camera for searching is to tap on the **Camera** icon to the right of the search box. When you do this an informational screen will be shown. Tap on **Get Started** to begin scanning.

After you have tapped on the **Get Started** button, your camera will become active with a view finder for you to use. Use your camera to move the view finder over your medication bottle. If the medication can be identified, it will be matched and shown in the list of medications. If there are multiple matches, a list of possible matches will be shown. You can select the appropriate one from the list. It is possible that it may not be able to be identified. If it cannot be identified, then you can tap on the **Search By Name** button to search by name.

You do not need to necessarily scan medicine bottles. The camera app can also detect text, so if you have a piece of paper from your doctor's office, or from a pharmacy, that has the name of the medicine that you take on it, the Health app may be able to use that to scan the name.

If the medicine that you have selected comes in more than one type, like a tablet, liquid capsule, or a chewable tablet, you will be brought to a Choose the Medication Type screen. Here you can select the proper type that you take. Once you have selected the proper type, tap on the **Next** button.

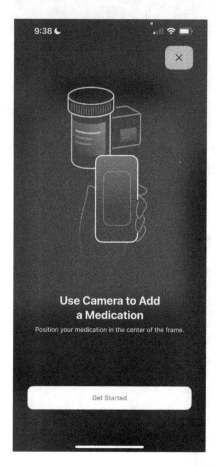

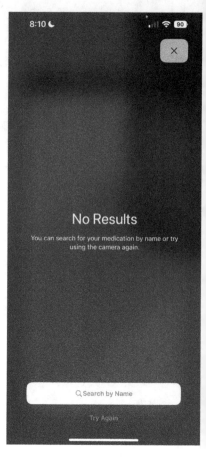

| Use Camera to Add a Medication | Search Results for medication search (Result is blanked out) | No Search Results when using the camera |

Choose the Medication Strength

Similar to the various dispensing methods of medication, it may also come in various strengths. If it does come in a variety of strengths you may be brought to the "Choose the Medication Strength" screen. In the case of Ibuprofen, it may come in 200 mg, 400 mg, 600 mg, or 800 mg varieties. You can tap on the strength that you take. Tap the **Next** button.

When Will You Take This?

The next screen you will see is the **When will you take this?** Screen. There are some medicines that you need to take at certain times throughout the day, while others you can take at any time. Along with the time of day, there is also how often you take a particular medicine. On this screen you can configure both.

The first thing you want to select is how frequently you take the medication. The default is every day. If you need to change this, tap on **Every Day** and a popup will appear. Here you will have three frequency options. These options are:

- At Regular Intervals
- On Specific Days of the Week
- As Needed

At Regular Intervals

If you select At Regular Intervals, you can select between any number of days, between every and 99, including Every other day. You select the interval needed by selecting it in the scrolling wheel. You will also be able to select the day that you want to start taking the medication.

On Specific Days of the Week

If you select the On Specific Days of the Week option you will be able to select which days of the week you need to take the specific medicine. This option also has the ability to select the day that you want to start taking the medication.

As Needed

The As Needed option does not have any options, because you only take the medicine as you need to. This option is good for allergy medicines where you might not take them very often, but might need to take them during specific times of the year.

Once you have finished selecting the frequency tap on the **Done** button. After you have selected the frequency you will then need to select the Time of Day that you take the medicine. This is done by tapping on the **+ Add a Time** button.

When you tap on this the nearest half hour will be be selected by default. You can change the time by tapping on it and selecting the new time. You can only select the time in five-minute intervals, meaning that you cannot choose the time of 6:03, but you can select either 6:00 or 6:05. On the same line you will also see a location to set the number of units that you need to be taken. Tap on this and enter in the number of units.

Frequency of Medication

If you need to add additional times you can add them as needed. After you have finished adding all of the times, you can tap on the **Next** button. This will bring you to the Choose the Shape screen.

Choose the Shape

After you have specified the frequency, times, and units, you will be brought to the Choose the Shape screen. This screen is designed to allow you to choose the shape that most closely matches the shape of the medication that you take. By selecting the shape, you can be reminded of the shape. Locate the shape that you want to use to identify the medication. Once finished, tap on the **Next** screen. Alternatively, you can skip selecting a shape if desired.

Choose Colors

Medications come in all sorts of colors. After you have selected the shape of your medication, you can select the colors to be used to help you identify the medication. You can choose the color for the shape you chose as well as a background color. The Shape colors closely match the ones that are actually used in medicines. Meanwhile the Background colors are ones that have a bit more contrast so you can see the shape's color a bit easier. After selecting the Shape and Background color, tap on the **Next** button.

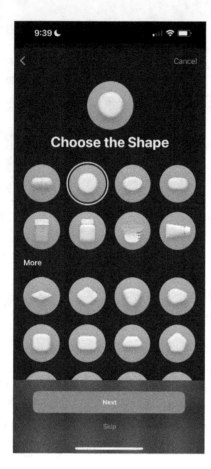

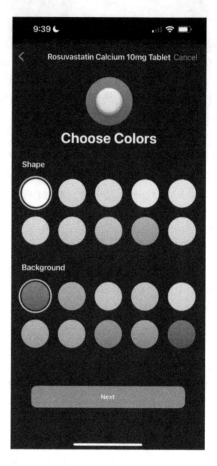

| Medication Shape | Medication Colors |

Optional Details

The next screen is the Optional Details screen. None of the items on the screen are required, but they are offered as a convenience. Here you can enter in a Nickname for the medication. This name will be used on both the list of medications as well as when you log that you have taken them. There is a second area on the screen for Notes. Here you can enter in any notes that you want for the medication. After you have entered in the optional nickname and details, tap on the **Done** button.

As soon as you have tapped on **Done**, the medication will be added to the list. Next, let us look at enabling reminders for medications.

Medication Reminders

Having your medications in the Health app is somewhat useful, but what is more useful is to be reminded of when to take the medication. This can be done by using the following steps:

1. Open **Health**.
2. Tap on **Browse**.
3. Tap on **Medications**.
4. Locate the **Log**.
5. Tap on **Options**.
6. Enable the **Dose Reminders** toggle to enable medication reminders.

After you have enabled Dose Reminders you will receive notifications when it is time to take your medication. Let us look at what happens when you get a reminder.

Logging Medication

When the time arrives for you to take one of your medications, and if you have enabled notifications, you should receive a notification on both your iPhone as well as a paired Apple Watch. For the Apple Watch if you are on watchOS 8 you will only receive a basic notification letting you know that it is time for your medications. You can then log your medication on iOS

On an iPhone

When you tap on the notification you will be brought directly to the medication logging screen.Here you can indicate how many units of each medicine that you have taken as well as the time. The default time is the time that you tapped on the notification.

You can modify the units and time by tapping on the "1 Unit at 6:10PM" item. If you do edit the units and time, you will be brought to the **Log Details** screen. Here you can select the number of units and the exact time. Once you have modified this information, you can tap on **Done** to bring you back to the Medications screen.

On this screen you can indicate whether you have taken a medication by tapping on the **Taken** button. If you have skipped taking the medication you can tap on the **Skipped** button.

If you have multiple medications that you take at the same time, you can tap on the **Mark All as Taken** to mark that you have taken all of the medications.

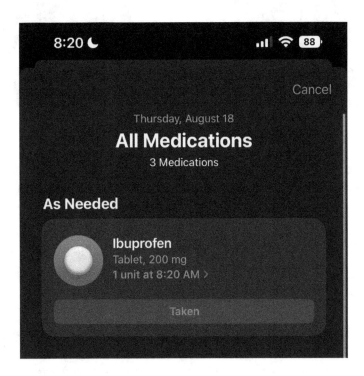

On an Apple Watch

If you have watchOS 9 on your Apple Watch you will get a slightly richer experience than on watchOS 8. With watchOS 9 you will be able to use these preset options:

- Log All As Taken
- Log All as Skipped
- Remind me in 10 minutes

These options allow you to quickly and easily mark whether you took your schedule medication, or delay it for 10 minutes. If none of these options work, you can use your iPhone to log your medications as needed.

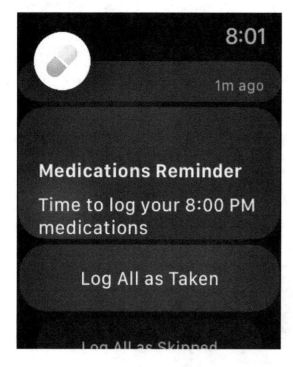

Medication Notification on watchOS

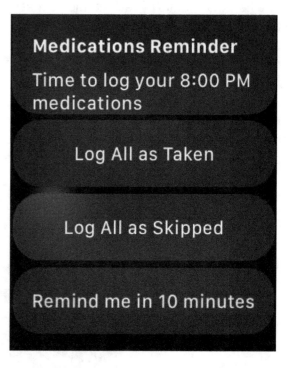

Medication Logging options on watchOS

If you are running watchOS 8 on your Apple Watch, you will get a notification when it is time to take your medication, but you will not be able to log it from the watch. Instead, you will need to log your medication on your iPhone.

After you have indicated whether each medication has been Skipped or Taken, tap on the **Done** button to enter in the information into your Medications logged.

Interaction Detection

If you watch any sort of television in the United States it is inevitable that you will hear an advertisement for medications. In all of these ads there is likely to be 10 seconds worth of legalese that has all of the side effects of the medication. Some of these side effects may be due to interactions with other medications.

If you only take one or two medications it is not likely that you will have any interactions between them. However, as you add additional medications it is possible that interactions between them may occur.

When you add a medication the Health app will use the information about your current medications that alert you to possible interactions that may occur between the medications that you are taking. These interaction alerts are only for those within the United States.

Medication Interactions

If there is a possible interaction between your medications it will have one of three levels, moderate, serious, or critical, depending on its severity. This way you can know about the possible interactions and discuss them with your doctor.

Archiving and Deleting Medications

There may be times when you only need to take a medication for a short while. In these instances you may not always want the alerts for the medication if you are no longer taking it. In these instances you have two options, you can either archive a medication or you can delete a medication. Each of these has different implications. Let us look at each.

Archiving, and Unarchiving, a Medication

When you archive a medication, all of the information regarding that medication like its log history and schedule will be preserved. This option is good for medications that you may need to take regularly but infrequently, like allergy medicines when you only take them during that particular allergy season. To archive a medication perform the following steps:

1. Open the **Health** app.
2. Tap on the **Browse** tab item at the bottom
3. Tap on **Medications**.
4. Under Your Medications tap the **Edit** button.
5. **Locate** the mediation that you could like to archive.
6. **Tap** the medication that you want to archive.

Once you have tapped on the medication it will be archived. You can set a medication to be active again by tapping on it in the **Archived Medications** list.

Rearranging Medication Order

The order that medications appear in the list of Your Medications is based upon the order in which they were added. This may not always be the best order for you. You can easily rearrange the order by performing the following steps:

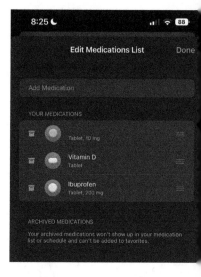

1. Open the **Health** app.
2. Tap on the **Browse** tab item at the bottom.
3. Tap on **Medications**.
4. Under Your Medications tap the **Edit** button.
5. **Locate** the mediation that you could like to move.
6. **Tap and hold** on the three bar icon on the right of the medication.
7. **Drag** the medication to the order that you would like.

When you order your medications the order will be updated on the Your Medications screen.

Re-arrange Medication List

Deleting a Medication

If you opt to delete a medication all of its information will be deleted. This includes the log history and schedule. Once you have deleted the information it cannot be retrieved. To delete a medication perform the following steps:

1. Open the **Health** app.
2. Tap on the **Browse** tab item at the bottom
3. Tap on **Medications**.
4. Under **Your Medications** locate the medication that you would like to delete.
5. **Tap** on the Medication to bring up its detail screen.
6. **Scroll down** to the bottom of the screen.
7. Tap on **Delete Medication** a pop up will appear.
8. Tap on **Delete Medication** to confirm that you want to delete the medication.

After you have tapped on the second Delete Medication, the medication and its history will be deleted. There is no way to retrieve this information.

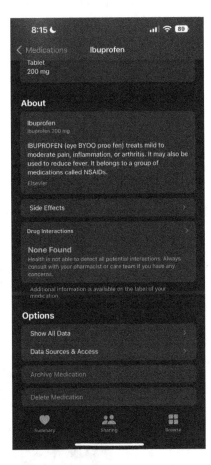

Archive and Delete Options for a medication in Health app on iOS

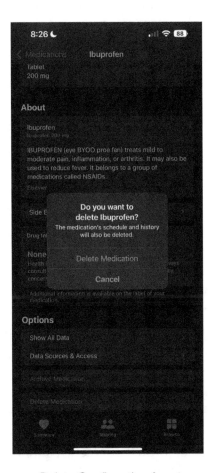

Delete Confirmation for a medication

Editing a Medication Schedule

When you first setup a medication you may have been prescribed one schedule, but as time goes on your may need to adjust the schedule for an individual medication. To do this perform the following steps:

1. Open the **Health** app.
2. Tap on the **Browse** tab item at the bottom.
3. Tap on **Medications**.
4. Under **Your Medications** locate the medication schedule that you would like to edit.
5. **Tap** on the Medication to bring up its detail screen.
6. Scroll down to **Schedule**.
7. Tap on **Edit** to bring up the Edit Schedule page.

On the Edit Schedule screen you can make any changes that you need to for the medication. If you change the time or frequency, you will receive a notification at the new time.

Medication Log Details

It is a fact of life that our memories are fallible. The things that we think we remember, we might not remember how they actually occurred. Instead of having to rely on memory, it is better to look at actual data. After you have been logging your medications for a while you may want to see how frequently you are taking certain medications.

Some medications that are prescribed are to be taken every day, while others may be less frequently, and some may just be on an as needed basis.Regardless of the actual frequency we may want to look at some details about the medications that we take. This can be done on the Medication Details screen. To access the details of any of your medications perform the following steps:

1. Open the **Health** app.
2. Tap on the **Browse** tab item at the bottom
3. Tap on **Medications**.
4. Under **Your Medications** locate the medication that you would like to see the details of.
5. **Tap** on the Medication to bring up its detail screen.

Once you have opened up an information screen, you will be shown a variety of information. The information that is provided includes a bar chart of logging history, details, the medication schedule, Highlights about logging history, information about the medication, and options. Let us look at a couple of these, specifically Charts, Highlights, and About. The others have been covered elsewhere.

Charts

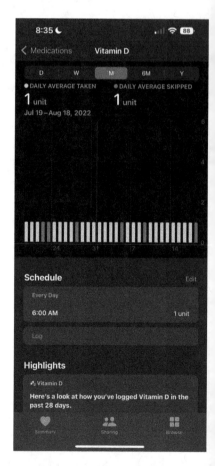

At the top of the medication detail screen is a bar chart. This chart shows how often the medication was logged. You can choose the date range to show by tapping on any of the time frames at the top of the chart. There are likely to be there different colors on the screen. A bright blue to indicate that the medication was taken, a more muted blue that indicates it was skipped, and if there is no item for a particular time frame, then there is no information logged at all.

Along the x-axis at the bottom is the individual interval for the selected time frame. Along the y-axis is the number of units taken or skipped. You can tap on any individual bars to get information about that time frame. This is a good way of being able to see overall trends.

Highlights

The Highlight section uses your logging information to provide a calendar view of your last 28 days so you can see which days you have logged that you have taken your medication. Unlike the Chart sections, either a day is bright blue to indicate that you did take the medication that day, or it is gray to indicate that you did not take it. Whether it was logged as skipped or no information was added will both appear as not taken.

About

The **About** section is used to provide you information about the medication

Monthly View with skipped doses

itself. At the top of the section is the name and any possible unit measurement for the medication that you take. Below this is a brief, but more detailed about the medication and its uses.

Underneath the description is a button where you can see possible side effects of the medication. At the bottom of both the description and the side effects will be the source for the information.

The last item in the About section is the possible drug interactions that may occur between this individual medication and the other medications that you are taking.

Exporting Medication List

It is possible that you may need to discuss what medications that you are taking with someone else, or just to have a list for yourself. You can actually export your medication list to a PDF. This can be done by performing the following steps:

1. Open the **Health** app.
2. Tap on the **Browse** button in the tab bar.
3. Scroll down to **Medications**.
4. **Tap** on Medications to open up the medication information.
5. Scroll down to the **Your Medications** section.
6. Tap on the **Export Medication List PDF** button. This will create a PDF.

When you tap on the **Export Medication List PDF** button the PDF is created. The PDF will contain some sensitive information that will be in the PDF. This includes your name, birthdate, and age. This information will be in the upper left corner.

The main portion of the PDF will have the list of medications that you are taking. The name of the medication, the medication type (tablet, capsule, drops, etc), and the dosage. Each medication will be on its own line. Once it is generated you can tap on the **Share** button in the upper right corner to share the PDF, via Messages, Files, or another app.

Closing Thoughts on Medications

The new medication tracking function of the Health app is a feature that many will utilize to keep track of their medications. The medication tracking is more than just a list, it will also provide reminders so you can be assured that you take your medication when you are supposed to, whether it be every day, every other day, a few times a week, once a week, once a month, or whatever frequency you need to take your medication, it is covered.

When you decide to add a medication you do not necessarily need to do so manually. You can add your medications by searching for them but you can also use your camera to scan your medications.

When you add a medication you will be able to set the frequency, shape, and color for the medication, and you can optionally set a nickname, all so that you can easily identify the medication in both your list of medications as well as when you log when you take the medication.

If you live in the United States you can receive possible interactions alerts between your medications. The severity of these interactions will be noted in the alert. Medication tracking is not the only new feature. Let us look at some enhancements to various aspects of fitness.

Fitness

Fitness is something that can come in a variety of ways. Sometimes this is by going on a brief walk just to get some exercise in for the day, partaking in an Apple Fitness program, or even by competing in an ultra-marathon, or anything in between. While the Heath app is the actual location where all of your health and fitness data is stored, it is likely the Apple Watch that is providing all of the data. However, that may not always be the case. There is a change that is going to make it a bit easier.

Fitness App

When someone mentions that they can do something with the Fitness app, you may attempt to try and find it, however you might not see it in the apps on your iPhone. You could go and search for it o the App Store and you would definitely find it, replete with an Open button, meaning it was already installed. However, if you try and open it you would see something that states

> "The Fitness app works with Apple Watch to keep track of your activity and workout history. To start using the app on your iPhone, first set up Activity on your Apple Watch."

That is not exactly conducive to being able to track workouts if you do not have an Apple Watch. In iOS 16 this all changes because you will be able to use the Fitness app right on your iPhone, even without an Apple Watch. As you might suspect, this will have some limitations.

Since it is an iPhone, it will not be able to track heart rate, because there is no sensor for it. However it will track both steps and distance traveled. If you take this and combine it with any third-party workouts that you might do, an estimation of the calories that were burned will be calculated. This amount will contribute to your daily move goal. While it is not going to be nearly as accurate as an Apple Watch, it does go a long way to allowing all users to keep track of their fitness goals. Now, let us look at some changes that are coming to fitness and watchOS 9, starting with Atrial Fibrillation History.

Atrial Fibrillation History

Back with watchOS 5.1 inDecember of 2018, Apple added two features, an Electrocardiogram, or ECG, app for detecting irregular heart rhythm. Along with this Apple also added the ability to be notified when it detects Atrial Fibrillation, or AFib. While the Apple Watch does not check this in an ongoing basis, it will check periodically and if it detects that someone is currently in AFib, it will provide an alert so they can seek medical assistance. While there has been notifications for when it happens, there has been no insight into how often it has occurred, or if there is any sort of pattern. This changes with watchOS 9.

Now there is a feature called AFib history. AFib history will allow you to possibly correlate lifestyle factors with the occurrences of AFib.

With AFib history you will be able to see the time of day, or the day of the weeks when AFib occurs. This has to be enabled by you, as it is not enabled by default.

Let us now turn to some changes with the Workout app on watchOS.

Workouts on watchOS

When you decide to perform some sort of exercise you are likely going to need to start a workout. The Apple Watch can sometimes detect that you are in a workout and retroactively start one, but this is not foolproof, so it is better to start it yourself. When you are in the middle of a workout you may want to look at how well you are doing with your workout. The Workouts app on watchOS has always provided some data, like current heart rate, distance traveled, and length of the workout. This information is good to know if you want an overall view, but the Apple Watch also tracks additional information for each workout, like elevation. Now, you can see some of the information while out in the middle of the exercise.

Custom Workouts

Apple has been regularly adding new workout types to the Apple Watch. With watchOS 8 there were 80 different workouts that you could add. For a significant part of the population these predefined workout types will suffice. However, there may be times when you are attempting to follow a specific workout routine, whether it be because it is recommended by your physician or trainer, or if you are just attempting to vary things from time to time, you may have wanted the ability to add some custom lengths of time.

For instance, let us say you like to start with a ten minute warm up, followed by doing five minutes worth of exercising, then two minutes worth of recovery, and you repeat this five times, and then do ten minutes worth of cool down at the end. You cannot configure any specific exercise to do this, so you may just put this into **Other** or if this is a run, it might fall into either Outdoor Run or Indoor Run. . Now with watchOS 9 you can use the new **Custom Workout** type to create just this scenario.

Custom

When you add a Custom Workout you can add as many different segments to it as you would like. Therefore, the scenario that is outlined above. When you create a custom workout you will want to start with a type of workout, like Outdoor Run, Indoor Walk, Yoga, or any other workout type. Let us create the above scenario as an Outdoor Run workout. To do just that perform the following steps:

1. Open the **Workouts** app on your Apple Watch.
2. Scroll down to **Outdoor Run**.
3. Tap on the "**...**" button to bring up the additional list.
4. Scroll down to **Create Workout**.
5. Tap on **Create Workout** to bring up the custom types.
6. Tap on **Custom** to create a new custom workout.

Create Custom

Once you create the custom workout you can then add the warm up time, the 5 minutes of work and two minutes of recovery. You can then have this repeat five times, and then set the cool down time. Once you have set the items, then you can set the title. After you have done this, you can then use the custom workout whenever you want. You can add as many custom workouts as you need.

Running

One of the groups that utilize the Apple Watch for tracking their exercises is runners. The Apple Watch is an ideal companion because it is lightweight, secured to your wrist, and you can connect a pair of bluetooth headphones so you do not need to bring your phone with you. The Apple Watch can provide a number of different metrics, including the four mentioned earlier, heart rate, distance traveled, pace, and length of the workout. Heart Rate and length of workout apply to all workouts. The other two metrics, distance traveled and pace can apply to walking, running, and cycling. There are three new metrics that are being added to your running workouts, let us look at these.

New Metrics

Runners are a different type of exerciser. When a runner exercises there may be running specific details that they want to know about. This might be how long they are in contact with the ground, how much they go up and down while running, and how long their stride is. All three of these are now available in watchOS 9. These three metrics are Ground Contact Time, Vertical Oscillation, and Stride Length.

Ground Contact Time

Ground Contact Time is the amount of time that a foot remains on the ground during a run. The lower the time, the faster one is traveling and therefore the quicker the pace. This is measured in milliseconds (ms), and more elite runners tend to have lower ground contact time, because they are moving a bit faster.

Vertical Oscillation

When you are running, you may think that you are only going laterally in the direction that you are traveling. However, as we have all noticed, or at least should have noticed, when we are running our bodies tend to move up and down. This includes the torso and the rest of the upper body. The reason for this is because the impact of your foot hitting the ground is transferred up the body. The amount of movement from this is Vertical Oscillation. Vertical Oscillation is an important metric and may have a possible correlation between injury and the amount of vertical oscillation that one experiences. The lower the Vertical Oscillation the less likely there are to be injuries related to that. The average vertical oscillation can be found while in a workout and it is measured in centimeters.

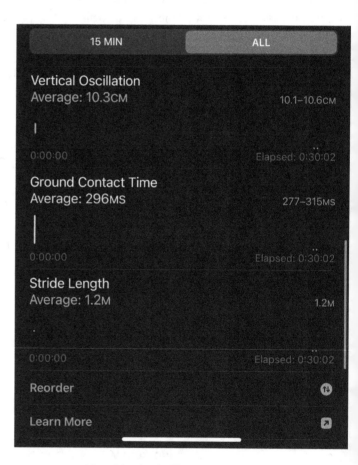

New Metrics in Fitness app on iOS

Stride Length

When you run you are putting one foot in front of the other. The amount of distance that you cover when you take one full step with both of your feet. This can be an important measurement for runners because the longer their stride, the more ground they can cover, the faster they can go. You will now be able to get stride length while you are in the middle of a workout as well as in the details at the end of a workout.

All of these metrics can be helpful when determining how well you are improving. There is another new metric that the Apple Watch will be able to help with.

Running Power

When you are on a run, you are exerting a lot of effort and burning a lot of calories. The amount of energy that you are expending may be a sustainable amount, at the same time it might be a bit more than you can sustain. There is a new feature called **Running Power** that will let you know how much energy and effort you are expending and it will let you know whether or not it is a sustainable amount. If you are going too fast, the Apple Watch will let you know, at the same time if you could go a bit faster, it might suggest that as well.

Race a Route

Often when you are training for a race, like a half marathon or full marathon, you may use the same route for your training. When you are finished with your route you will likely want to know how well you did. This is easily accessible at the end of a workout where watchOS will tell you the pace for your run. What is not easy is being able to compare your current pace to your previous pacing. With watchOS 9, you can now do just that.

When you are using the Outdoor Run or Outdoor Cycle workout you can now receive instant feedback on how you are doing on your current route as compared to the last time that you ran the route. This is called **Race Route**. When you use Race Route you will be given instant feedback with how you are doing as compared to both your last run, as well as your best run. This is a nice feature for those who want to try and beat their own previous pace and do so without having to manually keep track of their pace.

To start using Race Route, use the following steps:

1. Open the **Workout app** on your Apple Watch
2. Scroll down to **Outdoor Run**.
3. Tap on the "**...**" Button.
4. **Scroll down** to the Route that you want to race again.
5. **Tap** on the Route to bring up the information screen.
6. **Select the time** that you want to Race against. Either you Last or Personal Best.
7. Tap on **Start workout** to begin the workout.

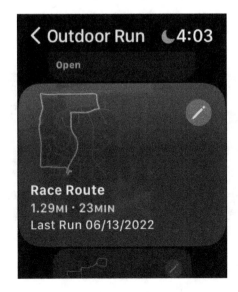
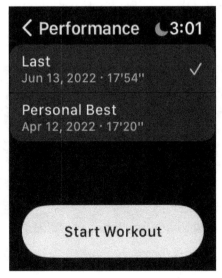

On this information screen each of the Last Race and Personal Best items will show the date of the route, as well as the overall pace for that date. There is one thing to mention about this. It is entirely possible that you may have information for routes before you upgraded your Apple Watch to watchOS 9. This makes sense given that the Apple Watch has been able to map your routes for a while, even so it is good to have some data to work with as soon as you upgrade.

Multisport Workouts

When many people do a workout they generally only do a single type of workout at a time. This could be running, cycling, volleyball, basketball, or any other exercise. There is one significant exception to this, Triathlons. In a Triathlon you actually compete in three different sports, Running, Cycling, and Swimming.

If you wanted to track how well you were doing in each of these sports, you would likely have to manually start and stop each workout, or ask Siri to stop your current workout and start another one. What would be more convenient is if the Apple Watch could easily switch between these three sports, so you do not have need to worry about it.

Now, with watchOS 9, it can do just this. The Apple Watch will be able to easily switch between swimming, biking, and running, so you no longer need to manually change between these during a triathlon. This means that you can now focus on the sport and not whether or not your exercise is being tracked or not, because it will be. This is done through the sensors built into the Apple Watch, where it will detect the various movement patterns, like your arm movements when your are running, the various swimming strokes, and the distance you are going while cycling. All of these will allow it to seamlessly transition between the various sports.

Most importantly is that each of the metrics for each of the different sports will be recorded separately so you can see each of them in relation to previous workouts. You can even swipe between the three so you can see information at a glance while in the middle of a workout.

To start a Multisport workout, use the following steps:

1. Open the **Workout app** on your Apple Watch
2. Scroll down to **Multisport**.
3. Tap on the "**...**" button to bring up customization options.
4. **Scroll down** to the type of multisport workout that you will run.
5. **Tap** on the multisport workout to start the workout.

 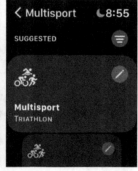   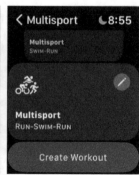

The options that are available for the multisport workout are:

- Triathlon
- Run-Bike-Run
- Swim-Bike
- Bike-Run
- Swim-Run
- Run-Swim-Run

Being able to select the exact triathlon that you are going to run and the not have to worry about the proper sport information being recorded can go a long way to making it easier to train and participate in triathlons. Let us now turn to another new feature, updated views of your Workouts.

Workout Views

With watchOS 8, when you are working out you can easily move between a few different metrics while in a workout. The metrics are different depending on the type of workout. For the outdoor running or indoor running workouts you can see the the aforementioned metrics of Heart Rate, Distance Traveled, Length of workout, and Pace. Now, while you are in a workout you can see more metrics.

Some of these views have already been mentioned, like Running Power and Heart Rate Zones. There are a couple of other ones that should be mentioned. The first is specifically for hikers. For workouts like Hiking you will be able to see your current elevation as well as the amount of elevation gained.

All of these can easily be seen by scrolling the digital crown while in a workout. When you scroll down you will see the various new views that will allow you to quickly glance at the information that you need.

The last view to mention is one that seems like it should have been there before, but it has not been. That view is the Activity Rings View.

Activity Ring View while Exercising

The Activity Rings view will provide you a glanceable look at your activity rings. This includes all three of the rings, Move, Exercise, and Stand hours. You no longer need to switch to the Activity app, or back to the Home Screen of your watch, if you have an activity complication configured. Now, you can simply use the digital crown to switch to the view. It is likely that this view will get the most usage out of all of them.

After you have completed a workout and you have rested and recovered, you may want to look back at how well you did. There has been some changes to the Workout Summaries as well, so let us look at those next.

Enhanced Workout Summary

When you complete a workout you may want to look back at how well you did with your workout. This is where the new Workout Summary information can be helpful. In order to view details of a particular workout you can use the following steps:

1. Open the **Fitness** app on your iPhone.
2. Under Workouts **tap** on a workout. This will show you the details for the workout.

On this screen you will see some additional details like workout time, elapsed time, active calories, total calories, and average heart rate. You can also see a graph of your heart rate over the course of your workout.

For the Heart Rate you tap on **Show More** to see even more details about your hear rate. What will be shown is how often you were in each Heart Rate Zone. As a reference here are the zones and the corresponding heart rates:

Zone 1 - less than 131 beats per minute - shown as bright blue
Zone 2 - 132 beats per minute to 143 beats per minute - shown as aqua blue
Zone 3 - 144 beats per minute to 155 beats per minute - shown as green
Zone 4 - 156 beats per minute to 167 beats per minute - shown as orange
Zone 5 - greater than 168 beats per minute - shown as red

Zones during a Running Workout

The total time for each zone will be shown, with the average being shown a the top of the screen. The heart rate chart will show your rate and zone over the length of your workout. Included in the chart is the color of the heart rate zone that you were in at that time.

In the workout summary view there is also a map of where your workout occurred. If it is an outside run, cycle, or walk, it will show the route. Next, let us look at another health related item Sleep, so let's see what has changed.

Sleep

Sleep is an important part of overall health, and even though it is important many people do not get enough sleep. Starting with watchOS 7 Apple introduced the ability for the Apple Watch to be able to track the amount of time that you were asleep. It was able to do this by using the heart rate sensor on the Apple Watch to be able to detect your heart rate for sudden changes. Along with this, the gyroscope is used to detect movement, which can indicate that you are not actually asleep but awake.

Being able to detect that you are asleep was a great start, but starting with watchOS 9 the type of data is being expanded to include additional sleep information. In particular, additional data around sleep.

There are three different types of sleep, these are REM, or Rapid Eye Movement, Core Sleep, and Deep Sleep. Here are the descriptions of each of the types of sleep directly from Apple's Health app.

REM

Studies show that REM sleep may play a key role in memory and refreshing your brain. It's where most of your dreaming happens. Your eyes will also move side to side. REM sleep first occurs about 90 minutes after falling asleep.

Core

This stage, where muscle activity lowers and body temperature drops, represents the bulk of your time asleep. While it's sometimes referred to as light sleep, it's just as critical as any other sleep stage.

Sleep Stages Descriptions

Deep

Also known as slow wave sleep, this stage allows the body to repair itself and release essential hormones. It happens in longer periods during the first half of the night. It's often difficult to wake up from deep sleep because you're so relaxed.

The Apple Watch with watchOS 9 is now able to track when you are in each of the various states of sleep. It does by tracking the time spent in each of the various sleep states, as well as when you are considered to be Awake. All of the information is gathered together in a set of graphs. An example is like the one below:

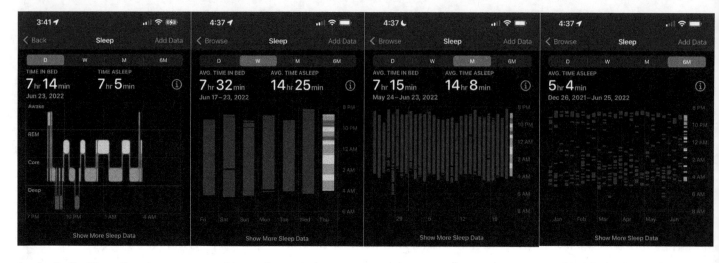

| Daily Sleep Graph | Weekly Sleep Graph | Monthly Sleep Graph | Six Month Sleep Graph |

Viewing Sleep Detail

You can view the detailed Sleep data in two different places, on your iPhone or on your Apple Watch. To access the Sleep Detail on the iPhone use the following steps:

1. Open the **Health** app.
2. Tap on the **Browse** button at the bottom of the screen.
3. Scroll down to **Sleep**.
4. Tap on **Sleep** to bring up the Sleep health data.

When you open the Sleep Data you will immediately be shown the graph for your sleep for the previous evening. Just like all other data within the Health app, you can look at the data for various time frames. You can view the data for the last day, last week, last month, and last six months.

By default the Day view will be shown and you will see the graph with each of stages and when it occurred. For week, month, and six months you will see the data in a stacked bar chart, meaning that each of the sleep stages will be stacked on top of each other. You can tap on any of the items and it will show the summary data. In order to get some more data, tap on the **Show More Sleep Data** link at the bottom.

More Sleep Data

The More Sleep Data screen will show additional information. For instance, you will be able to see the four sleep stages, Awake, REM, Core, and Deep, broken down by minute and percentage. You can tap on any of the sleep stages that indicate the time and that area of the graph will be shown.

Similarly, if you tap on any of the sleep stages with percentages, the information will be shown in a bar form and highlighted with appropriate color.

Sleep Data info

One thing to be aware of is that unlike the Race Route, where data may be available before you upgraded to watchOS 9, that is not the case with the more in depth sleep data. This is because watchOS 9 has algorithms to be able to detect this sleeping. The route being used for your racing was already being tracked previously, now it is just being displayed.

Even though this is only available after you upgrade to watchOS 9, is still a great enhancement to be able to see even more detailed sleep data. You may be able to correlate this data with how you are feeling the next morning and whether or not you feel rested, and if you do not, maybe the type of sleep you got can help indicate why.

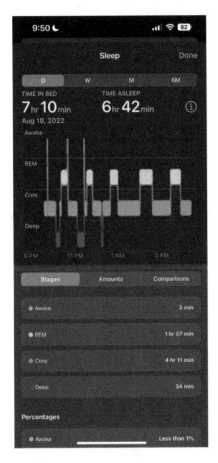 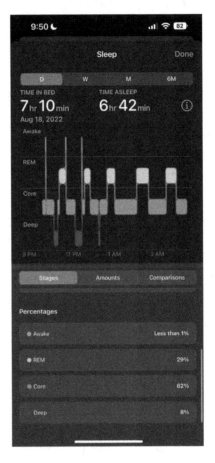

Sleep Data amounts   Sleep Data percentages

Closing Thoughts on Health and Fitness

Even though the primary purpose of the Apple Watch was not completely formed when Apple introduced the Apple Watch in 2015, today it is clear what use case the Apple Watch has become. The Apple Watch is used for quick and glanceable information, as well as for health and fitness tracking, along with notifications.

watchOS 9, in conjunction with the Health app on iOS 16, has a new app, Medications. After you have setup the medication in the Health app on your iPhone, you can use the Apple Watch to log your medications. This will help you easily keep track of what medications you take, when you are supposed to take them, and you can even export your medication list. All of these are a worthwhile addition to help people be a bit more healthy and keep track of their medications.

One of the main purposes of the Apple Watch is fitness and that has expanded with watchOS 9. You can now start a Multisport workout for triathlons, with various exercises. The new Race Route feature will allow you to race against yourself using a route that you have run in the past. This is a good feature if you want to try and improve your existing pace for that particular route.

There are those times that you want to be able to do a workout of your choosing. This is now possible with the new Custom Workouts option. You can add a number of stages for each custom workout, and even set it to repeat a specified number of times. You can then use that custom workout as needed.

There are more metrics being shown particularly for runners. Vertical Oscillation, Stride Length, and Ground Contact Time are all new measurements that are being taken so you can see this information post workout.

Sleep is an important part of your overall health. The Apple Watch can now track how much time you are spending in the four stages of sleep, Awake, REM, Core, and Deep. You need to upgrade to watchOS 9 for this to track this additional detail. But once you do upgrade you can see the detail and correlate it with other data.

One place where you may do some exercising is at home. Next, let us see what new features are available for the Home app and HomeKit.

Home App and HomeKit

Technology can both help and hinder us. Sometimes technological progress is beneficial, other times less so. It is often the intention to make things easier. Today's technology has provided a lot of modern conveniences. One of those conveniences is the Internet of Things, or IoT. Internet of Things devices take what were previously non-internet connected, and connects them to the internet.

Connecting devices to the internet is a double-edged sword. The positive part is that it does make life more convenient. When you connect an Internet of Things device, you can often access it from just about anywhere in the world where there is an internet connection. You could be in another town, across the country, or on the other side of the world. The downside to this though, is that any Internet of Things device needs to be secure in its connection, otherwise anyone would be able to gain access to your devices, which is not the intention.

Back with iOS 8 Apple introduced a new framework called HomeKit. HomeKit is designed to allow manufacturers to add devices securely to HomeKit. The way that this was done is by scanning a QR code. When the QR code was scanned it would pair the device with the HomeKit service, therefore allowing you to connect to the device. The way that you would manage your HomeKit devices was through the Home app. The Home app has seen a significant update, we will get to the details, but first, let us look at a brief history of HomeKit.

HomeKit

Even though HomeKit was introduced with iOS 8, it would require third-party developer's to create an app and integrate HomeKit into it. Many companies that developed accessories ended up creating an app to control their own devices. If they integrated HomeKit, an end user could use that company's app to control all of their HomeKit accessories. This approach did indeed work, but it actually created a very inconsistent experience.

In order to keep things consistent all HomeKit data was synchronized to iCloud. This synching allowed all HomeKit data to be kept up to date no matter what device, nor which app, they were using to control their HomeKit devices.

While allowing companies to integrate HomeKit with their own app did indeed work, it was not ideal, and there was no central place to control all of your HomeKit accessories. Apple introduced a way to do just that in June of 2016, That solution was the Home app.

Home App

The Home app was introduced in June of 2016 with the introduction of iOS 10. The Home app is designed to be your single view into your entire HomeKit database. When introduced the Home app was a pretty basic application. It would allow you to add devices via QR code and you could even perform some automations.

A home consists of a variety of rooms. You could assign a device to a particular room. This made it significantly easier to organize your home. This also made it much easier to look at single room and be able to turn on and off devices as needed. This was particularly needed if you had the same device type in a variety of rooms.

HomeKit also offered the ability to automate some tasks, like turning off items whenever the last person leaves the home. In order for these automations to work, it needs a device that can run the automations even when you are not home. For this you need a Home hub.

Home Hub

In order for the smart devices in a home to be remotely accessible they would have to have a Home Hub. A Home Hub is a device that is always connected and available in the Home where the HomeKit accessories are. At its introduction there were three devices that could be used as a Home Hub. These were an Apple TV HD (4th Generation), a HomePod, or an iPad.

Starting with iPadOS 16, an iPad is no longer available to be used as a Home Hub. You can still use an Apple TV, an original HomePod, or a HomePod mini as a Home Hub. This is a minor change, but one to be aware of.

Home app on macOS

From its introduction in 2014 through 2018 HomeKit was exclusive to iOS and tvOS. Beginning with macOS Mojave, the Home app that ran on the iPad was brought to the Mac through a technology called Mac Catalyst, which allowed iPad apps to run on macOS.

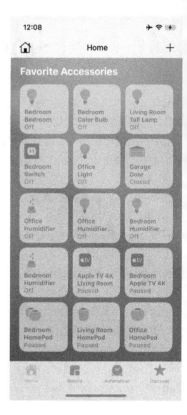

Home App in iOS 15

The Home app on macOS is the exact same one that is on the iPad, just with a different view for the controls, which are controls that are native to the Mac. This continues to be the case with macOS Ventura, including a complete redesign that is across iOS 16, iPadOS 16, and macOS Ventura.

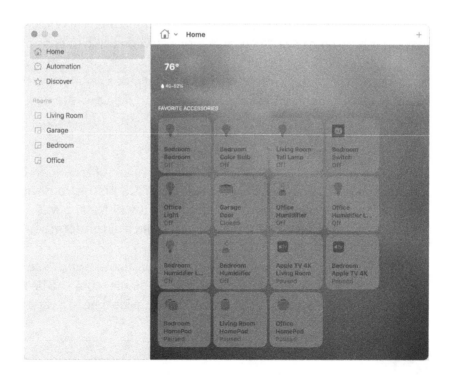

Home app in macOS Monterey

Redesign

With this year's releases of iOS 16, iPadOS 16, and macOS Ventura, the Home app has received a significant redesign. The app has gotten more than just a cursory improvement in the graphics. Instead there have been some very welcomed improvements. Let us look at the new look of the Home app starting with the various tabs. The Home app is divided into three tabs Home, Automation, and Discover. Let us look at each of these in turn.

Home Tab

The Home Tab is comprised of a few different sections. These sections are Summary View, Favorites, and Rooms. Let us look at each, starting with Quick View.

Summary View

At the top of the Home app there is now a row that gives you a quick look at the status of various groups of items. Some of the groups that you might see could include:

- Climate
- Lights
- Speakers & TVs
- Security

You may see different categories, depending on what HomeKit accessories you have configured. You can tap on any of these categories and all of the devices that match that grouping will be shown. Only the rooms that have devices that match the category will be shown. Along with this, a summary of the overall status for that group will be shown directly beneath the group name.

Home app on macOS Ventura

As an example, for Climate, it might show Temperature: 72 Humidity: 30% - 41%. Whereas for Lights, the summary might be "3 Lights on". You can tap on these summary items and each of the items that are contributing to the summary will be shown. You can then tap and hold on any individual item to see its detailed view and adjust the settings for the accessory as needed.

Favorites

Below the Quick View area is each of the rooms with their accessories included in the group. The first section is the Favorites section followed by each of the rooms in the home.

The Favorites section is where all of the items that you have indicated should be in your Favorites. The Favorites section is good for being able to get quick access to the items that you need to access the most.

Rooms

Below the Favorites section are each of the rooms that you have defined in your Home. In each room all of the items that are assigned to that room will be shown.

Regardless of which section an individual item belongs in, if there is any information that would be good to know about it, for example if a light is on, or if a humidifier is on, or if a garage door is open, that information will be shown within the tile for that item. This is the same way that it worked with previous versions of the Home app.

Item Tiles

In previous versions of iOS, iPadOS, and macOS each of the item tiles were all the same size and could accommodate up to four lines of data. The first line of the tile would have an icon representing the type of item. The second line would be the room. The third line would be the name you gave the item. The fourth line would be the current status for the item. The fourth line could be the light percentage, the intended humidity, or in the case of a HomePod, it might be playing.

Home app on iOS 16

When you first open the Home app on iOS 16, iPadOS 16, or macOS Ventura, all of the tiles in the Home app are the same size, albeit they are a bit wider than the previous versions. These also show the same information as outlined above, but in a different configuration. On the left is the icon representing the type of item. Next to this are three lines of text the room name, the name of the item, and the items current status.

There are a couple of new features about organization that are worth knowing about.

Reordering Sections

One of the new features of the Home app is the ability to rearrange the sections so they can be organized in a way that works for you. You can rearrange the sections by performing the following steps:

1. Open the **Home** app.
2. Tap on the "**...**" Icon in the upper right corner.
3. Tap on **Reorder Sections**. A popup will appear.
4. **Tap and hold** on the rearrange icon on the right side of the row that you want to rearrange.
5. **Drag** the row to the position that you would like to place it.
6. After you have finished rearranging the sections tap on the **Done** button to save your changes.

As soon as you tap on the **Done** button the sections will rearrange. Rearranging the sections are not the only organization that you make in the Home app. You can also modify the Home view itself.

Modifying the Home View

A feature that many have requested of the Home app is the ability to rearrange the items for each room so they could be put in an arrangement that makes sense for them. This is now possible with the Home app in iOS 16, iPadOS 16, and macOS Ventura. In order to edit the Home view, perform the following steps:

1. Open the **Home** app.
2. Tap on the "**...**" Icon in the upper right corner.
3. Tap on **Edit Home View**. The Home view will enter into jiggle mode.

Home app Menu View

Once the Home view has entered into jiggle mode you can then tap and hold on the tile for an individual item and you can then drag it to the location that you want, provided it is within the same section (room). You can also rearrange the Favorites section as well. But rearranging is not the only customization you can make.

Changing Tile Sizes

The item tiles have two different sizes, a compact, which is the default, and a larger view. You can set any item tile to be either size that you prefer. In order to adjust a tile's size perform the following steps:

1. Open the **Home** app.
2. Tap on the "**...**" Icon in the upper right corner.
3. Tap on **Edit Home View**. The Home view will enter into jiggle mode.
4. **Tap on the tile** you want to resize. An adjustment icon will appear in the upper right corner.
5. Tap on the **adjustment icon** and the tile size will toggle to the other size.

When you adjust the size of a tile the other tiles in the same room will rearrange to accommodate the new tile size. You can resize any number of tiles that you would like. Let us presume there are four items in a room, you could set two of the items to be larger sizes, and keep the other tiles the compact size, and have them alternating to where in the top row you have a large tile and a small tile, and in the second row is a small tile and then a large tile. Or you can have any other arrangement that you would like.

Room Views

The Rooms tab is no longer in the tab bar at the bottom of the screen. Instead, this has been moved to one of two locations. On iOS the room list will be under the "**...**" button. Meanwhile on iPadOS and macOS the rooms has its own section of the sidebar. You can tap or click, on any individual room to bring up the specific room.

When you open a room you will see a similar layout as the Home view, but it is subtly different. The first row of each room is a Summary row. Similar to the Home View this will show a summary of each of the various items in the room. However, the key difference is that items are not grouped together, each summary item is listed out. You can still tap on the item and a popup will appear. This will be the items that are contributing to the summary. If there is only one item it will be the items Details screen. If there are multiple items they will be shown and then you can tap on an individual item to show its detail view.

The remaining items will be the various groups of items that are present in that room. You can tap on any item to see the details for that individual item.

Room Tiles

The way that you edit a Room view is the same as with the Home view. You tap on the "**...**" button in the upper right corner and tap on **Edit Room View**. The Room will then enter jiggle mode and you can make your changes as desired.

Just as with the Home view you can also rearrange the individual tiles to your preferred order. The organization will only apply to the current room. Even though the organization applies to the current room, it will synchronize across devices.

Similarly, you can adjust the size of the item tiles in the Room view. Be aware that the size of the tile will also change the size in the Home View.

The last item that you can modify for any room is the background. This is done by tapping on the "**...**" button in the upper right corner, then tapping on Room Settings. You can then either take a photo, use a suggested color, or choose an existing photo for your room.

Automations

The Automation tab has remained the same as in previous operating systems. You can add automations for the following circumstances:

Room View in Home app

- People Arrive
- People Leave
- Time of Day occurs
- Accessory is controlled
- Sensor Detects Something

You can have as many automations as you would like, but be aware that if they are too complicated you may inadvertently end up setting up competing automations that will not have the desired results.

Discover

The Discover tab is a good place to learn about HomeKit in general as well as get suggestions for various HomeKit accessories that might fall into various categories. There is one last thing to discuss regarding HomeKit and that is standards.

Matter Standard

There are countless Internet of Things accessories from a variety of companies that can help you automate various tasks in your home. The problem with so many options is that there are undoubtedly going to be competing standards. There are a number of standards including Zigbee, Z-Wave, Amazon Alexa, and of course HomeKit, just to name a few.

One of the downsides to these competing standards is that rarely do they interoperate with one another. Therefore, this means that you have to either stick with a single standard or deal with having to use multiple apps or accessory ecosystems. These competing standards should be a thing of the past with a new standard called **Matter**, previously known as Connected Home over Internet Protocol, or CHIP.

The thing that makes Matter different than other previous standards is that there are multiple companies behind the standard. Some of these companies include Amazon, Apple, Google, Samsung, and the Zigbee alliance. With Amazon, Apple, and Google all joining forces, the Matter standard should actually become the de facto standard.

The Matter standard should be released sometime in late 2022. It was anticipated that Matter would be released earlier in the year, but there was enough interest by companies that additional time was needed. With Matter becoming the accepted standard, this means that you should be able to use accessories from multiple companies on whichever platform standard you choose.

For instance, this means that you could possibly add a Google Home speaker to HomeKit, or even an Amazon Ring doorbell to HomeKit. Not every accessory will be compatible with the Matter standard, but once it is available it should be helpful for everyone involved.

Closing Thoughts on the Home App and HomeKit

The redesigned Home app provides a number of new features. In particular the Home and Room views have both been redesigned to allow you to see a summary of your home or room. Within both the Home view and Room view you will see the summary line. This will provide you with a way to quickly glance at the status of various items in your home or room.

On the Home Tab you can see all of your favorites at the top of the screen so you can quickly control the items that are considered your favorites. On the Home view you can rearrange any of the tiles to the order that you would like. Beyond the order you can also choose between the compact size or the larger size. When you make a change the tile will also be modified to keep everything up to date.

The new Matter standard should allow additional accessories to be used within HomeKit and therefore the Home app. Once this standard is finalized and released, companies should be able to begin adopting it and you should get access to more accessories.

Siri

Back in February 2010 a new app was released for the iPhone. That app was called Siri. A mere two months after launch Apple purchased the nascent app. The Siri app was used to perform some actions, like opening a search, getting a table at a restaurant, and answers to questions. On April 29th, 2010 it was announced that Apple had purchased Siri. Siri did not become integrated into iOS until iOS 5 in October of 2011. In the intervening 11 years Siri has become more and more useful. One of those set of enhancements was through a purchase that Apple made.

On March 22nd, 2017 Apple purchased an app called Workflow. Workflow allowed for automating various aspects of iOS. Even though it was through an app and not integrated into the system, there were still a number of useful tasks that the Workflow app could accomplish. In 2018 with the release of iOS 12 the Workflow app received a new name, Shortcuts. Because it was an Apple app, it now had additional access to system functions as well as system settings. With the release of iOS 13 in 2019, Shortcuts became integrated into iOS which unlocked a slew of possibilities. One of the enhancements with iOS 13 is a feature called Siri Shortcuts.

Siri Shortcuts

With iOS 12 there was a new concept introduced to Siri called Siri Shortcuts. Siri Shortcuts are a way of being able to easily ask Siri to perform a task that is offered up by an app. This is done through what are called Siri Intents.

Developers need to setup these intents, but when they do the system can easily identify what actions are available to Siri through the app. When you added a Siri Shortcut, you would be able to assign a phrase that would trigger the action for the app.

With iOS 16 and iPadOS 16 you still have the option of assigning a trigger phrase, but now the system will be able to use any of the Siri Shortcuts as soon as the app is installed. This means that you no longer need to setup Siri actions by yourself. You can simply ask Siri "**What can I do**", while within an app, and Siri will present all of the possibilities to you. If you already know that an app can perform a particular action, you can ask Siri to perform the action, with that particular app, and Siri should be able to accomplish the task.

This is a great advancement for Siri and should make it easier for users to find out what they can do with Siri. That is not the only enhancement in regards to Siri. There is now some enhanced offline support as well.

Expanded Offline Support

When Siri was first introduced a vast majority of the requests that you made of Siri needed to be sent to Apple's servers to process the request, then retrieve the information, and the response was returned to your device. This configuration worked, but if you had unreliable internet or if the Apple servers were overloaded it could take a significant amount of time to get the response from the server, which lead to users complaining about the reliability of Siri.

Apple responded to this by improving the server component of Siri. Beyond this they have also moved a significant amount of the processing to be on your device. The reason that they were able to do this is was due to the increased processing power of the chips that are inside of their devices, and in particular, the inclusion of the Neural Engine, which can handle some of the language processing directly on the device. A secondary reason is actually due to privacy. If the processing is done on the device, this results in less data that needs to be sent to Apple's servers, which means less data that Apple needs to have. All of this results in faster response times for users.

Even though there are only a couple of actual features for Siri, the ability to start using Siri actions without needing to perform manual setup is a huge step for all users and should allow for more users to utilize the features of apps that have Siri intents integrated into them.

That concludes all of the direct user-facing features, it is now time to turn to what is new for Developers.

Closing Thoughts for Users

This year's releases of Apple's operating systems, iOS 16, iPadOS 16, macOS Ventura, and watchOS 9 all bring their own set of improvements and features. Each operating system has its own strengths and tradeoffs when compared to others. watchOS is designed for the extreme portability and can easily be with you all day, but it is designed for glanceability and fitness. On the opposite end of the spectrum, the Mac is designed to provide you the most power out of any device, as well as the largest screens, but that comes at the cost of portability (in some models). The iPad is designed to be portable, but much like a portable Mac, requires a bag or case to be able to tote it along with you, but you do get the big screen. The iPhone is intended for portability but this portability means that the devices has a smaller screen. Each of these devices got its own set of enhancements.

The biggest feature for the devices with the largest screens is Stage Manager on iPadOS and macOS. With Stage Manager you can now keep focus on a few window groups and easily switch back and forth between them. Along with this, you can move windows between groups. On both the Mac and iPad you can have up to four windows in a app group and up to four groups on the screen. Stage Manager on the iPad brings something else with it, enhanced external display support. With external display support you can also have four app groups and up to four apps in a group on an external display, as well as on the built-in display.

Stage Manager requires a higher end iPad, specifically at minimum an iPad with an M1 processor and 256GB of storage. This is needed for a new feature that is new to the iPad, but not to the Mac, Virtual Memory. Virtual Memory allows some of the storage space to be used for memory when switching between App Groups when in Stage Manager. This may be disappointing to some, but tradeoffs sometimes have to be made in order to provide the best experience. Stage Manager will change the way that some people interact with both the Mac and the iPad. Having the same experience on both will allow users to be comfortable on both platforms.

While the iPhone did not get Stage Manager it did receive a new feature of its own, a customizable Lock Screen. The Lock Screen on iOS is designed to allow you to easily glance at items, similar to complications on the Apple Watch. In fact, the complications that are designed for the Apple Watch can be brought directly to the Widgets on the Lock Screen. The same technology is used for both. Having widgets right on the Lock Screen will allow users to stay up to date on a variety of different things throughout the day. Beyond this is the ability to fully customize the wallpaper for the Lock Screen and Home Screen.

One area where people may want to stay up to date on something is when it comes to sports scores. Coming later in 2022 is a new feature called Live Activities. Live Activities will allow anyone to have the latest score of a game right on their Lock Screen, so they no longer need to receive a slew of push notifications to stay up to date on a game. Beyond this you can also stay up to date on the arrival of your ride sharing request.

When you need to focus, you can link a particular Lock Screen with a Focus, which will automatically switch to that Lock Screen when a particular Focus is enabled. There have been some enhancement with Focus this year as well, with a new Focus Filter feature. If supported by an app, a Focus Filter will allow you to filter content within an app so that only items related to that particular Focus are shown. One app that does not support this, but where it might be handy is the Notes app.

The Notes app has received a few new features like organization by date. The biggest change for the Notes app though is when it comes to filtering with the app. There are now some powerful filters that will allow you to precisely dial into exactly what you want. By combining metadata like tags, creation date, and even which folder to include, you can a filter to find exactly what you want.

Notes are great for working on your own, but sometimes you need to collaborate with others. This can be done in a variety of ways using Apple's own apps like Mail, Messages, or FaceTime, all of these have seen some improvements as well. Mail has added support for Focus Filters, but also the ability to detect if an attachment is missing, which can save those follow-up emails that we have all had to send. In addition to this you can now cancel sending an email within a few seconds of hitting the send button. If you need to send an email later, you can now schedule an email to be sent at a particular date and time. This can make it useful for following up on email or sending out an email at a specific date and time.

Messages get an Undo Send feature for a specific message as well as the ability to edit messages. When you do this, there will be annotations below the message to indicate that it has either been unsent or edited. If you edit a message and it gets sent to an older device, a second message will be sent with the new edit and it will also be indicated that it was edited. There is a limit to how long a message can be edited or unsent, but it is beyond the few seconds to cancel sending an email.

FaceTime gets some new functionality like having the ability to use your iPhone camera as the camera for your FaceTime call on your Mac. This goes beyond just using the camera itself, but also allow you to use the features of the phone, like Portrait Mode.

There is also a new feature called Desk View. Desk View will use the UltraWide lens on your Camera to show your desk. This can be a boon for those who need to be able to show someone how to do something physically on their desk when they cannot be together. Alongside all of this is the ability to handoff FaceTime calls from one device to another. This means that you can go between your iPhone and Mac, or even your iPhone and your iPad, depending on your needs.

There is one last place to discuss collaboration and that is within Safari. Last year Safari introduced a new feature called Tab Groups. Tab Groups allow you to have a variety of different tabs. Now, you can have a Shared Tab Group. When you share a tab group everyone will have full access to all of the tabs. Anyone can add or remove a tab group. Also with Safari any extensions that you have enabled, will sync its current enabled status, whether it is enabled, or disabled. There is one requirement for this, you must have already have had the extension installed. Being able to collaborate with anyone is good, but sometimes the group that you need to collaborate with is a bit closer and the items that you want to focus on are not Safari Tabs, but photos.

Photos has seen some changes as well with the biggest enhancement in years, Shared iCloud Photo Libraries. You can now have a Shared iCloud Library with your iCloud family. This is a separate Photos library. Everyone has full access to add, remove, and edit photos. You can even have some photos automatically shared to the library, so you do not have to remember to do so. But that is not all of the changes, if you use the Hidden or Deleted folders, by default you will need to authenticate with your passcode, Touch ID or Face ID in order to show the items in those folders.

The Home app has seen a complete visual overhaul. The app is now reorganized to provide easy access to your favorite items as well as seeing the overall status within each category. You can organize the tiles as you would like and all of that information now synchronizes across all of your devices so everything will remain up to date.

Life can be hectic at times and we can all use some assistance in some ways. One way might be with staying healthy and sometimes that requires taking medications. If you do need to take medications on a regular basis you can use the new Medications section of the Health app to schedule a reminder each time you need to take your medication. When you do this you will get a reminder on your iPhone and Apple Watch and you can then log the fact that you took, or skipped taking, the medication.

One way that many stay healthy is by exercising. You can now use the Fitness app on your iPhone even if you do not have an Apple Watch. This will not be nearly as accurate as if you did pair it with an Apple Watch, but you can still get credit for your steps as well as any third-party health apps that add to the Health app. If you do have an Apple Watch you can use the new Multisport workout which will allow them to keep track of their exercise during a triathlon and it will automatically detect and switch tracking for each sport.

There are a number of features specifically for runners including new metrics like stride length, vertical oscillation and ground contact time. Runners can also do a new workout type called Race Route, which will allow them to race against themselves, either using their last workout with the same route or against their best time.

Before you go out on your run, be sure to check the weather with the enhanced Weather app. The Weather app now provides additional detail including charts, graphs, and more depending on what you investigate.

This concludes the users portion of the book, now time to focus on Developers.

Developers

There is a symbiotic relationship between Apple and its developers. This has always been the case, but it is truer today more than ever. While Apple did create the modern app based economy with the introduction of the iPhone in 2007, it was ultimately the third-party developers who made it thrive. Apple does have its own core set of applications, that are required to make the devices function properly, but it would be impossible for Apple to create even 0.01 percent of the applications that are available within Apple's ecosystem.

While Apple does have its own app, they primarily create the hardware that is used by end users, as well as the frameworks that are used to create the apps, but it is up to third-party app developers to create the overall experiences that bring users to the platforms.

Apple's modern set of frameworks are pretty robust and can be used for creating new experiences, but each year there seem to be even more new features added. In order for developers to be able to take advantage of these features Apple needs to create the APIs that developers can utilize. This year there are a lot new features for developers.

These range from new features to the Swift language itself, like the @**available** keyword for Async/Await functions, to Window and MenuBarExtra, and the all new NavigationSplitView, and NavigationLink enhancements in SwiftUI.

Along with these comes an entirely new framework, WeatherKit, which will allow you to incorporate the weather into your app and replaces the old DarkSky API previously available. WeatherKit also has a web component to it as well for those who need to incorporate the Weather on their site.

Beyond WeatherKit, there is a whole new SwiftUI Charts framework that will allow you to build a wide variety of charts based upon the data that you provide.

One thing that many developers do not like doing is documentation. However, if you document your app while you add new features the enhancements to DocC might be able to help you out there. There is an updated look to the documentation that DocC outputs as well as some enhancements to static sites, but this also applies to any hosting site.

When you build your app, you are likely going to use Xcode, which has seen a nice set of enhancements including function header changes, significant improvements to SwiftUI Previews, and even changes to Continuous Integration of your app, including deployment of your app to TestFlight.

Before we delve deep into some of the new frameworks and enhancements, there are a few things that we need to cover

Privacy and Security

It would not be a stretch to say that both user privacy and device security are important. Many developers strive to make sure that their apps only get the information that they need to provide a great user experience. Even with this, there are those developers who might try to take advantage of information. Similarly, there may be some nefarious entities that may try to get users to install apps on their devices. Apple has implemented a couple of changes related to this. Let us look at both Developer Mode and Device Names.

Developer Mode

One of the areas that Apple focuses on is related to security. Security can come in many forms, like a read only volume for macOS system files, security updates, and general bug fixes. Nefarious actors have been known to get users to unwittingly install apps on their devices. In order to help stop these types of things, Apple has created **Developer Mode**.

Developer Mode is a specific mode that is needed for debugging applications. It should be noted that you do not need to enable Developer Mode for apps that are from the App Store nor for apps that come from TestFlight, because apps installed from both of these methods are considered **release** builds, not debug builds.

When you do enable Developer Mode what is actually occurring is that your iPhone, iPad, or Apple Watch is entering into **Reduced Security** mode, which is the same mode that is used on macOS when you need to install certain extensions.

Developer Mode is disabled by default, because most users do not need this mode, but can be enabled by using these steps:

1. Open the **Settings** app.
2. **Scroll down** to Privacy & Security.
3. Tap on **Privacy & Security** to open the Privacy and Security Settings.
4. **Scroll down** to Developer Mode.
5. Tap on **Developer Mode** to open up developer mode settings.
6. Tap on the **toggle** next to Developer Mode to enable the settings. A popup will appear.
7. On the popup tap on **Restart** to restart your device. You device will restart.
8. **Unlock your device** by entering in your passcode. A popup will appear.
9. On this popup tap on **Turn on** to verify you want to enable Developer Mode.
10. Enter in your device's **passcode** to fully enable Developer Mode.

Only after you have completed all of the steps above will your device be enabled to use Developer Mode. At this point you can run any apps on your device that you need to, particularly while in development. If you have any apps that were installed on your devices while under iOS 15, iPadOS 15, or watchOS 8, these will still be installed but you will need to enable Developer Mode before these can be run.

Another area where Apple tends to focus is related to security and that area is privacy. There is a change related to privacy that developers need to be aware of, and that is related to the UIDevice class.

| Developer Mode Off | Restart after enabling Developer Mode | Enter Password to enabled Developer Mode | Confirm enabling Developer Mode |

Device Names

There are times when you need to be able to get information about the device that your app is running on. This could be information like state of the battery, battery level, orientation of the device, or current interface idiom. One thing that has been available since the first iPhoneOS SDK, version 2.0, is the ability to get the name of the current device.

The device name is considered personally identifiable information and could easily be used to track a particular device. As an example if someone has named their iPhone as "John's iPhone", that is not that unique of a name for an iPhone. However, if an iPhone is named "John Smith's iPhone", then that might be a bit easier to narrow down, although John Smith is a common enough name. If someone were to name their iPhone "John Smith's iPhone 13 Pro Max", it is even more specific. The more unique the name, the easier it becomes to determine the exact user.

A single company being able to determine that an iPhone is a particular one is not always that helpful. There is a group that could use this information and are data aggregators. Data aggregators can easily correlate all sorts of data and if they have a unique identifier, like the unique name of an iPhone.

The way that you can access the name of a device is by calling UIDevice.current.name. In order to minimize the likelihood of this happening, there is going to be a change when you call this function. Starting with iOS 16, iPadOS 16, macOS Ventura, and tvOS 16, calling to this will now return the type of device.

As an example, instead of getting "John Smith's iPhone iPhone 13 Pro Max" you will now get "iPhone". Obviously, this significantly improves privacy for end users. A vast majority of developers never need to know the exact name of a device, and therefore will not be impacted.

If you do need the exact device name you will need to request an entitlement that will allow you to get the exact name. The process for this has not been formalized as of this writing, so it may be best to contact Apple developer support to see how to do this.

This is a good change for user security but may provide a bit of a headache for some developers who need this information. Let us now look some information regarding Interface Frameworks.

Interface Frameworks

When you are building an app there are three things needed, a programming language, a user interface framework, and a tool to build the interface. For a majority of the time at Apple this has been through using Objective-C or Swift for the programming language, AppKit or UIKit for the user interface framework and by using Interface Builder to build the interface, or doing it entirely through code.

When you are looking to build a new app you may continue to use these to build applications and it will remain so for many years yet. However, it might be worthwhile to start looking at using some newer tools, like Swift for the programming language, SwiftUI for the user interface, and Previews for SwiftUI.

SwiftUI is still a relatively young frameworks that is still lacking some features that developers are asking for. Some of these have been added to this year's release of SwiftUI, you can read all about those changes in the dedicated chapter on SwiftUI. Even with SwiftUI being a somewhat nascent User Interface Framework it is production ready. There may still be times that you might have to rely on using UIKit, or App Kit, and possibly even Objective-C, with that you cannot do entirely with just Swift and SwiftUI. However those things are getting to be fewer and fewer as time goes on. On the topic of Swift, let us look at some changes with Swift.

Swift

No active programming language is every fully complete. As a language ages, the amount of change to the language my slowdown, but it never fully stops. Swift is now eight year old, but it is still very much a language that is evolving.

Unlike some other languages, Swift is entirely open source and enhancements to the language can be suggested by the community of Swift developers. If their proposals are accepted, they are implemented in a future version of Swift.

Swift is designed to work across a wide variety of operating systems. Of course it will work on all of Apple's own operating systems, iOS, iPadOS, macOS, tvOS, and watchOS. However, it also runs on Microsoft Windows 10, as well as a variety of Linux versions, like CentOS 7, Amazon Linux 2, and Ubuntu 18.04 and 20.04.

In order to maintain functionality across all of the operating systems, there needs to be a consistent base set of functionality across all of the various operating systems. This is called the Swift Standard Library.

The Swift Standard Library is composed of three parts, the Core, the Runtime, and SDK Overlays. The first two of these, Core and Runtime, are consistent across all platforms that support Swift. However, the SDK Overlays are only available on Apple's operating systems. The SDK Overlays "provide Swift-specific additions and modifications to existing Objective-C frameworks to improve their mapping into Swift. In particular, the Foundation overlay provides additional support for interoperability with Objective-C code.".

From time to time new features are added to the Standard Library through the Swift Evolution process. Let us look at some of the additions to the Standard Library.

Swift 5.6 Features

Swift 5.6 was release on March 14th, 2022. There were a total of ten additions to Swift with Swift 5.6. We will only cover a couple of these, including Unavailability Condition and Temporary Uninitialized Buffers. So let us look at those now.

Unavailability Condition (SE-0290)

When you are building a Swift app, library, or framework, you often need to support multiple operating system versions and be able to conditionally support, or not support, depending on your need. Beginning with Swift 2, the language has had the ability to provide availability checking. There are two different availability conditions. `@available` and `#available`.

`@available` is typically use for declaring an entire function, or class, as only being available with a specific iOS version. Meanwhile, `#available` is normally used within a function to check for particular version or for API availability.

Swift 5.6 extends the `#available` check with its opposite, `#unavailable`. The new #unavailable keyword will allow you to more explicitly indicate how to handle a condition if a particular operating system version, or API, is unavailable.

This is possible using the #unavailable conditional. If there were actually a !#available, the #unavailable conditional would be its equivalent.

The explicit inclusion of the #unavailable conditional is quite useful when it comes to readability. In Swift 5.5 and earlier you could have to use this type of approach:

```
if #available(iOS 15, *) { // Perform iOS 15 and newer action
} else { // Perform iOS 14 an earlier action }
```

While this approach would work, it does leave open the possibility that you might error and forget to properly handle things. Instead, now you can use something a bit simpler.

```
if #unavailable(iOS 15, *) { // Perform iOS 14 and earlier action }
```

This version of the code is a lot easier to read and much earlier to parse and follow when you are looking at it.

Beyond this, the `#unavailable` condition does also bring Swift inline with Objective-C, which supports an unavailable checker. This will make it a bit easier to move existing Objective-C code to Swift, if necessary.

You can read a bit more in-depth information about this at the Swift Evolution page for SE-0290, available at https://github.com/apple/swift-evolution/blob/main/proposals/0290-negative-availability.md. On the topic of better integration between Swift and Objective-C, there is also the integration between Swift and C, or C++. There is a new feature that helps in this. That feature is called Temporary Uninitialized Buffers.

Temporary Uninitialized Buffers (SE-0322)

Swift is designed to be a type-safe language. What this means is that you can rely on the compiler to be able to accurately determine a variable's type when it is instantiated. When a variable is instantiated the amount of memory needed to store the variable's data is calculated and that amount of data is requested from the system.

The reason that this occurs is because all Swift values need to be declared before they can be used. While this does add to the type safe nature of Swift, this can become problematic when calling between Swift and C, or C++ libraries.

Within C and C++ it is possible to initialize a variable, but not generate a size for the value. Furthermore, the place where the memory is allocated may depend on the size needed. For instance, there maybe sufficient memory already allocated to work with a variable. However, additional memory may be needed. When the latter occurs a call to allocate memory from the heap may be needed.

Prior to Swift 5.6 there is no way to handle this within Swift. There is a new function called **withUnsafeTemporaryAllocation**. This function is typically when you need to temporarily allocate a buffer. When this is run, the compiler will attempt to allocate the memory on the stack, if possible.

There are two implementations of withUnsafeTemporaryAllocation with two parameters each. The first accepts a byteCount, which is an integer, as well as an alignment, which is also an integer. The alignment is the new, temporary region of allocated memory, in bytes. As a note, the alignment must be a whole power of 2.

The second implementation is where you declare the type, along with a capacity.

The withUnsafeTemporaryAllocation function is designed to be limited in scope and when used within a closure, it can allow the compiler to be more aggressive since it knows that the memory allocated will not leave the closure.

Next, let us turn to a couple of enhancements to Swift 5.7.

Swift 5.7 Enhancements

Features that are accepted into Swift do not have to wait an entire year before they are deployed. Typically Swift sees two releases a year. One in the spring and another in the fall. This release cadence allows the language to keep evolving and changing as needed. Swift 5.7 is to be released in the fall of 2022 and with it brings some new features. These include enhancements to "If let" and limiting Async, and Sendable.

if let Shorthand for Shadowing an Existing Optional Variable (SE-0345)

When writing Swift code it is quite common to do conditional checks on optional variables to make sure that they exist before using them. Typically the is done using an"if let" pattern. This approach is not needed for non-optionals because they already exist. But for non-optionals it looks something like this:

```
let someLengthyVariableName = Foo?
let anotherImportantVariable = Bar?
if let someLengthyVariableName = someLengthyVariableName,
   let anotherImportantVariable = anotherImportantVariable  { ... }
```

What is actually occurring when you use this pattern is that you are declaring a local variable that is equal to the type. The "if" conditional is indicating that as long as the base variable exists, then perform an action in the closure. This works as written above, but you may notice that it can become cumbersome when you use long variable names. It is possible that you could use shorter, variables name, like the following:

```
if let a = someLengthyVariableName, let b = anotherImportantVariable { ... }
```

When you do this, it does indeed work, but it doing this can break readability of your code. Starting with Swift 5.7 this syntax can be shortened to this:

```
let someLengthyVariableName: Foo? = ...
let anotherImportantVariable: Bar? = …

if let someLengthyVariableName, let anotherImportantVariable { ... }
```

What is actually happening is that the compiler will automatically synthesize the extra variable declarations as was done in Swift 5.6. the actual functionality does not change, but this does have a couple of the implications. The first is that your code still remains very readable. This is just better overall.

Secondly, this is not limited to "if let", but actually applies to all of the similar patterns, including:

```
if let foo { ... }
```

```
if var foo { ... }

else if let foo { ... }
else if var foo { ... }

guard let foo else { ... }
guard var foo else { ... }

while let foo { ... }
while var foo { ... }
```

While this is mostly a syntactic change and is purely additive, it should allow developers to write not only less code, but more readable code.

Unavailable from Async Attribute (SE-0340)

Swift 5.5 introduced a whole new concept called Async/Await. This was a major addition to Swift. Async/Await is a pattern that significantly reduced the amount of code needed for calling functions that may be long lived. With Async/Await you would no longer need to have nested closures, instead you can make calls to multiple Async calls simultaneously and wait for all of their data to be returned before processing and returning some sort of result.

When you have an asynchronous function it is possible that its execution will be paused for one reason or another. When execution of an asynchronous function is paused it may not resume on the same thread, depending on availability of system resources. In a vast majority of cases when this happens it is not a problem at all. However, there are times when resuming an asynchronous function on another thread can break functionality and create corrupted data.

For instance, let us take this example.

```
func badAsyncFunc(_ mutex: UnsafeMutablePointer<pthread_mutex_t>, _ op : () async -> ())
async {
  // ...
  pthread_mutex_lock(mutex)
  await op()
  pthread_mutex_unlock(mutex) // Bad! May unlock on a different thread!
  // ...
}
```

The example function above will end up producing an undefined result. This is because a mutex must continue on the same thread that created it. That is the entire point of a mutex. In these instances, you would want to be able to indicate that a particular function is not available to call from an asynchronous context. That is where the new noasync availability attribute can come in handy. Here is an example of how to use it.

```
@available(*, noasync)
func pthread_mutex_lock(_ lock: UnsafeMutablePointer<pthread_mutex_t>) {}
```

When you add this availability to a function it will tell the compiler that it cannot be used within an asynchronous context. Attempting to do so will produce an error. There may be instances when you want to provide a possible alternative without someone explicitly having to do the research to determine the exact replacement. In these situations you can add a message, as outlined below.

```
@available(*, noasync, renamed: "mainactorReadID()", message: "use mainactorReadID
instead")
```

```
func readIDFromThreadLocal() -> Int { }

@MainActor
func readIDFromMainActor() -> Int { readIDFromThreadLocal() }
```

In the example above, the alternative is being run on the **@MainActor**, which therefore means it will be run in an asynchronous safe manner. There may also be instances when you want to be able to indicate that a function that is not safe to call in an asynchronous context has been renamed to one that is safe to use asynchronously. For those instances there is an option, as shown in the above example. Providing a "renamed" will make it easier for developers to be able to update their code, as necessary.

You can read the all of the motivation at the SE-0340 proposal page, available at https://github.com/apple/swift-evolution/blob/main/proposals/0340-swift-noasync.md.

Next, let us cover a new keyword, Sendable.

Sendable and @Sendable closures (SE-0302)

Swift 5.5 introduced a huge change to Swift, with the Async and Structured Concurrency. Structured concurrency is designed to provide a standard means of performing asynchronous calls. One aspect of structured concurrency is a feature called an "Actor".

Actors are designed to be the controlling aspect for various asynchronous calls. There is a "MainActor" type, which is the global shared actor type. It is equivalent to dispatching on the main queue. All actors are designed to work on value types and do not permit access to their values from other actors. This is intentional in its design so that a core principle of Swift, a single source of truth, is maintained.

In many cases you may not need to cross actor boundaries and send data between them, but there may be instances when this needs to be done. Prior to Swift 5.7 it was not possible to send data between actors, but now it is. This is made possible through two items, conformance to the "Sendable" protocol or by using an "@Sendable" attribute, for functions. Let us look at both of these in turn, starting with the Sendable protocol.

Sendable Protocol

When you conform to the Sendable protocol your types will be allowed to safely move between various Actors. Whether or not a custom type conforms depends on its usage. If all public APIs for a type conform to Sendable then the entire type can conform to Sendable. Another example is if all public mutators come to copy-on-write, or have an internal locking mechanism.

There are a number of built-in Swift types that automatically conform to Sendable. Anything that creates an immutable value automatically conforms to Sendable, because there is no way to modify the value of the object. Some of these include:

```
extension Int: Sendable {}
extension String: Sendable {}
extension Optional: Sendable where Wrapped: Sendable {}
extension Array: Sendable where Element: Sendable {}
extension Dictionary: Sendable where Key: Sendable, Value: Sendable {}
```

It is important to note that Error and CodingKey both inherit from Sendable, so any types that conform to these will automatically conform to Sendable and useable across Actors.

It might be a bit easier to understand given an example, so let us look at the following structs:

```
struct MyMovie : Sendable { var name: String, year: Int }
struct MyNSMovie { var name: NSMutableString, year: Int }
```

The "MyMovie" struct is sendable because both String and Int are Sendable because they are value types that are stored as copy-on-write. Meanwhile, the MyNSMovie struct cannot conform to Sendable because the name variable is an NSMutableString, which is passed by reference and can be modified in place.

Where possible it is important to try and remove any extraneous boilerplate. This is also the case with Sendable. The compiler is able to automatically determine which types can automatically conform to Sendable and will only provide a compile time error if it is unsure or if it the native types, or associative types, cannot conform to Sendable. Implicit conformance to Sendable is only available for non-generic types and for generic types whose instance data is guaranteed to be of Sendable type.

There might be instances when you are aware that the types cannot automatically conform to Sendable, but they might still be safe to send between Actor domains due to internal checks. In these instances, you can use the `@unchecked` attribute. Setting this attribute will tell the compiler that it should not perform any checking for conformance to Sendable.

There is another item to keep in mind, should you want a have a struct or enum be able to conform to Sendable, that must be done within the same source file where the struct or enum is defined. This is required so the stored properties are visible so that their types can be confirmed to be able to conform to Sendable. This required can be bypassed by using the `@unchecked` attribute.

One type that has not been discussed thus far is Classes. Any class can declare conformance to Sendable with an `@unchecked` attribute. However, there is one limitation for unchecked Sendable classes. These classes cannot inherit from any other classes, except NSObject. Additionally, these types of classes need to be defined within the same source file, just like Structs and Enums.

Now that Structs, Enums, and Classes have been covered, let us look at making individual functions confirming to Sendable, with `@Sendable`.

@Sendable

Functions that need to conform to Sendable must be marked with the `@Sendable` attribute. The largest limitation to this is that all captures within a function must also conform to Sendable.

There are some other types that need to have notes regarding them.

- ManagedBuffer: is meant to provide mutable reference. It must not conform to Sendable, even unsafely.

- Unsafe(Mutable)(Buffer)Pointer: these generic types unconditionally conform to the Sendable protocol. This means that an unsafe pointer to a non-concurrent value can potentially be used to share such values between concurrency domains. Unsafe pointer types provide fundamentally unsafe access to memory, and the programmer must be trusted to use them correctly, enforcing a strict safety rule for one narrow dimension of their otherwise completely unsafe use seems inconsistent with that design.
- Lazy algorithm adapter types: the types returned by lazy algorithms (e.g. as the result of array.lazy.map { ... }) never conform to Sendable. Many of these algorithms (like the lazy map) take non @Sendable closure values, and therefore cannot safely conform to Sendable.

You can read more about the Sendable protocol and the @Sendable attribute in the SE-0302 proposal, which is available at https://github.com/apple/swift-evolution/blob/main/proposals/0302-concurrent-value-and-concurrent-closures.md. The additions to Swift 5.6 and 5.7 are by no means the only additions. There are actually a large number of additions to both versions of Swift.

Everything that has been covered so far is part of the Swift Standard Library, so they can be guaranteed to be part of every Swift installation. However, there are instances when you might need to add some functionality that is not part of the Standard Library. For these occasions you might want to add a third-party library to your application. There is a mechanism designed just for these occasions, that mechanism is called Swift Package Manager.

You can add any number of Swift Packages as dependencies to your apps intended for Apple's Operating Systems, but you can also add packages to your Linux or Windows-based applications as well. There is one Swift Package that needs to be discussed, that package is Swift Async Algorithms.

Swift Async Algorithms

Swift Async Algorithms is a package that takes some familiar synchronous algorithms and packages them up in a single library that is comprised of the asynchronous versions. These asynchronous versions all work using the Async/Await pattern as well as with Structured Concurrency.

There are a number of algorithms in in the package, but let us look at just a few of them. These are zip, debounce, and async.

Zip

There are instances when you want to be able to combine a number of items into a tuple, but you may not be able to do it in a synchronous manner. Typically, when you use Zip, you want to combine two Sequences. Zip does this in an asynchronous manner and will take two asynchronous sequences and combine them.

Debounce

When you are going through, or retrieving, data, you may want to artificially introduce some delay. In order to do this you can use the ".debounce" function comes in handy. Debounce can take a parameter for a specific duration. For example, if you want to delay something at least a half second, you can use something similar:

```
for await value in input.debounce(for: .seconds(0.5)) { }
```

This is great way of being able to add a delay to calls.

Async Modifier

There are instances when you want to be able to combine a synchronous item and asynchronous item. This is now possible with the async modifier. Here is an example:

```
let preamble = [
    "// This is source file comment
].async
let lines = chain(preamble, URL(fileURLWithPath: "/tmp/Sample.swift").lines)
for try await line in lines { print(line) }
```

Being able to easily make a synchronous item, like a string, and then combine it with an asynchronous item should come quite handy for a number of apps and projects. These are just a few of the algorithms available in the Swift Async Algorithms package. Next, let us move onto another Swift Package related item, the Swift Package Manager. There have been some changes for that as well

Swift Package Manager (SwiftPM)

Not every part of Swift can be contained within the Swift Standard Library. Doing so would make the standard library explode in size. If everything was built into the standard library, not every application would need to use every aspect and it would be wasted.

Instead of putting everything together, you may want to pull in various libraries. In order to be able to pull in libraries across various operating systems, there needs to be a consistent way of defining the packages. In the world of Swift, this is called the Swift Package Manager.

The Swift Package Manager allows you to import various libraries from anywhere, as long as they are defined in a manifest file. There have been a couple of additions to the Swift Package Manager in Swift 5.7. These changes are the Extensible Build Tools and Command Plugins. Let us look at each of these in turn, starting with the Extensible Build Tools.

Package Manager Extensible Build Tools (SE 0303)

SwiftPM is still a nascent package management framework, and due to this, there are many features that can be added to the framework. One of these features is a way to be able to perform actions before or after a package is built. There are a number of items to tackle in order to make this happen.

The SE-0303 proposal, which was implemented with Swift 5.6, defines a new type called plugin. A plugin is a standard way of being able to create commands that should be run at build time. A plugin is invoked in an on demand manner by having targets opt into using a particular plugin. It should be noted that these plugins are only available during building, not outside of it. The plugin can be thought of as a procedural way of configuring commands.

The initial implementation of Extensible Build Tools only allows for one type of plugin, a buildTool. As the name indicates, these are designed to be plugins for when you are building a Swift Package.

Build Tool plugins are designed for use with code generation, in particular converting from one type of source to Swift.

Security should no longer be considered a secondary item to tackle after something has been created. This is especially the case for plugins. Some aspects of security are already inherent in SwiftPM. That feature is sandboxing. All SwiftPM builds are done in a sandbox which limits which directories the build can write to. Furthermore, SwiftPM plugins should not have access to the network, meaning that all needed libraries or files should be defined in the manifest and downloaded in order to use.

The full specification can be found at https://github.com/apple/swift-evolution/blob/main/proposals/0303-swiftpm-extensible-build-tools.md. Let us look at a similarly related item, Command Plugins.

Command Plugins (SE-0332)

Command Plugins are similar to build tools, with a few exceptions. The first is that Command Plugins are not invoked automatically. Instead, they are explicitly invoked by the user. The second differentiation is that command plugins carry out the functionality of the plugin when they are invoked.

As mentioned in the build tools section above, security is not a secondary concern. Instead, security is at the forefront. Because command plugins have access to all files, they are provided with a read-only snapshot of of the package, before being able to perform any processing on it.

Beyond the read-only snapshots there has been another change specifically to SwiftPM.

"To increase the security of packages, SwiftPM performs trust on first use (TOFU) validation. The fingerprint of a package is now being recorded when the package is first downloaded from a Git repository. Subsequent downloads must have fingerprints matching previous recorded values, otherwise it would result in build warnings or failures depending on settings." Let us now look at one last item related to Swift Package Manager, documentation.

Swift DocC Updates

At WWDC 21 Apple announced that there was a new documentation generation tool available that can automatically generate documentation for libraries and Swift Packages, directly from the source. That documentation generation tool is called DocC.

When you generate documentation with DocC you can use it directly within Xcode's search or you can host the generated documentation on a website. Initially, DocC was only available from within Xcode. Now, with Swift 5.6 this changes because DocC is now available as a Swift Package.

What this means is that you are now able to include the swift-docc-plugin into your Swift Package, so that documentation for your package can be generated.

As mentioned above, you could host the documentation on your generated documentation on your web server. This would require some additional configuration and setup in order to accomplish. Now, with the new DocC Swift Package you can generate documentation that can either be hosted on your own website or even on static sites, like GitHub pages. You can check out the getting started guide, which is available at https://apple.github.io/swift-docc-plugin/documentation/swiftdoccplugin/publishing-to-github-pages/. Next, let us look at something related to Swift, and that could not be possible with Swift, SwiftUI.

SwiftUI Changes

SwiftUI is Apple's Swift-only User Interface framework. SwiftUI is a significant shift from AppKit and UIKit in that it uses an entirely different style of programming. When you are using AppKit or UIKit you are using an imperative style, telling the app how to do something as well as actively changing the state of a program. With SwiftUI you are using a declarative style. This means that you define your interface and it will change when the underlying source data changes. If you have been using AppKit or UIKit for a while using SwiftUI can take a while to wrap your head around.

SwiftUI's declarative nature means that you can learn the syntax just once and it can be used everywhere. There may need to be some minor platform specific tweaks, as well as controls, but for any shared controls you only have to learn it once and you can apply it to almost anywhere.

As mentioned a couple of chapters back Swift and SwiftUI are the future of programming languages and interface building on Apple's platforms. Apple has continued to iterate on both Swift and SwiftUI. We covered the Swift changes last chapter. This chapter we are looking at the changes for SwiftUI. There have been a few including Multiple Windows, SplitView, and integrating SwiftUI into your UITableviews. Let us look at each starting with Multiple Windows.

Multiple Windows

When you develop for macOS the ability to have multiple windows for a single application is commonplace. The various windows could be any number of windows. You have your main content, but you could also have additional ancillary windows that might be useful, like a toolbox for selecting various tools. These types of windows are known as Auxiliary windows. While these have been possible on macOS using AppKit, it has not been possible with SwiftUI, but that now changes.

Starting with macOS Ventura there is a new struct, the **Window** struct. This struct allows you to define a Window that is outside of the main WindowGroup. Window is similar to most other primitives in SwiftUI, except that you need to specify a couple of parameters. These are the title for the window, which can be either a Text or a LocalizedStringKey. Here is an example of what that might look:

```
Window("Auxilary View", id: "aux-view") { AuxView() }
```

You can declare this in your struct that conforms to the **App** protocol. When you run an app with a Window defined, it will automatically appear in the Window menu item on macOS. You can define as many Windows as are needed for your app.

If it makes sense to only have an Auxiliary View but not a main view, you can declare a single Window as your entire view. This may be useful in some contexts, like when you have an app that runs in the background and only has a limited user interface, like a Menu Bar Extra app. Let us look at those next.

MenuBar Extras

There are a variety of utility apps that do not necessarily need a full application window to show. Only a few examples of this are iStatMenus by bjango (bjango.com), AirBuddy by Guilherme Rambo (airbuddy.app), and SwitchGlass by John Siracusa (hypercritical.co) are just three that come to mind, but there are hundreds. Previously if you had a SwiftUI app that also had a MenuBar Extra you would need to create the MenuBar extra in Swift, or Objective-C. Now, with macOS Ventura you can do this just in SwiftUI.

There are a couple of different approaches for creating MenuBar Extras. You can either create a MenuBar Extra as its own Scene that is included with your main app, or you can create a utility app that is only a MenuBarExtra. Let us look at both.

With an App

If you have an existing app that you are looking to add a MenuBar Extra to, or move an existing one to SwiftUI you can declare the MenuBar extra like this:

```
@main
struct AppWithMenuBarExtra: App {
  @AppStorage("showMenuBarExtra") private var showMenuBarExtra = true
  var body: some Scene {
    WindowGroup {
        ContentView()
    }
    MenuBarExtra( "App Menu Bar Extra", systemImage: "star", isInserted:
$showMenuBarExtra) {
        StatusMenu()
    }
  }
}
```

With the code above you define your Main app's view plus the view of MenuBarExtra . If you need to declare a MenuBarExtra on its own, you can use the following example:

```
@main
struct UtilityApp: App {
  var body: some Scene {
    MenuBarExtra("Status Utility App", systemImage: "gear") {
      StatusMenu()
    }
  }
}
```

The code above will create a utility app that is only a MenuBar Extra. When using the Utility App approach, the extra will terminate if the user removes the MenuBar Extra from the menu. By default Utility apps that only define a MenuBarExtra will not show a window, if you need to show a window as well, you can use the ".menuBarExtraStyle(.window)" modifier, applied to the **MenuBarExtra** struct to indicate that there needs to be a window as well. This will appear directly below the Menu Bar. One last item to note. Typically, Utility Apps that only have a MenuBar Extra do not show in the Dock or the App Switcher, to enable this type of behavior you will need to add the LSUIElement property with a Boolean of true in your app's info.plist file.

The ability to create MenuBar Extras right from within SwiftUI provides even more capabilities of SwiftUI on the Mac. Let us look at some changes around navigation.

Navigation

One of the more common ways of navigating within a SwiftUI app is to use a **NavigationView**. When you use a NavigationView you are able to push any type of content that you would like. You can use NavigationView to create single column, two column, or three column layouts, depending on the number of views that you define within the NavigationView. As an example, you could use something like this:

```
struct ContentView: View {
    var body: some View {
        NavigationView {
            Column1()
            Column2()
            Column3()
        }.navigationViewStyle(.stack)
    }
}
```

NavigationView has been deprecated and it has been replaced with NavigationStack and NavigationSplitView. These both have their own usage. NavigationStack is used with one column views. NavigationSplitView is used for multi-column displays. Let us look at NavigationSplitView in depth.

NavigationSplitView

When the iPhone was first released there was only screen size and only one app could be running at a time, with the exclusion of the Phone and Music apps. All other apps would be pushed to the background if you switched to another app and all of this was within a 3.5-inch screen.

It was not until the release of the iPad in April of 2010 when it was possible to have different screen sizes. The iPad introduced the possibility of having a second screen size with the 9.7-inch screen on the iPad. With that much space you would likely need new ways of displaying data. Apple made this possible with the introduction of a new user interface element called a Split View. There are a number of ways of displaying data and sometimes doing so in a hierarchical manner makes sense.

Sometimes you only need to have your information displayed in two columns, other times it might make sense to have three columns. These are aptly named the Double Column layout and a Triple Column layout, respectively. Previously, this was not possible to do, at least not easily, with SwiftUI. Now with all of Apple's platforms there is a new control, called NavigationSplitView.

NavigationSplitView is a Swift native control for being able to create a two or three column view, depending on your need. The code you would use for a three column layout is:

```
NavigationSplitView(sidebar: { Text("Sidebar") }, content: { Text("Content") }, detail:
{ Text("Detail") })
```

You can also have a two column layout using this code:

```
NavigationSplitView { Text("Sidebar") }, detail: { Text("Detail") })
```

When you show a View that has a NavigationSplitView in it, you may not always want to show certain columns. This can be achieved by providing a binding that is a NavigationSplitViewVisibility item. NavigationSplitViewVisibility has four options:

- automatic - provides default behavior based on the current device.
- all - shows all of the columns.
- doubleColumn - will show the content and detail columns and hide the sidebar, in a three-column layout. In a two column layout, this is equivalent to **.all**.
- detailOnly - will show just the detail view with the other columns hidden.

If you are setting visibility on a device that does not display SplitView columns, or if your app is in a context where it would, the columns would be hidden, such as in SlideOver on iPad, or on an iPhone in portrait orientation, the visibility setting will be ignored.

Apple provides a default size for each of the column widths, this is possible using the NavigationSplitViewColumnWidth modifier. You can specify the min, ideal, and max widths for each column. An example would be: NavigationSplitViewColumnWidth(min: 150, ideal: 175, max: 200). You would need to apply this to the view inside of the column.

Having a native SplitView navigation within SwiftUI will allow for additional developers to possibly move to SwiftUI from UIKit or AppKit, because **NavigationSplitView** is available on all of Apple's platforms. NavigationSplitView is great for providing navigation and the way that you move between views is using NavigationLink. There have been some changes to NavigationLink as well, but that is because of a new navigation primitive, the NavigationStack.. Let us look at those next.

NavigationLink

App hierarchies can be very complex. When you develop with Interface Builder and UIKit, or AppKit, you can easily see the layout of your app in Interface Builder. This can be done by zooming out on your storyboard and looking at each of the segues that you have created. This zoomed out view can help you figure out how everything fits together. This it not as easy to do with SwiftUI and its compositional nature. Even though it cannot be easily mapped out does not mean that they are any less complex. In reality, they could be even more complex due to the reusable nature of SwiftUI Views.

NavigationLinks are used for navigation between multiple views. This could be within a **List, NavigationSplitView,** or even just between two **Views.** When you are using a List, you can define a NavigationLink using something similar to this:

```
NavigationLink { NextView() } label: { Text("Link Text") }
```

In the example above you define the destination View, and the Label to use for the link. This is pretty standard use case. However, if you want to navigate from a button you will need to do something a bit different. You need to define a Boolean, and use the "isActive" parameter to bind to that property. Here is what that might look like:

```
@State private var showLink: Bool = false
NavigationLink(destination: NextView(), isActive: $showLink { EmptyView() }
.isDetailLink(false).labelsHidden().hidden()
```

In order to navigate via a button, the button would need to set "showLink" to be true. Once this happens, then the view will be pushed onto the stack. The first method, from within a List or anywhere within a NavigationView, will push that view onto the stack and the view would be displayed. The overarching approach to NavigationLinks has changed a bit.

SwiftUI is a framework that works on value types, not reference types. The use of value types enables SwiftUI's declarative nature in that a particular view will only update if the value of something within the view changes.

If you had previously declared a NavigationLink using the "isActive" approach, you should be able to use something akin to this:

```
@State private var path: [Color] = [] // Empty stack by default.
var body: some View {
  NavigationStack(path: $path) {
    List {
      NavigationLink("Purple", value: .purple)
      NavigationLink("Pink", value: .pink)
      NavigationLink("Orange", value: .orange)
    }
    .navigationDestination(for: Color.self) { color in
      ColorDetailView(color: color)
    }
  }
}
```

The top line in the example above will hold the array of colors, that you have pushed to the path. Now, instead of needing to define an individual link for each of your links, you can now define a destination for each type of data that might be pushed onto the stack.

Having two distinct types for the different navigation approaches makes sense because having distinct types will make code more understandable for everyone. One last thing to note about the stack of items. If you need to jump back to the root view, you can easily accomplish this by using **path.removeAll**(), which will remove all of the elements on the path and therefore will remove all of them from the stack, jumping back to the root view.

One place where you might use a NavigationLink is within a List or NavigationView. Either of these is equivalent to a UITableView in UIKit. There has been a slight change to UITableView and SwiftUI that needs to be covered, so let us move onto that.

UITableView and SwiftUI

SwiftUI is a great way of being able to quickly build interfaces for all sorts of use cases. One place where you need to build views is within a UITableView. UITableView is a UIKit element that is used for a table view, similar to the List primitive in SwiftUI.

UITableView has a lot of customization options and you may have an existing UITableView that you have optimized over time. One of the trickier things to handle when it comes building a UITableView is the UITableViewCell. UITableViewCells are elements that make up actual table and what is shown to users when they interact with the table.

Now, you can use SwiftUI in place of a pre-configured UITableViewCell or UICollectionViewCell, using the new UIHostingConfiguration primitive. The way that you would do this is as follows:

```
cell.contentConfiguration = UIHostingConfiguration {
  HStack {
    Image(uiImage: currentAd.image)
      .resizable()
```

```
      .scaledToFit()
      .frame(maxWidth:100, maxHeight: 100)
    Spacer()
    Text(currentAd.text)
  }
  .background(Color(UIColor.secondarySystemBackground))
  .frame(maxHeight: 150)
}.margins([.leading, .trailing], 5.0)
```

The UIHostingConfiguration item is all you need, along with importing the SwiftUI framework, to get started. Once you declare the UIHostingConfiguration you can then begin writing your SwiftUI code to accommodate for various aspects. Since you are declaring this in the same class as your UITableView, you can access any properties needed. In the example above the code is being written right inline. However, you can also use existing SwiftUI Views if you have also used them elsewhere in your SwiftUI Code. UIHostingConfiguration can only be used on iOS 16, iPadOS 16, and tvOS 16. It is not available for macOS 13 Ventura nor watchOS 9.

Margins

When you use a UIHostingConfiguration it will automatically inset the edges. This may not be what you intend for your view. You are able to adjust the margins on the UIHostingConfiguration by applying the margins modifier. The last line in the example above shows one method of setting the margins. This specifies which edges to apply the margin to and specifies a Float, technically a CGFloat, value. The other option is to use a EdgeInsets struct to specify the insets for each edge.

This is a great addition that will allow you to start experimenting with SwiftUI, if you have not previously done so, or even allow you to use your existing code all within a UITableView or UICollectionView.

Table

Tables are a great way of being able to show multiple columns of related items in a single view. Tables may not make sense on a device like the Apple Watch, but they absolutely make sense on the Mac or the iPad. You could try and build your own table type in SwiftUI by using an HStack to define your different columns, but this can become quite cumbersome to maintain. This can be accomplished with the **Table** primitive. **Table** was introduced last year with Swift 3, but it was only available for macOS. Starting with Swift 4 you can now use Table on iPadOS as well. Let us look at a refresher of what is possible with **Table**.

When you define a Table you pass a collection of items, just like you would in a List. You can define each column using the TableColumn primitive. Each TableColumn is defined by a name, and can be a value or binding that can be passed based on the model of your data. You can customize each TableColumn with a ".width" modifier, if you want to define a fixed width.

Selection

It is quite possible that you may want to be able to select certain rows within a table, and the Table primitive can support this by passing a binding to the selection parameter when you initialize a Table element. Here is an example:

```
@State var icons = getAppIcons()
@State var selection = Set<AppIcon.ID>()
var body: some View {
    Table(icons, selection: $selection)  { } }
```

When you declare the binding, you will then be able to tell the Table which rows are currently selected. You need to pass a Set because there may be more than one row that is selected at a time.

Besides selection, another feature common to tables is the ability to sort. This is also provided for.

Sorting

Users are likely to expect the ability to sort a Table. While your users may want to be able to sort every column, that does not always make sense. Therefore, you can determine which columns are sortable.

Similar to selecting rows you need to provide a binding for your sort order. However instead of being a set, this needs to be an array of KeyPaths to the field names that you want allow for sorting. This binding is passed to the "sortOrder" initialization parameter on Table. Here is an example of how to create a Sort Order.:

```
@State var icons = getAppIcons()
@State var sortOrder = [KeyPathComparator(\AppIcon.name)]
@State var selection = Set<AppIcon.ID>()
var body: some View {
    Table(icons, selection: $selection, sortOrder: $sortOrder) { }
}
```

Being able to add sorting is a great way of extending capabilities on a Table. There is another way to extend the capabilities of a Table, and that is **through search.**

Searching

If you want to be able to add search to a Table, List, or any other item, you can do so with the new ".searchable" modifier. When you add this modifier, you will need to provide some sort of filtered results, based upon the entered search term.

Unlike Table, Searching is available on all of Apple's operating system. Once you add the ".searchable" modifier, the searching will be placed appropriately for the specific platform. By doing this there is less that you need to worry about and the searching will feel native to the specific platform.

Let us cover a brief change to an existing SwiftUI primitive called Stepper.

Stepper

When you are building an app there may be instances when you need to specify a quantity of something. This could be the number of items to order, number of items delivered, or number of times to perform an action. When you know that you want to specify a number, you could use a TextField and then process the user's input to remove anything but numbers. However, there is a more appropriate control, a Stepper.

A Stepper allows you to, as the name indicates, provide step values for input. The step values can be any Float, Double, or an Integer value. The Stepper primitive has been available on iOS, iPadOS, macOS, and MacCatalyst since Swift 1. The one platform that has not had the Stepper is watchOS. Now with watchOS 9 you can use Stepper on watchOS and it will look native on the platform. This is a small change but one that can allow developers to remove any custom stepper like code they may have previously created and use the native Stepper in its place. Let us look at another item that has seen some enhancements, Date Pickers.

Date Picker

If your app has anything to do with dates, you are likely going to end up displaying a Date Picker. The DatePicker primitive view is an elegant way of being able to choose a date and use it within your app. Using a DatePicker to select a single date is helpful, but it is not that useful if you need a bunch of dates. You could work around this by presenting a couple of alternative date fields, that each have their own binding and then aggregating those dates into an array or set. Starting with Swift 4 you no longer need to do this. Instead, you can use the new **MultiDatePicker** primitive. Before we dive into **MultiDatePicker**, let us have a quick refresher on **DatePicker**.

DatePicker

```
struct ContentView: View {
  @State private var selectedDate: Date = Date()
  var body: some View {
    DatePicker("Day Off", selection: $selectedDate)
  }
}
```

As you can see, it is quite simple to declare a date picker. When you declare a default DatePicker it is an inline element comprised of two components, one component for the date and another for the time. When you tap on either of them it will show the appropriate control to select the date, or time. Here are a couple more examples of what you can do with DatePicker:

```
DatePicker("Day Off Calendar", selection: $selectedDate, displayedComponents: .date)
.datePickerStyle(.graphical)
```

The above code will show a graphical calendar where you can select the date. Similarly, if you just need the hour, you can do this:

```
DatePicker("Hour Only", selection: $selectedDate, displayedComponents: .hourAndMinute)
```

With DatePicker you have a variety of options. There are a few more, but we will look at those in context of MultiDatePicker. Let us now turn to MultiDatePicker.

MultiDatePicker

The MultiDatePicker will allow you to, as the name indicates, select multiple dates. Let us look at how to use MultiDatePicker with an example.

```
struct ContentView: View {
  @State private var selectedDates: Set<DateComponents> = []
  var body: some View {
    MultiDatePicker("Days Off", selection: $selectedDates)
  }
}
```

In the above code, you will see that in the body property of our Swift View there is a MultiDatePicker element defined and it has a binding to the selected dates. This is an empty set of DateComponents. The default view of a MultiDatePicker is a calendar, or graphical, view. This makes sense because you want to select multiple dates, therefore a calendar view is the easiest. In fact, that is the only view available. If you try to apply the **datePickerStyle** modifier it will be ignored.

With a standard DatePicker you are able to select the type of element, hourAndMinute or date to be shown. There is no displayedComponents parameter, so this is not even a possibility.

Limiting Date Selections

Having the ability to provide a multi-date selection control is a great enhancement, but it may also be useful to be able to limit what dates can be selected. Let us say that you are providing historical data only from 2010 up to yesterday (in our example we will make it June 5th, 2022), being able to select anything before 2010 or after yesterday would not make sense. You are able to accomplish this by using the "bounds" parameter in the MultiDatePicker function declaration. There are actually three different ways of specifying the bounds for a MultiDatePicker. These are the PartialRangeUpTo<Date>, PartialRangeFrom<Date>, and Range<Date>. Let us look at all of these.

Below is all of the code needed to create three multi-date calendar pickers that limit the range of dates, based upon the computed property for each different type of date range.

```swift
struct ContentView: View {
  // Declare env variables of calendar and timeZone used in the computed properties
  @Environment(\.calendar) var calendar
  @Environment(\.timeZone) var timeZone
  // Create the Set of selected dates
  @State private var selectedDates: Set<DateComponents> = []
  var upToBounds: PartialRangeUpTo<Date> {
    let endDate = calendar.date(from: DateComponents(timeZone: timeZone, year: 2022,
month: 06,day: 05))!
    return ..<endDate
  }
  var fromBounds: PartialRangeFrom<Date> {
    let startDate = calendar.date(from: DateComponents(timeZone: timeZone, year: 2010,
month: 01, day: 01))!
    return startDate...
  }
  var dateRange: Range<Date> {
    let fromDate = DateComponents(calendar: Locale.current.calendar, year: 2010, month:
1, day: 1)

    let toDate = DateComponents(calendar: Locale.current.calendar, year: 2022, month: 6,
day: 6)
    return fromDate.date!..<toDate.date!
  }
  var body: some View {
    ScrollView {
      // Create a MultiDatePicker up to 2022-06-05
      MultiDatePicker("Up to Date", selection: $selectedDates, in: upToBounds)
      // Create a MultiDatePicker up to from 2010-01-01
      MultiDatePicker("From Date", selection: $selectedDates, in: fromBounds)
      // Create a MultiDatePicker with dates between 2010-01-01 through 2022-06-05
      MultiDatePicker("Between Dates", selection: $selectedDates, in: dateRange)
    }
  }
}
```

The code above creates three different computed properties, which will be used as the end date, start date, and date range, respectively for each of the different types. You can also omit the "in" parameter and every date will be selectable.

The ability to add a MultiDate Picker is a very welcome change and being able to limit the date range is one that should be helpful to a number of apps.

Transferable Protocol

Apps comes in many different varieties. Some apps keep all of their data contained within the app and there is no easy way to get the data out. While other apps allow you to share the data within the app quite easily. When data is transferred between two apps binary data is being handled. One aspect that needs to be determined is the type of data. There are a slew of common data types. These are all defined using the UniformTypeIdentifiers.

If your app has support for either drag and drop or opening other files of specific types, then you are likely aware of the UniformTypeIdentifiers. **UniformTypeIdentifiers** are way of being able to identify various types of data. Here are a few examples:

```
UTType.json
UTType.movie
UTType.plainText
UTType.image
```

These are just a few examples out of the nearly 200 system defined types. It is possible to define your own types as well. The reason that you might need to do this is because the data for your app cannot fit into one of the standard types. This is a common occurrence, particularly if you have a custom data format. Below is an example of how to declare your own UTType

```
extension UTType {
    static var myMovie: UTType = UTType(exportedAs: "com.example.myMovie")
}
```

This will allow you to use a dot notation to access your custom type, just like you can with the system defined types. Beyond defining this in your code you will also need to define this within your Info.plist file, so that the system knows that your app can support your custom type.

It is possible that you are wondering how this can be used. If you have your own data type it is likely that you want to be able to share it from your SwiftUI app, you will need to make sure that your model code conforms to the new Transferable protocol.

Transferable is a new protocol that can be used in a declarative way to support features like the Share Sheet as well as drag and drop. With Transferable you are able to provide all of the functionality needed. In order to use Transferable you may need to make a few modifications to your models. One thing that you will need to do is declare a type identifier, which is discussed above.

A lot of the standard types, like String, URL, Data, Image, and Attributed String already conform to the Transferable protocol, so if your app only uses these, then there is no work that you need to necessarily do. However, if your data does not already conform to these then you will need to have your models conform to Transferable. Let us use a model called MyVideoModel as an example:

```
struct MyVideoModel: Codable {
    var id: UUID
    var name: String = ""
    var rating: Rating = .nr }
```

This is just a very simple model that contains an identifier, the video name, and the rating, which is just an enum of various ratings. In order for your model to conform to transferrable you will need to implement a single property, the **transferRepresentation** property. Here is how you can have the above model conform to the Transferable protocol.

```
extension MyVideoModel: Transferable {
  static var transferRepresentation: some TransferRepresentation {
    CodableRepresentation(contentType: .myMovie)
  }
}
```

There are three different Representation types available, Codable, Data, and File. Each has their own use case, but for our simple model, the CodableRepresentation will work. If we were transferring an actual file, then the FileRepresentation would be appropriate.

Due to the fact that our custom model already conforms to Codable, it makes sense to use the CodableRepresentation. By default CodableRepresentation uses JSON encoder and decoder functions to represent the data. You can implement your own encoder or decoder if necessary. After you have declared the CodableRepresentation, the above model now fully supports Transferable. That is all that needs to be done.

As mentioned above there are two other types, DataRepresentation and FileRepresentation. Each of these has its own unique needs. For instance, with DataRepresentation, you will need to provide the methods for exporting and importing data. It might look something like this:

```
static var transferRepresentation: some TransferRepresentation {
  DataRepresentation(contentType: .commaSeparatedText) { archive in
      try archive.convertToCSV()
  } importing: { data in
      try MyVideoModelArchive(csvData: data)
  }
}
```

Likewise for a file, using the FileRepresentation, it might look something like this:

```
struct Video: Transferable {
  let file: URL
  static var transferRepresentation: some TransferRepresentation {
    FileRepresentation(contentType: .mpeg4Movie) {
      SentTransferredFile($0.file)
    } importing: { received in
      let destination = try Self.copyVideoFile(source: received.file)
      return Self.init(file: destination)
    }
  }

  static func copyVideoFile(source: URL) throws -> URL {
    let moviesDirectory = try FileManager.default.url(
      for: .moviesDirectory, in: .userDomainMask,
      appropriateFor: nil, create: true
    )
    var destination = moviesDirectory.appendingPathComponent(
      source.lastPathComponent, isDirectory: false)
    if FileManager.default.fileExists(atPath: destination.path) {
      let pathExtension = destination.pathExtension
```

```
        var fileName = destination.deletingPathExtension().lastPathComponent
        fileName += "_\(UUID().uuidString)"
        destination = destination
        .deletingLastPathComponent()
        .appendingPathComponent(fileName)
        .appendingPathExtension(pathExtension)
    }
    try FileManager.default.copyItem(at: source, to: destination)
    return destination
  }
}
```

The new Transferable protocol is a great way of being able represent your data in a declarative way that works well with SwiftUI. If your custom types conform to Transferable they will be able to be used with Drag and Drop, or even the new PasteButton inSwiftUI. On the topic of the PasteButton, let us look at that.

PasteButton

PasteButton is a new control that you can add to your app which will allow your users to easily paste things into your app from the PasteBoard. You can declare a PasteButton like this:

```
PasteButton(payloadType: String.self, onPaste: { strings in
  self.pastedText = strings[0]
})
```

The **payloadType** parameter must conform to the Transferable protocol. Due to the conformance to the Transferable protocol, if the data on the PasteBoard cannot be pasted in the current context, then the PasteButton will be set to disabled, but only on iOS and iPadOS, but not on macOS. This is a nice touch. The PasteButton is defined by the system, but you an add some modifiers like the **buttonBorderShape**, **labelStyle**, and **tint** modifiers.

Closing Thoughts on SwiftUI

Swift, SwiftUI, and the use of Xcode Previews is the future of building on Apple's platforms. While this has been apparent in the past, is it has been explicitly stated. Apple has pushed SwiftUI forward this year by adding the new NavigationSplitView primitive. With NavigationSplitView you can declare either two or three column layouts for your data. When you do this it will automatically display the data. Furthermore on platforms, or in contexts, where separate panes cannot be shown, the NavigationSplitView will be collapsed into a stack.

NavigationView has been deprecated and replaced with two more appropriate types, NavigationStack and NavigationSplitView. NavigationStack is used for one-column views, while NavigationSplitView can be used for two or three-column navigations. When you do create a NavigationLink, you can now use new .navigationDestination modifier to specify the different types of links that will be put onto the stack.

The Stepper can now be used on watchOS which will allow developers to possible remove older code. Similarly, there is a new MultiDatePicker for iOS, iPadOS, macOS Catalyst apps, that will allow you to create a calendar that permits selecting multiple dates, with the option of providing date ranges.

The new Transferable Protocol, will allow you to have your own custom types conform to the protocol, with only a single property. This pairs nicely with the new PasteButton, which will provide a system-level way of allowing data to be pasted into your app, and if the data is not of the right type, it will be disabled, at least on iOS and iPadOS.

We covered the MultiDatePicker primitive. One place where even a basic date picker would be helpful is when you need to select a date to put into a field, or fields, to specify dates and where to pull dates to display in a chart. If you wanted to create a chart using Swift you would have to create your own implementation, but that all changes with a new Swift only framework called SwiftUI Charts.

SwiftUI Charts

Charts are a great way to be able to convey a lot of information in a compact area. The manner in which data can be organized can be quite varied depending on the source and the way you intended on displaying the data. SwiftUI Charts is a new View in SwiftUI that allows you to create a variety of charts including Bar Charts, Line Charts, Stacked Bar charts, and more. Charts has a variety of modifiers that allow you to customize your chart. Let us look at a basic example.

```
struct ValuePerCategory: Codable, Identifiable {
  var id: String
  var value: Double
}

let data: [ValuePerCategory] = [
  .init(id: "A", value: 5),
  .init(id: "B", value: 10),
  .init(id: "C", value: 8)
]

struct ChartView: View {
  var body: some View {
    Chart(data) {
      BarMark(x: .value("Category", $0.id), y: .value("Value", $0.value) )
      .foregroundStyle(.green)
    }
  }
}
```

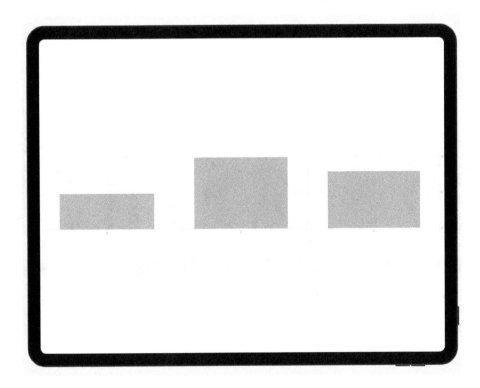

SwiftUIChart - Basic Bar Chart

The code above would create a a three bar chart with the category along the x access and the value along the y-axis. This is a very basic example, but they can become even more complex. Take the following Chart as another example:

```
struct AllTimeBarChart: View {
  @State var bookType: BookTypes
  var body: some View {
    Chart(SalesData.allTime.filter({$0.type.type == bookType }), id: \.id) {
      BarMark(x: .value("Year", $0.year, unit: .year), y: .value("Sales", $0.sold) )
      .foregroundStyle(by: .value("Title", $0.title))
    }
  }
}
```

The above chart is similar to the first example in that it will also create a Bar Chart, however this one will organize it based upon the Year of the sales and the units sold. The **foregroundStyle** modifier will actually select a different color based upon the title of the book. The resultant chart might look something like this:

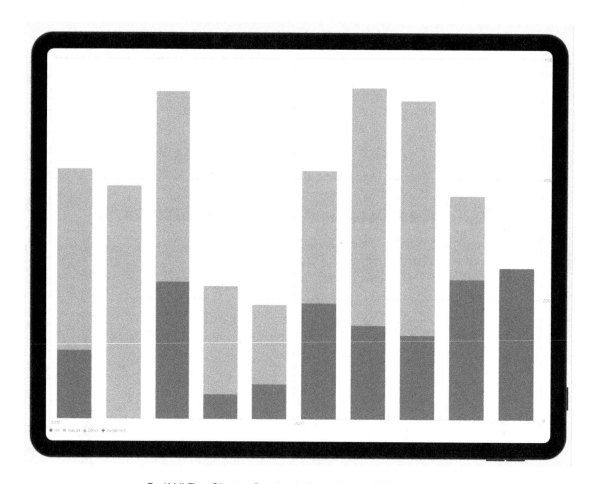

SwiftUI Bar Chart - Stacked -Book Sales 2012 to 2022

Bar Charts at not the only chart type. In fact you can create the following types:

- Bar Charts
- Line Types
- Plot Area
- Points

Each of these has its own use case, but all of them have the same basic construction with the x-axis and y-axis. For some chart types, like the Line Chart you can add a series label as well, where appropriate. It will take a bit of time to be able to determine which chart type is best for your particular data.

There is one item that is definitely worth mentioning. By default charts will take up the entire screen. Therefore, it is likely that you will want to limit the height or width, so be sure to apply the **frame** modifier on your Chart views.

SwiftUI Charts are a great way of being able to display various types of data. The only thing that might make them even better would be the ability to generate them and export them as images, but maybe with the next release that will be possible.

Xcode Changes

In order for developers to be able to build their apps they need some sort of interface to do so. If you are building a web based application it is entirely possible to use a text editor and Safari to be able to build a website. While it is certainly possible to use a text editor to modify Swift files, particularly if the text editor supports the Language Server Protocol (LSP). LSP is a protocol that allows for things like language keyword highlighting, autocomplete, and go to definitions. Even though it is possible to use a text editor and LSP to write applications most Apple developers will use the tools provided by Apple. That product is Xcode. Xcode is an all-in-one editor, compiler, and debugging tool. Each new release of Xcode brings some new features and enhancements. Xcode 14 is no exception to this. Some of the changes with Xcode 14 include floating Class and function definitions, improved DocC support, and updates for SwiftUI Previews, among a couple of other changes. We will begin with changes when installing Xcode.

Installing Xcode

Xcode is chockfull of features and capabilities. Xcode can be used to develop on all of Apple's platforms, as well as a number of versions of those operating systems. By default Xcode 13 included support for iOS, iPadOS, macOS, watchOS, and tvOS. Not every developer needs to develop on watchOS and tvOS. Therefore, now when you install Xcode only iOS, iPadOS, and macOS support will be installed by default. You do have the option of installing watchOS and tvOS at install time, but they are not included by default.

When you first startup Xcode 14 you will be presented with a screen like the one below.

Runtime installation with Xcode 14

The screen will ask which platforms you would like to install. By default iOS 16.0 and macOS 13.0 will be selected, and cannot be disabled. Here you will also be able to install watchOS 9.0 and tvOS 16.0 by simply clicking on the correspond checkboxes. Next to each of the operating systems will be how much space it will take to download and install.

This change has two implications. The first is that Xcode is approximately 30% smaller, because only the most common code is downloaded with Xcode. The second implication is that Xcode does not take up nearly as much space on disk as it has previously, because there is not as much installed.

Downloading and installing the tvOS 16 within Xcode 14

If you do opt to install watchOS or tvOS it will take a bit to download, but once it is downloaded and installed you can then begin working with Xcode 14, which has its own changes. Let us look at one of them, which is a change with class and function headers while using the Xcode editor.

Class and Function Headers

It is entirely possible that while you are building your app you may have a class or function that can contain a lot of functions. There are those instances when you may want to be able to quickly jump up to the top of the function or class. Of course this can be done by using the command + up arrow. This works well for classes, but what about functions because sometimes you just need to jump to the top of current function.

With Xcode 14 when you are looking through your code you may notice that the class and function definitions are pinned at the top of the editor window. These are the full definitions of the class, including protocol conformations. For functions it including all of the parameters as well. For functions specifically, this can be quite helpful when it comes to knowing the name of parameters that are passed to the function.

```
14   struct ContentView: View {
23       var body: some View {
25           Image(systemName: "timelapse", variableValue: value)
26               .scaledToFill()
27               .font(.system(size: 72))
28               .border(Color.gray)
29
30
```

Function headers displayed in Xcode 14

It's not only the class or function definition that you will find in the row. You will also see the line number. You can click on either of these and it will jump you to that definition. This is not limited to just classes and functions. It also applies to SwiftUI Views as well, including computed properties. This is a nice update and one that should help many developers, especially if you have a complicated function. There is another feature, related to functions that needs to be covered, and that is function completion.

Function Completion

Xcode has long had the capability of helping you complete functions by helpfully displaying them when you start writing a function header. If you find one that matches you can complete it. One of the features that is quite useful with Swift is the ability to overload functions. In case you are not aware,'s when you overload a function you are able to define the same function name with different parameters to be able to keep code a bit more organized.

Because Swift supports the ability to overload functions it is possible that you might have multiple definitions for the same function. With Xcode 13 in order to see all of the possibilities you would have begin enter in the name of the function and all of the possibilities would be listed. This would not be an issue if there were only two or three possibilities, but what if there 10 or 12. You may have been able to see the one that you wanted, but it was also equally possible you would not.

Now with Xcode 14 all of an overloaded function definitions will be collapsed into a single listing with the ability to expand the definition list. This tidies up the completion list a bit, but beyond this it also allows you to still easily expand the list should the definition you are looking exist in the collapsed list. Next, let us look at a change to Assets.

Assets and Icons

When we build an app we have an idea for how we want to represent our app. One of the more important ways of representing our app is the icon. When you start out you may have one icon or even offer the possibility of two icons. After a few years it may be time for a redesign of your app and during that redesign you decide to redo your app's icon as well. This is not always an easy task to accomplish. It's not just the design process, which does take some time on its own, but actually adding that icon to your app. If you support all of Apple's platforms in your app you can have up to 61 different icon sizes. This includes some 1x, 2x, and 3x assets, and 18 for iOS and iPadOS, 2 for CarPlay, 15 for watchOS, and 10 for macOS, and 18 for tvOS. That is a lot of icons, particularly if your icon is the exact same, just at different sizes.

Now with Xcode 14 you can let Xcode handle all of the heavy lifting, at least for iOS and watchOS. There is a new option for AppIcons for these. You can use the "Single" icon option, which is 1024x1024 and Xcode will create all of the necessary images for you. You cannot retroactively convert your current AppIcon asset definition, but you can add an addition one. For new projects, the default will be to use the "Single" size option.

To add a new App Icon set, perform the following steps:

1. Open **Xcode 14**.
2. **Open the app** that you would like to add a new App Icon set to.
3. Click on the **Assets** Catalog
4. **Right Mouse click** in an empty area.
5. Scroll down to **iOS**. A menu should show.

6. Click on **New iOS App Icon**. A new AppIcon set should be added.

This should create a new app icon set for you. Now you can add your 1024x1024 icon for your iOS app. Here you can also add a macOS icon set or a watchOS icon set as well. tvOS is still its own entire thing due to its unique nature of icons. The ability to have just a single app icon should make development even simpler than it was before because you only need one icon instead of the various sizes as before. Even though this only applies to iOS, iPadOS, and watchOS, it is a great start. Maybe it will come to macOS and tvOS one day as well. Let us now look at some changes to SwiftUI Previews.

SwiftUI Previews

As outlined earlier in this book, Apple has given a definite answer to the question of what tools and languages should be used when building apps going forward, that answer is Swift, SwiftUI, and SwiftUI Previews. SwiftUI Previews provides a way of allowing you to quickly and easily iterate on your SwiftUI Views.

Under the hood, SwiftUI Previews is powered by the Xcode Simulator. When you select a device to preview your SwiftUI view on, a simulator for that device is spun up and you can preview your SwiftUI view. The goal of SwiftUI Previews is to allow you to make a modification to your View and then have it update in near-realtime.

When SwiftUI Previews were first introduced, they could be a bit slow to render with changes. In some cases it was so unbearably slow that many paused the previews made their changes, and then resumed the Preview so it would actually render the changes. Apple has since fixed the issues, and SwiftUI Previews works pretty well on all SSD-based Macs, but could still be a bit sluggish on spinning hard drive Macs.

SwiftUI Previews in Xcode 14 has gotten some enhancements like Live rendering, View Switching, and easier variant switching. Let us start with Live Rendering.

Live Previews   Selectable Mode

Live Rendering

SwiftUI Previews are designed to show you near-realtime changes. With SwiftUI Previews under Xcode 13 you could enter into Live Preview for a single view. This would allow you to see how a single view will function. What would be even more helpful is being able to view how the entire app might function, including moving between views. This is now possible with Xcode 14. When you are in Live Preview mode, you will be able to move between views, just as if you were running the app on a device.

Actually, under Xcode 14 you no longer even need to start a Live Preview, because this is now the default. When you are previewing a SwiftUI View it will be running live, so you can interact with it as you might expect if you running a simulator or on device.

There are a couple of things to note. First, if you make any change to your SwiftUI code, the Live Preview will be recompiled and your preview will reset back to the first view. This makes sense since it needs to recompile your entire view hierarchy to incorporate the change. The second thing to note is that if you move away from that view, the Live Preview will stop. This makes sense because you do not want to keep a Live Preview running if you may not come back to it for a while. The last thing to note is that you you can stop the Live Preview by entering into the **Selectable** mode. Let us now move onto another new feature, Multiple Views

Multiple Views

When you are creating a SwiftUI View it is very likely that you may end up having multiple views within a single view. For instance, you might have two or three VStacks within a single View body. With Xcode 13 when you had this a new SwiftUI preview would be generated in the Preview canvas. This would allow you to view each of the views. This would allow you to look at them individually, which is helpful, but if you have a lot of VStacks, or other elements, it could create a large number of previews. You could mitigate this a bit by enclosing multiple views by multiple views into another VStack, but the entire idea is to preview the app as it will be.

With Xcode 14, the behavior of creating different previews for each individual element, like a VStack remains the same, but the presentation itself has changed. Now instead of being a scrolling list of views, each view is in its own tab at the top of the Preview window. You can click on each of the tabs and that portion of the preview will be shown. This is a small change, but one that will make things a bit easier to manage. There have also been some changes regarding previewing items, let us look at that next.

Variants

Apps are designed to be used on a variety of devices, with various font sizes, both in light and dark modes, and in various orientations. With Xcode 13 it was possible to set various aspects of an individual preview. For instance, let us say you have a view and you wanted to preview it in Dark Mode with the text size of Extra Small, all while viewing it horizontally with the notch on the left. You could modify your preview to be something like this:

```
ContentView()
  .previewInterfaceOrientation(.landscapeRight)
  .preferredColorScheme(.dark)
  .environment(\.sizeCategory, .extraSmall)
```

You would then need to modify this for each of the various sizes, or add additional previews. Even on the fastest machines, like the Mac Studio, it might take a bit to render all of those previews, and if you had more than one view, it could be even more problematic. What would be more convenient would be the ability to view all of the variants at once. This is possible, but with only one item at a time.

In the Preview Canvas there is a button labeled **Variants**. The Variants button will allow you to view all the variants for **Color Scheme**, **Orientation**, and **Dynamic Type**, on a per View basis. This means that if you have two different views you can have different variant views for each. Plus, those variants will stay applied, until you switch away from the file.

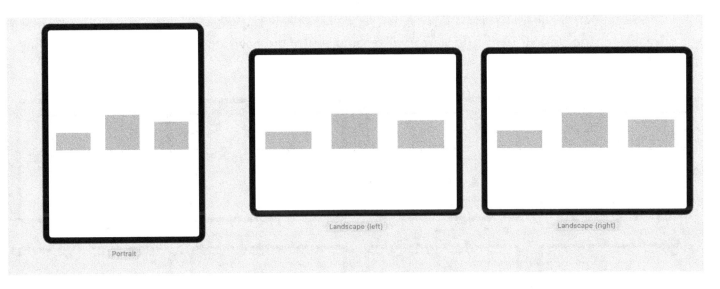

SwiftUI Previews - Orientation Variations

For Color Scheme you can preview a single view in both Light and Dark mode. One caveat with this is that your preview is set to Dark, both of your views will be in Dark mode. When you select the orientation the view will be to preview the variants in all of the various orientations, but only those defined in your project's Info.plist file. Therefore, if you do not have the **upside down** option selected, it will not be shown in the preview. For Dynamic

SwiftUI Previews Color Variations

Type, the view will be shown in each of the 12 variants, from X-small to AX 5, where AX 5 is the largest size when the Larger Accessibility Sizes option is enabled in Settings on iOS and iPhoneOS.

When you are viewing any of the variants you can click on a single variant and that one will zoom in so you can investigate it further. You can click on the back button to return to the grid of variants.

There are two items to be cognizant of regarding viewing variants. The first thing is that you cannot do this while in Live Preview, meaning you can still only run one Live Preview at a time. Not all systems would be capable of running three or four simultaneous Live Previews, so it is limited to one. The second thing to keep in mind is that if you do make a change to your SwiftUI Preview, it will recompile all of the views, so it is quasi-live, at least for that specific view.

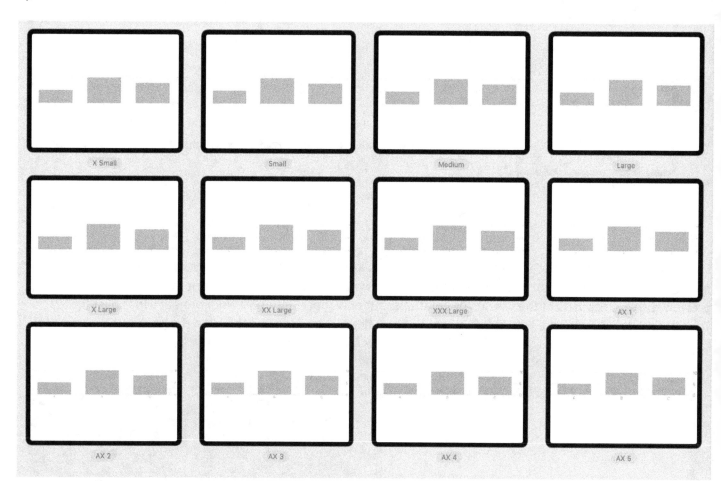

SwiftUI Previews - Dynamic Type Variations

Widgets and Complications

There is one other variant item to discuss, but this is only for Widgets and Complications. When you develop a Widget or Complication you have the option for **Widget Family Variants**. If you enable this you will be able to see all of the possible Widget Family variants. All of the possible variants, even if your extension does not explicitly indicate that the widget supports the widget family. The last thing to note about this is that only the widget families that are supported on the currently selected device will be shown. As an example, the Extra Large widget will not be shown on an iPhone, similarly the Accessory Corner option will only be shown on the Apple Watch.

Also when you are developing for complications there is the **Presentation** variant. This is used for viewing Normal, Placeholder, and Sensitive variants. This is great for developing your various widgets in all of the necessary contexts.

Device Settings

There is one last thing to discuss and that is the **Canvas Device Settings** button. The Canvas Device Settings button will allow you to make modifications to the Canvas, without needing to create a different preview. For example, let us presume you are running a Live Preview of your app, when you click on the Canvas Device Settings button you will be able to specify which Color Mode, Orientation, and Dynamic Type you want set on the Canvas. This will allow you to quickly change the settings and the Canvas will update accordingly.

This is not limited to just Live Previews, you can use also use this in Selectable mode, and even when viewing different Variants. When you change device settings while viewing a specific variant, the options for that variant will not be shown. As an example, if you are looking at a view in the Color Scheme variants view, you will not be able to modify the Color Scheme, because you have already set that option. Even so, you can set the Orientation and Dynamic Type and all of the Variant Previews will update.

The changes to SwiftUI Previews in Xcode are ones that almost every developer will use at some point. Now that we have covered previewing, let us move to building on a device or simulator.

Building on Device

There has also been a minor change when it comes to building on device. As you are likely aware when you select a simulator or device to test your app on, it needs to be chosen from the Target dropdown. If you only have a couple of devices and simulators the list may not be that long. However, most apps support multiple versions back and you may need simulators for each. When this is the case the list of simulators can get rather large. There have been a couple of changes to help with this, filtering and recents.

Filters

If you know the particular simulator, or device, that you want to run your app on, you can now use the Filter option at the top of the Target Simulator/Device list to quickly filter the list. For instance, if you want an iPhone mini, you can type in mini, and you will get just the devices that match that, meaning likely an iPhone mini and an iPad mini.

Recents

If you are switching back and forth between a couple of devices during development you may want to quickly switch back and forth. The new Recent area may be able to help. If you run an app on a particular simulator or device it will appear in the new Recent section of the Target Simulator/Device dropdown. This should be at the top, just below Filter. This new Recent section should make it much quicker to find and run an app on your most recently used devices.

Let us now move onto another build related item, but this one is not local, it is in the cloud specifically Xcode Cloud.

Xcode Cloud

Any app that you build is likely to be run on a variety of devices and various operating systems. If you are a part of a large company, it is quite possible that you will be able to get the devices you need, with the operating systems on them, but not everybody has the means to be able to do this. Instead, it may be possible to use Apple's continuous integration system, Xcode Cloud, to do this.

Xcode Cloud was introduced at Apple's World Wide Developer Conference in June of 2021. Xcode Cloud allows you to build, test, and distribute your app to testers and users.

When Xcode Cloud was introduced it was considered a beta, and only a limited number of developers could use the service, because it was available on an invite only basis. Now, Xcode Cloud is out of beta and available to all developers. With Xcode Cloud there are four actions:

- Archive
- Analyze
- Build
- Test

When you define an Xcode Cloud Workflow these are the four steps that occur. All of these actions will occur in the order above, for each target. The process of building each is done in parallel. What this means is that there are actually two numbers, the duration and then there is the usage. The Duration time is the length of time for the longest action to complete. The Usage value is the total time for all actions to finish.

One thing to note about the Build Phase, if you define a post action to send to Test Flight, that will all be included in the overall usage.

Pricing

Due to the nature of continuous integration services, Xcode Cloud is not free. It does have a monthly subscription cost. The way that Xcode Cloud is billed is on the amount of time it takes to complete the job. The cost structure is as follows:

- 25 hours per month: $14.99
- 100 hours per month is $49.99
- 250 hours per month is $99.99
- 1000 hours per month is $399.99

The Usage value is what is used to determine what should be billed to the account. You can view all of your usage within the Xcode Cloud tab for the app in App Store Connect. It should be noted that Apple has indicated the 25 hours per month plan will be free for all development teams through December of 2023.

If your team wants to be able to automate a number of tasks, like providing continuous integration, Xcode Cloud may be a way of making that happen. During your development one thing that it is hoped that you are doing is documenting your code. Let us look at some changes with automatic documentation generation using a technology called DocC.

DocC Updates

There are many aspects to development that some consider to be tedious. In some cases this might be tracking down a bug that is difficult to replicate, for others it might be writing useful and comprehensive release notes (you know who you are), and for others it is something like documenting their own code. If you are writing a Framework or Library you might have some additional motivation to do so with the introduction of a feature introduced with Xcode 13. That feature is Documentation Catalog, or DocC.

DocC is similar to an Asset Catalog, in that it is a collection of all of the elements that are needed for documentation. DocC uses a custom variant of the Markdown syntax that is used with the DocC compiler to generate documentation from your code. After you build your documentation it can be viewed from right within Xcode. This includes the ability to search.

DocC is not limited to just code. You can also create Articles explaining the concept behind the Framework or Library. Along with these you can also add tutorials to allow people to follow along with how to use your framework or library.

As you might expect a new feature that was just released last year will get some enhancements to it the following year. DocC is definitely one of those that has seen some enhancements. There are two areas to cover, Documentation enhancements, and Hosting enhancements.

Documentation Enhancements

With the first iteration of DocC in Xcode 13, there was a limited scope in terms of what could be documented. The limitations were in both languages and projects. Xcode 13 allowed you to document Swift and SwiftUI code only. In terms of an initial release focusing on the newest language made sense. What else made sense was limiting the types of projects that were supported. Last year only Frameworks and Libraries could have documentation automatically generated. Both of these have expanded capabilities.

Starting with Xcode 14 DocC can now generate documentation for apps as well. This is a huge advancement, particularly for large projects or large teams where you want to be able to provide documentation but manually creating documentation for new features can be problematic. Now, as long as your documentation is in the code, it can be generated automatically. When you generate the code for your app, you can view that right within Xcode's Help just like you could previously with Frameworks and Libraries.

But that is not all, as mentioned above with Xcode 13 you could only document Swift and SwiftUI views. This year that list has expanded to include Objective-C and C APIs. Now, all of your code can be documented consistently.

The documentation that you have generated is also getting some enhancements as well. Now on the left hand side of documentation window. This will allow you to view all of the documentation in a single spot, you can expand on each group and even click on an item and it will expand or show that item. You may want to be able to quickly find what you are looking for, this can also be done with the new search bar which is located at the bottom of each page. The search will automatically filter based upon your search terms. The search bar should allow you to quickly find what you are looking for and is a significant help.

If you have code that is callable from either Objective-C or Swift, there will be a toggle in the upper right corner that will allow you switch between the languages. Given the there are different languages you might think that you would have to learn a slightly different syntax when documenting Objective-C or C APIs, but this is not the case. All of the formatting is the same for all languages.

A great example of all of this in action is the latest Apple Developer documentation. As an example here is a link to the SwiftUI documentation: developer.apple.com/documentation/SwiftUI.

After you have generated your documentation, you may want to host it. There have been some changes to that as well. Let us look at those next.

Hosting Enhancements

Hosting DocC archives is not necessarily a straight-forward process. It will likely require some configuration changes on your server. This is doable if you have your own server, but in today's environment it is likely that you may be using a hosting service, like GitHub, that does not provide access to the configuration. In order to help accommodate these situations, DocC can now be used to generate documentation that could be hosted on GitHub pages, or even any other site, including your own. There has been a big improvement here.

There is a new build setting called **DocC Archive Hosting Base Path**, it can be easily located by going to Build Settings and typing in **DocC arch** and it will be the only setting. This setting can be set globally for all of your Schemas, or you can modifying it a per schema basis, depending on your use case. A good example of this might be if you use an internal server for debug builds and documentation gets pushed to a different path as compared to your release builds, which may go to GitHub Pages.

This parameter is for the relative path, based upon the root of your server. For instance, for GitHub pages it would be something like **repository-name**. Once you set this it will be used whether you build documentation as part of your overall build process or whether you build it manually. Even if you build the documentation manually, you can then deploy the documentation as needed.

This is a major improvement over last year where you would need to perform some server configuration. This is now no longer necessary, provided you set the base path.

Closing Thoughts on Xcode

Xcode 14 provides some significant improvements, like the new improvements to SwiftUI Live Previews as well as the ability to view the variants for Color Scheme, Orientation, and Dynamic Type, to more subtle changes like the floating headers at the top of the Xcode Editor.

The ability to use one App Icon for your app and have Xcode automatically generate the necessary versions should be a significant improvement for many developers. They can now spend time building their apps instead of having to worry about making sure they have all ,of the necessary variants. For now, this only applies to iOS, iPadOS, and watchOS apps, but it is a great improvement none-the-less.

While you are in your development phase you may want to use continuous integration to make sure all of your builds are working as expected. This is possible with Xcode Cloud. Xcode Cloud is now out of beta, meaning it is ready for production with a variety of pricing ranges, depending on needs. The 25 hours per month plan will be free until December 2023 so you can test it out and see how well it works within your overall continuous deployment workflow.

When you are ready to release, this might include documentation. With DocC in Xcode 14 you can now not only generate documentation for Swift Framework and Libraries, but you can now also generate documentation for Objective-C and C, and you can generate the documentation for your app as well. When you are ready to publish your documentation you can do quickly and easily to static hosting environments like GitHub Pages, or even your own server.

There is one thing that Xcode supports that needs to be covered. Well, it is not directly in Xcode, but something you might use while using Xcode. That feature is native support for regular expressions. Let us go through that in the next chapter.

Regex

Data can come in a variety of formats. Sometimes this is a JavaScript Object Notation, or JSON, string, other times it might a comma-separated value, or CSV, file. When it comes in these data formats it is easy enough to separate out because these are standard formats. The tough part comes when it is not in a standard format.

It might be a minor change that could require a single-time change to the file and it might make sense to put in the effort to programmatically, or even manually, manipulate the file to be in a usable format. The hard part comes when there might be small variations. There are a variety of ways that you could tackle this problem. However, there is an existing approach called Regular Expressions, sometimes shorted to regex.

Regular Expression Literals

There are two ways of being able to use Regular Expressions strings within Swift. Either directly within code, or by using the runtime compiler. Here are two examples of how to create a Regular Expression that will be matching only digits.

```
// Regex literals
let digits = /\d+/
// digits: Regex<Substring>

// Run-time construction
let runtimeString = #"\d+"#
let digits = try Regex(runtimeString)
// digits: Regex<AnyRegexOutput>
```

Both of these examples above show how to create a regular expression that will match only digits. The Regex Literal is integrated into the Swift compiler. What this means is that as you create your regular expression the compiler can find syntax errors. These will show as all other code errors would appear in Xcode.

Regex Builder

For some, Regular Expressions are like a second language, they can easily look at a regular expression and parse it in their head. However, for others being able to ascertain exactly what actions a regular expression is performing can be difficult. For those individuals the new Regex Builders may work well. Given our example of looking for one or more digits above, here is what that might look like with a Regex Builder.

```
// Regex builders
let digits = OneOrMore(.digit)
// digits: Regex<Substring>
```

The Regex builder allows you to build complex regular expressions in an expressive way. The reason for this is that Regex Builder is using a Domain Specific Language, or DSL. Here is an example from Apple's World Wide Developer conference slides:

```
private var ledger = """
KIND        DATE          INSTITUTION                    AMOUNT
----------------------------------------------------------------
```

```
CREDIT    03/01/2022    Payroll from employer    $200.23
DEBIT     03/05/2022    Doug's Dugout Dogs       $33.27
"""""
// Declare a field separator of two or more spaces, or a tab.
let fieldSeparator = /\s{2,}|\t/
let transactionMatcher = Regex {
  // Capture to a variable whether it is credit or debit
  Capture { /CREDIT|DEBIT/ }
  // Match on a field separator
  fieldSeparator
  // Capture the date for the current locale
  Capture { One(.date(.numeric, locale: Locale(identifier: "en_US"), timeZone: .gmt)) }
  fieldSeparator
  // Capture one or more field separators
  Capture {
    OneOrMore {
      Lookahead(negative: true) { fieldSeparator }
      CharacterClass.any
    }
  }
  fieldSeparator
  // Capture the currency to a variable
  Capture { One(.localizedCurrency(code: "USD").locale(Locale(identifier: "en_US"))) }
}
// Extract the first match from the ledger string using the transactionMatcher regex.
if let match = ledger.firstMatch(of: transactionMatcher) {
  let (_, kind, date, institution, amount) = match.output
  print("Kind: \(kind)")
  print("Date: \(date)")
  print("Institution: \(institution)")
  print("Amount: \(amount)")
}
```
If you were to run the above code within a Swift Playground you would see the following output:

```
Kind: CREDIT
Date: 2022-03-02 00:00:00 +0000
Institution: Payroll from employer
Amount: 200.23
```

The comments in the code above should explain what is happening. There is one item to cover explicitly, **Lookahead**. Within Regular Expressions a lookahead will test the characters ahead of the match to see if they match, without capturing them. In effect it pulls everything up to the next match and then works backward until it gets to the current match.

Using the **ledger** variable above. The first match is the first row. For the **Institution** variable that is captured it initially matches "Payroll from employer   ", including the six spaces after the phrase. The Negative Lookahead in the example above will start at the six space and match the **fieldSeparator** "two or more spaces, or a tab", and work backwards until it no longer finds that match. What should remain is just the phrase "Payroll from employer".

This just scratches the surface of what is possible with the new Regex Builder. There is a lot more that you can do and could be worth investigating if you need to use Regular Expressions within your code. Let us now move to a new framework and API, WeatherKit.

WeatherKit

Available: iOS 16, iPadOS 16, REST API Web Service

One of the more popular services Dark Sky was purchased by Apple in March of 2020. At the time, it was announced that the Android app would stop functioning on August 1st, 2022. The Dark Sky iOS app continued to be sold until December 31st, 2022. When Apple bought Dark Sky many speculated what would become of the service, given that Apple has been known to shutdown services.

There are two parts to WeatherKit. There is the native WeatherKit framework as well as the REST API. Each of these will be covered in-depth, starting with integrating with your app. But before we do that, let us look at what type of information that the WeatherKit API can provide.

Data

The WeatherKit API provides a variety of different items related to weather. WeatherKit can provide you the following data:

- Current weather
- Daily forecast
- Hourly forecast,
- Forecasts broken down by minute
- Weather alerts

Current weather, daily forecasts, hourly forecasts should be available for all supported regions. However, forecasts broken down by minute are only available in certain regions. Weather alerts should be available in most areas, but there may not be any weather alerts for a given area.

Apple has accounted for the fact that not every feature is available in every area. In order to be able to determine what information is available, Apple has provided an "Availability API".

Availability API

As mentioned above, not every piece of weather data is available in every location. In order to allow an easy way for developers to ascertain what information is available Apple has included an Availability API. The Availability API will provide the following data points that are available:

- Alerts
- Minute Forecast
- Current Weather
* Daily Forecast
* Hourly Forecast

Some of this data endpoints are optionally available. For instance, when building an app that incorporates WeatherKit, you can only check for availability of alerts and the minute forecast. The other three, Current Weather,

Daily Forecast, and Hourly Forecast, do not have an availability check. This means that you should be able to reliably presume that these three items will always be available.

App

Apple has created a great sample code project, available at https://developer.apple.com/documentation/weatherkit/fetching_weather_forecasts_with_weatherkit. We will not dive too deep into this demo project, but we will look at certain aspects.

App Setup

In order to use WeatherKit you need to do some setup on the Developer account portal. Specifically the following things need to be configure:

1. An explicit profile needs to be setup
2. Add WeatherKit capability to app.
3. The WeatherKit App Service needs to be enabled for the profile.

Each of the above steps needs to be completed before you will be able to receive WeatherKit data.

Explicit Profile

If you have been developing apps on Apple's platforms for a while you may recall the days of needing to explicitly configure a profile for each app. Luckily, those days are behind us. This process can be handled by Xcode when you assign a Team and bundle identifier within the Signing & Capabilities tab of your project.

Add WeatherKit Capabilities

This step has to be done from within Xcode. To add the WeatherKit capability perform these steps:

1. **Open** the Xcode project you want to use.
2. In the **Project Navigator** click on your project file.
3. Under **Targets**, select the appropriate target.
4. Click on the **Signing & Capabilities** tab.
5. Click the **+ Capabilities** icon to bring up the Capabilities search.
6. Type in **Weather**.
7. Click on **WeatherKit** to add WeatherKit capabilities to the app.

Now the WeatherKit capabilities have been added to the app, but there is still one additional step.

Add WeatherKit Service to the App

The last step, and the most crucial, is to add the WeatherKit app service to the profile. This is done via the Developer portal. To add the WeatherKit App service perform the following steps:

1. **Login** to the Apple developer portal.
2. Navigate to **Certificates, Identifiers & Profiles**.
3. Once on the Certificates, Identifiers & Profiles page, click on **Identifiers**.
4. **Locate** the profile for your app. If Xcode configured it for you, its name may start with XC.

5. **Click** on the profile to open the App Edit Configuration editor.
6. Once the editor opens, click on **App Services**.
7. Click the checkbox next to **WeatherKit**.
8. Click the **Save** button.

Once you have saved the profile, Apple will begin to tell the WeatherKit APIs that your app now has access. This make take up to 30 minutes to complete. If you do not perform this third step, you will not receive any weather data within your app.

Shared Weather Service

The WeatherKit framework has a class that is the starting point for accessing WeatherKit. You will likely want to create a shared object within your class for this. There is a shared instance which is accessible by using the **WeatherService.shared.** property.

Obtaining the Weather

All calls within WeatherKit require the use of a Core Location, CLLocation, object. The simplest object is one that consists of a latitude and longitude. Here is how to create an object for Apple Park.

```
let applePark = CLLocation(latitude: 37.334679, longitude: -122.008980) // Apple Park
```

You can obtain the weather using the following line of code:

```
let weather = try? await WeatherService.shared.weather(for: applePark)
```

The first thing that you may notice is that there is the **try await** syntax in the call to the function. This indicates that this call is an asynchronous call. All of WeatherKit's functions are asynchronous. It is not that they support asynchronous calls. Those are the only calls that are available. There are no synchronous calls.

When the result is returned it will be a Weather object. A Weather object contains a lot of data. The object that it contains are:

- var availability: WeatherAvailability
- var currentWeather: CurrentWeather
- var dailyForecast: Forecast<DayWeather>
- var hourlyForecast: Forecast<HourWeather>
- var minuteForecast: Forecast<MinuteWeather>?
- var weatherAlerts: [WeatherAlert]?

Each of these objects has its own properties which can all be found at https://developer.apple.com/documentation/weatherkit/weather.

You may not always want to retrieve all information. Sometimes you may only want some information. Let us presume you want to get only the current weather for Apple Park. This would be done by using the following code:

```
let current = try? await WeatherService.shared.weather(for: applePark,
including: .current)
```

You can actually include up to six different sets within your query. You can mix and match the available datasets to get just the data you want. Let us look at how you can determine what datasets are available.

Availability

Not every location will support all of the available sets of data. You can make a request to see which items are available. This is possible using the following line:

```
let available = try? await WeatherService.shared.weather(for: applePark,
including: .availability)
```

This will return an array with the type availability for some sets. You can access these by attempting to access the property. For example you can use:

```
if(available?.minuteAvailability == .available) { }
if(available?.alertAvailability == .available) {}
```

The possible availability types are available, unknown, unsupported, or temporarilyUnavailable. You can check the availability using any of those types and act accordingly.

Go through Results

Let us take a look at a couple of examples of how you can use the results. We are going to use the Weather result that returns all of the available weather data for our tests.

Let us say that you want to get the current temperature at Apple Park. You could do this using:

```
let current = weather?.currentWeather.temperature //21.94 °C.
```

The value would come back as something like 21.94 °C. As you can see, the values returned from WeatherKit are all in metric. Fear not, you can easily convert any value to the desired temperature scale. This can be done like this:

```
let fahr = weather?.currentWeather.temperature.converted(to: .fahrenheit) //71.49 °F
```

You can get the feels like temperature as well, like so:

```
let feels = weather?.currentWeather.apparentTemperature.converted(to: .fahrenheit)
```

The current weather is just one item. You also get a 10 day forecast, which contains a lot of information on its own. Let us presume you want to get the high temperature for 2 day from now, you can do just that by using this code:

```
let highTemp = weather?.dailyForecast[2].highTemperature
```

You would not likely access the index directly, but for this example it works fine. You can also get some additional data like:

Sunrise: .weather?.dailyForecast[2].sun.sunrise
Sunset: .weather?.dailyForecast[2].sun.sunset
Day's Forecast Symbol: weather?.dailyForecast[2].symbolName

These are just a few examples of what you can get out of the data for a particular location.

Closing Thoughts on WeatherKit Framework

The WeatherKit Framework is a great addition to the available options for features in your app. The WeatherKit Framework is a Swift-only framework that utilizes async/await to be able to provide you with a variety of weather data to your app using Apple's new WeatherKit service. You can use WeatherKit in more than just your app, there is also an API available over the web. Let us look at that next.

WeatherKit REST API

It is not often these days that an app is built that is does not require some sort of web access. Of course, it is entirely possible, but unlike the early days of iOS app development, it is not something that is commonplace today. Typically, a web service has a means of being able to communicating with other servers or clients through an application programming interface. The method employed by most web services these days is a technique called a RESTful, or REST, web service.

The term RESTful does not mean that the API just sits there and does nothing. The term REST means that the API does not need to keep a constant channel open to each and every client. Instead, the client can make its request, the API can respond appropriately, and the client can continue on its way.

WeatherKit is not Apple's first web-based API. In fact Apple has a few of them, including MusicKit, MapKit, and ShazamKit.

Setup

There are a few steps to setting up access to the WeatherKit REST API. These steps include:

1. Generate a WeatherKit key.
2. Create an App Profile for use with WeatherKit.

Each of the above steps needs to be completed before you will have access to the WeatherKit REST API.

Generate a WeatherKit Key

If you are going to use the WeatherKit REST API, you will need to generate a key. This key is used to sign each of your requests. This key is one half of a cryptographic public/private key pair.

The overall process is that when you generate a key, is as follows:

1. You request that a WeatherKit key be generated.
2. Apple's developer portal generates a public/private key pair along with a unique id for the key.
3. Apple stores the key id in its own databases somewhere
4. Apple stores the public key in its own database.
5. You download the private key.

You can then begin using that private key to sign requests. We will get to that entire process in a bit. First, let us look at the actual steps for generating a key. The steps to follow are:

1. **Login** to the Apple developer portal.
2. Navigate to **Certificates, Identifiers & Profiles**.
3. On the left-hand side click on **Keys**.
4. Click the "**+**" button next to the Keys header at the top of the page. This will bring you to the Register a New Key page.
5. On the Register a Key page enter in the **Key Name**. This is a readable name for you to easily identify the key.
6. In the list of services click the checkbox next to **WeatherKit**. Alternatively you can also just click on WeatherKit and it will enable the checkbox.
7. Click the **Continue** button. This will bring you to the Register a New Key confirmation screen.
8. On the Register a New Key confirmation screen click on the **Register** button to register the key. Once you click on the Register button your key is registered and the public/private key pair is generated and you are brought to the Download Your Key page.
9. On the Download Your Key page click the **Download** button to download the private key.

As the Download Your Key page indicates, you can only download the key once. If you lose the key, it cannot be retrieved and you will need to generate a new one. What happens when the key is generated and how Apple stores the information is proprietary to them.

After you have generated a WeatherKit key, you will also need to create an App ID for you to use for your WeatherKit REST API requests.

Create an App ID

Note: If you plan on using WeatherKit in both an app and a website. You do not need to create a second profile. You can use the same App ID for both, and you can skip this step.

However, If you are only going to use the WeatherKit APIs via a website, you will need to create an App ID. To create an App ID perform the following steps:

1. **Login** to the Apple developer portal.
2. Navigate to **Certificates, Identifiers & Profiles**.
3. Once on the Certificates, Identifiers & Profiles page click on **Identifiers**.
4. Click the "**+**" button next to Identifiers to add a new App ID. This should bring you to the Register a new identifier screen.
5. On the Register a new identifier screen click the **App IDs** option. This will bring you to the Register a new identifier page.
6. On the Register a new identifier page select the **App** type.
7. Click on the **Continue** button. This will bring you to the Register an App ID page.
8. On the Register an App ID page **select** an App ID, likely your Team ID.
9. In the Description field enter in a readable **Description** for your service.
10. Under Bundle ID select **Explicit**.
11. In the **Bundle ID** box enter in an identifier for your service. This should be unique and in Reverse Domain format. An example of this would be com.example.weatherkit.
12. Under **Capabilities** select WeatherKit.
13. Click on the **Continue** button. This will bring you to the Confirm your App ID page.
14. Click on **Register** to complete the registration. If your App ID is not unique, you will receive an error.

Once you have clicked the Register button, your App ID has been registered and you can begin actually making requests. Before we get to actually making requests let us discuss the format of the API, starting with the overall API construction

API URL Construction

Every web based REST API is comprised of a full URL. The format of a URL use for the WeatherKit REST API is:

> https://weatherkit.apple.com/api/v1/availability/{latitude}/{longitude}?country={code}

Let us break this down into its constituent parts.

Scheme	Base URL	API Version	Endpoint	Latitude	Longitude
https://	weatherkit.apple.com/api/	v1/	{endpoint}/	{latitude}/	{longitude}

The **Scheme** will always be https, because https is now the default expectation for website request.

The **Base URL** for all WeatherKit API calls is weatherkit.apple.com/api/.

The **API Version** is "v1". If Apple deems it necessary to change this, because they significantly rework the API, this will change.

The **Endpoint** is the actual information that we are trying to retrieve.

The **Latitude** field is latitude for the location we are trying to retrieve data for.

The **Longitude** field is the longitude for the location we are trying to retrieve data for.

The last part, "?country={code}" are what is called the Query Parameters. Query Parameters are fields that the server can read to help decide on what information you are trying to retrieve. In this example the ISO Alpha-2 country code, which is a standard two-letter code to indicate the country. You are very likely familiar with them, but just in case here are some examples are:

- AU: Australia
- CA: Canada
- CN: China
- DE: Germany
- ES: Spain
- GN: Guinea
- GB: United Kingdom of Great Britain and Northern Ireland
- HK: Hong Kong
- KE: Kenya
- NE: Niger
- NZ: New Zealand
- RO: Romania
- UA: Ukraine
- US: United States

The country code is used for retrieving air quality index levels as well as weather alerts. These codes also match the top-level domain names for most countries.

Note: Throughout this chapter we will use Apple Park as our example. The latitude for Apple Park is **37.334679** and the longitude is **-122.008980**. Refer back to data if needed.

Endpoints

One aspect that must be taken into consider of when developing a modern web API is how to structure the API endpoints that clients use to request data. The approach that one would take depends on the data it is trying to present.

In the case of retrieving weather data, we know that we would likely want to retrieve the information for a particular place on earth. Humans have already come up with a system that works, the latitude and longitude system. Each latitude and longitude indicates a specific point on the planet, so this makes it ideal for weather data.

As for actually retrieving data using the WeatherKit REST API, you will use one of two endpoints, **availability** and **weather**.

Available Data Sets

As mentioned above there is certain information provided when you make a call to WeatherKit. In the case of the REST API, you will need to specify which sets of data that you would like to retrieve. The possible data sets that you can retrieve are outlined in the App Data section above. But since we are using a REST API, we need some easily identifiable names. The mappings of the possible data sets that you can retrieve using the WeatherKit REST API are:

- currentWeather will retrieve the Current weather
- forecastDaily will retrieve the Daily forecast
- forecastHourly will retrieve the Hourly forecast
- forecastNextHour will retrieve the Forecasts by minute for the next hour.
- weatherAlerts will retrieve any Weather alerts.

These are the actual data set names that you will need to specify in your request. But you need to know what type of data is available for a given latitude and longitude. That is where the availability endpoint is used.

Availability Endpoint

The availability API endpoint is used to request what dataSets are available for a given latitude and longitude. Here is an example of the url you would need to use to see what data is available for Apple's Headquarters, Apple Park, in Cupertino, California. Let us plug that into our URL.

> https://weatherkit.apple.com/api/v1/availability/37.334679/longitude=-122.008980?country=US

This will provide us with a JSON response with which data sets are available. This will be an array of strings, with the data set names outlined above. For Apple Park the response is:

```
["currentWeather","forecastDaily","forecastHourly","forecastNextHour","weatherAlerts"]
```

Therefore, we should be able to retrieve all of the information available. Some locations will not have forecastNextHour and they may not have weatherAlerts.

Weather Endpoint

The weather endpoint is where you actually retrieve data about a given location. The URL is slightly different than the availability API url. An example of getting the current weather for Apple Park would look like this:

```
https://weatherkit.apple.com/api/v1/weather/en/37.334679/-122.008980?
dataSets=currentWeather&timezone=America/Chicago&country=US
```

You will notice that the schema, base url, and version are the same as a call to the availability endpoint. The weather endpoint is used to retrieve the actual weather data. What information is returned depends on the dataSets query parameter. In the example above, only the currentWeather dataset is being returned.

After the weather endpoint is a language code. This is a two-character code to specify the language that any text should be in. The text that might be returned includes the conditions, and other localizable data.

The latitude and longitude are the latitude and longitude of the location where you want weather data for.

The query parameters are what are used to specify the data that you want to retrieve. The list of query parameters includes:

- **countryCode** - The ISO Alpha-2 country code for the requested location. This parameter is necessary for air quality and weather alerts.
- **currentAsOf** - The time to obtain current conditions. Defaults to now - using Date Time format, eg "2022-06-18T14:00Z", which is 2pm on June 18th, 2022.
- **dailyEnd** - The time to end the daily forecast. If this parameter is absent, daily forecasts run for 10 days.
- **dailyStart** - The time to start the daily forecast. If this parameter is absent, daily forecasts start on the current day.
- **dataSets** - A comma-delimited list of data sets to include in the response.hourlyEnd - The time to end the hourly forecast. If this parameter is absent, hourly forecasts run 24 hours or the length of the daily forecast, whichever is longer.
- **hourlyStart** - The time to start the hourly forecast. If this parameter is absent, hourly forecasts start on the current hour.
- **timezone** - string - (Required) The name of the timezone to use for rolling up weather forecasts into daily forecasts.

You can combine the above query parameters to create a query specific to your needs. There is one last endpoint to cover, the Weather Alerts endpoint.

Weather Alerts

There is one last REST API endpoint to discuss, the **weatherAlerts** endpoint. This endpoint is used to obtain additional information if there are any weather alerts for a particular location. You can obtain the alerts for a location by requesting the **weatherAlerts** dataset. If there are any alerts, you will receive a response similar to this:

```
[weatherAlerts] => Array (
  [detailsUrl] => https://weather-data.apple.com/alertDetails/index.html?
ids=baf0a5e2-d721-5652-840b-f06357f0c739,8655a69a-
df11-5ffb-8587-93205ba030f0&lang=en-US&timezone=America/Chicago
  [alerts] => Array( [0] => Array (
      [name] => WeatherAlertSummary
      [id] => baf0a5e2-d721-5652-840b-f06357f0c739
      [areaId] => fz_azz101
      [areaName] => Lake Mead NRA/Colorado River-AZ side
      [countryCode] => US
      [description] => Red Flag Warning
      [effectiveTime] => 2022-06-18T18:00:00Z
      [expireTime] => 2022-06-19T04:00:00Z
      [issuedTime] => 2022-06-18T17:43:00Z
      [eventOnsetTime] => 2022-06-18T18:00:00Z
      [eventEndTime] => 2022-06-19T04:00:00Z
      [detailsUrl] => https://weather-data.apple.com/alertDetails/index.html?
ids=baf0a5e2-d721-5652-840b-f06357f0c739&lang=en-US&timezone=America/Chicago
      [precedence] => 0
      [severity] => severe
      [source] => National Weather Service
      [eventSource] => US
      [urgency] => expected
      [certainty] => likely
      [importance] => normal
      [responses] => Array ( )
    )
  )
)
```

In this particular response there are two alerts. This happens to be for Lake Mead in Arizona. In each of the alerts is the id field. This is the field that is needed to be used for the request to the weatherAlerts endpoint. The weatherAlerts endpoint will allow you retrieve specific information about the alert.

The URL for the weatherAlert endpoint is really straightforward. Here is an example.

```
https://weatherkit.apple.com/api/v1/weatherAlert/{language}/{id}
```

There are only two path items, the language, and the alert id. These two items can be substituted to get the actual information with the substituted information. Here is the weatherAlert url for the alert above:

```
https://weatherkit.apple.com/api/v1/weatherAlert/en/baf0a5e2-d721-5652-840b-
f06357f0c739
```

When you make a call to that URL you should the response below. It should be noted that some of the data has been removed from brevity.

```
[name] => WeatherAlert
[id] => baf0a5e2-d721-5652-840b-f06357f0c739
[areaId] => fz_azz101
```

```
[areaName] => Lake Mead NRA/Colorado River-AZ side
[countryCode] => US
[description] => Red Flag Warning
[effectiveTime] => 2022-06-18T18:00:00Z
[expireTime] => 2022-06-19T04:00:00Z
[issuedTime] => 2022-06-18T17:43:00Z
[eventOnsetTime] => 2022-06-18T18:00:00Z
[eventEndTime] => 2022-06-19T04:00:00Z
[detailsUrl] => https://weather-data.apple.com/alertDetails/index.html?
ids=baf0a5e2-d721-5652-840b-f06357f0c739&lang=en-US&timezone=UTC
[precedence] => 0
[severity] => severe
[source] => National Weather Service
[eventSource] => US
[urgency] => expected
[certainty] => likely
[importance] => normal
[responses] => Array ( )
[area] => Array ()
[messages] => Array ( [0] => Array (  [language] => en
    [text] => ...RED FLAG WARNING REMAINS IN EFFECT UNTIL 9 PM PDT /9 PM MST/
THIS EVENING FOR STRONG WINDS AND LOW HUMIDITY FOR MOST OF
SOUTHERN NEVADA AND NORTHWEST ARIZONA...
* AFFECTED AREA...In Nevada...Fire weather zones 461, 462, 463,
464, 465, and 466. In Arizona...Fire weather zones 101 and
102.
* WIND...Sustained winds of 20 to 30 mph with gusts to 50 mph.
Stronger wind gusts possible across the Southern Great Basin.
* HUMIDITY...Minimum relative humidity values of 5 to 12 percent.
* IMPACTS...A combination of strong winds...low relative
humidity...and warm temperatures can contribute to extreme
fire behavior. Any fires that develop will likely spread
rapidly.
        )
    )
```

The weatherAlert endpoint contains a lot of data, but the most useful is likely the actual text for the alert, which in contained within the message array. You can extract this and display it as necessary.

Now that we have covered all of the endpoints, let us look at actually make a request.

Making Requests

Each request to the WeatherKit REST API needs to include which developer and application is being used. This is accomplished by create a signed JSON Web Token.

Creating a JSON Web Token

The next step in your WeatherKit journey is the creation of a JSON Web Token. There are many libraries that can be used to create a JWT. Depending on the language you will need to determine the best way to generate your JWT. There is more information about JSON Web Tokens, and links to various libraries at JWT.io. After you have generated your JWT, you can then begin actually using your JWT to start using WeatherKit. When you generate a token there is an expiration, so you may need to refresh the token at certain intervals, otherwise any request will fail.

While the exact way that you create the signed JSON Web Token will differ, here is a general layout of how the payload should appear:

```
headers {
    "alg": 'ES256',
    "kid": [KEYID],
    "id": [Team_ID].[App_ID]
}

payload  {
    "sub": [APP_ID]
    "iss": [TEAM_ID],
    "exp": [EXPIRATION_TIME]
    "iat": [ISSUED_AT_TIME]
    "jti": [SERVICE_ID],
}
```

You can use any library or method you want to to create a signed JSON Web Token. The resultant token may look something like this:

```
eyJhbGciOiJIUzI1NiIsInR5cCI6IkpXVCJ9.eyJzdWIiOiIxMjM0NTY3ODkwIiwibmFtZSI6IkpvaG
4gRG9lIiwiYWRtaW4iOnRydWV9.dyt0CoTl4WoVjAHI9Q_CwSKhl6d_9rhM3NrXuJttkao
```

The resultant signed and base64-encoded data is what is called a Bearer Token. This token must be sent in the header of each request. This signed header information is how the WeatherKit API identifiers your app.

After you have checked availability, you will likely want to make a request for actual weather data. When you make a request to the weather endpoint, you will need to use a GET to full URL that you have constructed. If any data is received you will receive a response. Let us look at what that might look like:

Response

For our example we will presume you are getting the current conditions for Apple Park. The response you will get will be in JSON format. Since you specified the currentWeather, you will receive that information. Here is what a response might look like:

```
[currentWeather] => Array (
    [name] => CurrentWeather
    [metadata] => Array (
        [attributionURL] => https://weather-data.apple.com/legal-attribution.html
        [expireTime] => 2022-06-18T19:00:49Z
        [latitude] => 37.335
        [longitude] => -122.009
        [readTime] => 2022-06-18T18:55:49Z
        [reportedTime] => 2022-06-18T16:43:48Z
        [units] => m
        [version] => 1
    )
```

```
[asOf] => 2022-06-18T05:00:00Z
[cloudCover] => 0.14
[conditionCode] => MostlyClear
[daylight] =>
[humidity] => 0.68
[precipitationIntensity] => 0
[pressure] => 1013.65
[pressureTrend] => rising
[temperature] => 14.54
[temperatureApparent] => 13.9
[temperatureDewPoint] => 8.78
[uvIndex] => 0
[visibility] => 23615.34
[windDirection] => 306
[windGust] => 7.28
[windSpeed] => 2.78
)
```

The response for the request is shown above. Apple's documentation explains what each of the values means. But It should be noted that the values returned are metric for the following fields:

- temperature
- temperatureApparent
- temperatureDewPoint
- visibility (meters)
- windGust (kilometers)
- windSpeed (kilometers)

One last field to make note of is the windDirection field. This will range from 0 to 360. You can then use this number to determine the actual direction of the wind.

Therefore, it may be necessary to convert the values, depending on the preferences of where you are displaying information.

Attribution

One of the requirement for using both WeatherKit and the WeatherKit REST API is that you must put attribution in for where the data came from. This is provided with each API call. The attributionURL value in the metadata property has the link to the attribution information.

Costs

Unlike MusicKit, ShazamKit, and MapKit, WeatherKit is not entirely free. Each developer account does receive 500,000 WeatherKit calls per month, for free. After this though there is a charge for calls. Here is a breakdown of the cost as for this writing:

- 500,000 calls/month: included with membership
- 1 million calls/month: US$ 49.99
- 2 million calls/month: US$ 99.99
- 5 million calls/month: US$ 249.99

- 10 million calls/month: US$ 499.99
- 20 million calls/month: US$ 999.99

Apple only shows 20 million calls, but it is reasonable to presume that the costs rise linearly at $50 per million calls per month. The reason that Apple needs to charge is that weather data is not free in general, neither are the costs for hosting services. Weather data needs to not only be reliable but fast, in particular with weather alerts.

For those who were using the Dark Sky API, it had cost $0.0001 per call, where as Apple's WeatherKit API costs approximately $0.00005 per call. This is half the price, which is great for developers. These costs will apply not only WeatherKit REST API calls, but also for queries using the WeatherKit framework.

Closing Thoughts on WeatherKit

When Apple purchased DarkSky in 2020, and Apple announced that the API would continue to function through the end of 2021, many speculated on whether Apple would the Dark Sky API available for others to use. They have done just that with the WeatherKit API.

Of course, WeatherKit can be used natively in iOS, iPadOS, and macOS apps using the new WeatherKit framework. Alternatively, you can use the WeatherKit REST API for your website or other non-Apple platform product.

The WeatherKit framework is a Swift only asynchronous framework that you can use in your app. There is no Objective-C for synchronous set of APIs for the WeatherKit framework.

If you need to use WeatherKit in Objective-C, on the web, or within a non-Apple app, you can use the WeatherKit REST API to accomplish this. Be sure to add an App ID and enable the WeatherKit service under App Services in order for your WeatherKit REST API requests to be able to return data.

Beyond just receiving weather data, you can also obtain weather alerts, and their details, so you can present timely information to your users, regardless of platform.

There is a sample project for you to use as a guide or to explore various aspects of the possibilities of WeatherKit. WeatherKit is not free, but the price is less than what many were paying previously. This is a great addition not have for anybody who might need to provide weather data to their own application.

SFSymbols

Apple created its own font, San Francisco, for use on its platforms. When they did this they created an icon set that can be used by anyone on their platforms. That icon set is called SFSymbols. SFSymbols is designed to allow you to incorporate a variety of symbols into your apps. Each new release of SFSymbols brings with its some new functionality. This year's release SFSymbols 4 brings some new icons, as well as some additional features.

There are over 700 new symbols, including things like lights, blinds, furniture, applicants, fitness related items, and various objects. This brings the total number of icons to over 4,000 different symbols. There are a variety of ways to represent a color, let us look at those.

Rendering Modes

In SFSymbols 3 there are four rendering modes, Monochrome, Palette, Hierarchical, and Multicolor.

- **Monochrome** is grayscale icon, with some icons being black and white where it is appropriate and creates a uniform and consistent look to all icons.
- **Palette** is a rendering mode that provides the most customization and allows you to use your own color palette for the icons.
- **Hierarchical** is a rendering mode that subtly emphasizes a single color and highlights the most important shape of the symbols
- **Multicolor** is the rendering mode that represents a lot of color, with a variety of color options. This mode is useful when you need full color and prominent symbols.

With SFSymbols 3 the default rendering mode was monochrome. This changes with SFSymbols 4 because there is a new option, automatic. Automatic is enabled by default and will choose the rendering mode that makes the most sense for the given context. Even though there is the default, you can override it and select whichever rendering mode you would like for a given icon.

These rendering modes are great, and the new automatic as the default should choose the proper icon, but sometimes you need to convey some information in a symbol. For that there is a new concept called Variable Color. Let us look at that.

Variable Color

Variable Color is not a rendering mode on its own, but a way of being able to convey some information by changing the percentage value and having that percentage affect part of the symbol. You can actually use variable color with all four of the rendering modes. As you might suspect, this can be done within code, but you can also look at how this works in the SFSymbols app.

SFSymbols app

You can view all of the Variable Color compatible icons by using these steps:

1. Open the **SFSymbols** 4 app.
2. In the sidebar click on the **Variable** group. This will filter the icons. This will show all of the compatible symbols, there should be about 150 of them.
3. Click on the icon named **speaker.wave.3.circle.fill**.
4. Click on the **Gallery View** button in the toolbar.

When you click on the Gallery View button you will be able to see the icon in a large view. Next, click on the Multicolor rendering mode from the inspector. This is the one all the way to the right.

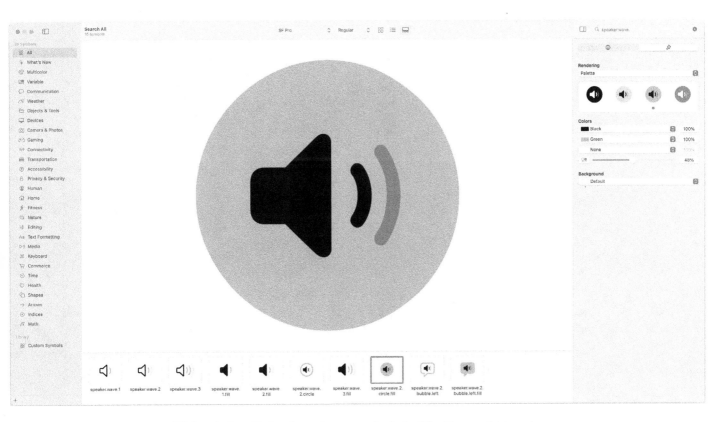

SF Symbols with the "speaker.wave.3.circle.fill" with a variable value

Underneath the color dropdown is a slider. If you slide the slider to the left it will start to change the color of the waves on the speaker. For this specific icon the breakpoints are 51% to 100% both waves will be filled. Between 1% and 50% one of the waves will be filled. At 0% both waves will be less prominent. This behavior occurs for all of the symbols that support Variable Color, but the percentages are going to be different. Technically, the percentages are up to 0.5% because when it comes to percentage values, all values are rounded to the nearest full digit.

Another example is the **badge.plus.radiowaves.forward** symbol This icon has three waves and the breakpoints for these are 0% will have all three waves be less prominent, 1% to 34% only one will be filled, 35% to 68% will show two filled, and anything above 68% will have all three filled.

These two examples are pretty easy to understand, but the thing with Variable Color is that there can be a lot more layers. Take for instance the **touchid** icon. It has six layers and the breakpoints are 1% to 17% for one layer, 18% to

33% for two, 34% to 50% shows three, 51% to 67% shows four, 68% to 83% shows five layers, and anything above 84% will show all of them as being filled.

Using the percentage is a good way of being able to indicate how full something is. But this also has a second application, you can use the percentages to show progress. The last example we will use is the **rays** symbol. There are eight layers to this icon and the breakpoints for this symbol are 1% to 13% shows one, 14% to 25% shows two, 26% to 38% shows three, 39% to 50% shows four, 51% to 63% shows five, 64% to 75% shows six, 76% to 88% shows seven, and anything above 89% shows all eight as being filled. The rays symbol is good for being able to show progress, but the **timelapse** icon is even better because it has 24 layers.

Let us now look at how to do this in code.

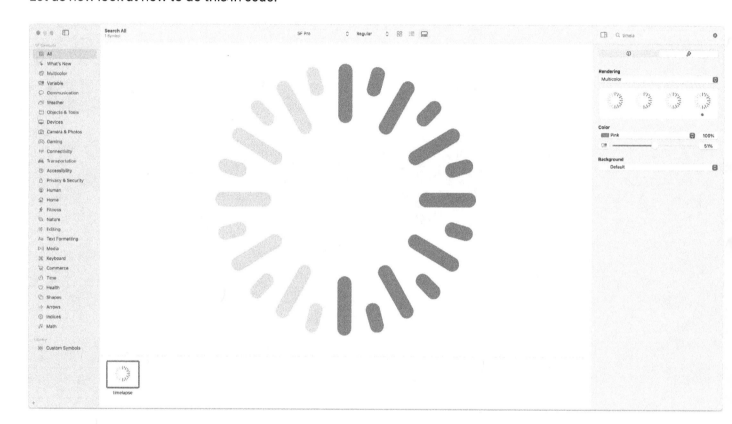

SF Symbols with the "timelapse" symbol with variable value

In Code

Using SFSymbols in code on their own is as simple as using Image(systemName: "timelapse"). To specify a percentage all you need to do is add the variableValue parameter, like this:

```
Image(systemName: "timelapse", variableValue: value)
```

Where **value** is your percentage value, between 0 and 1. If you specify that value, the Variable Color will be appropriately applied to the symbol.

Closing Thoughts on SFSymbols

The new gallery view with SFSymbols 4 will allow you to easily preview how a symbol will look at a specific percentage. Similarly, if you specify the **variableValue** parameter you will be able to set the value. When using SwiftUI, if you pair this with a binding as the binding's value changes, the Variable Color will change too Let us look at some changes with Widgets and Complications in the next chapter.

Widgets and Complications

In iOS 14 Apple released a whole new item that developers could include in their apps, Widgets. Widgets can be placed on the Home Screen on both iOS and iPadOS. For macOS you can place Widgets in the Notification Center, but they cannot be placed on the Desktop, or anywhere else in the system.

Widgets are extensions to their apps that allow developers to provide glanceable information that can be updated on a schedule. The declarative nature of SwiftUI, and the fact that views only updates when a value changes, allows for Widgets to be updated when they need to be, instead of constantly. This approach provides for better battery life. Now with iOS 16 Widgets are coming to the Lock Screen.

Widgets on iOS and iPadOS, as well as Complications on Apple Watch share a lot of similarities. Both work off of the idea of providing a timeline for when content should be updated.

With Widgets on the Lock Screen there are three new widget families that join the four existing families. These new families are:

- accessoryCircular
- accessoryRectangular
- accessoryInline
- accessoryCorner

All three of these are available for use on both iOS as well as watchOS, but these are not available on iPadOS, because there are no Lock Screen widgets on iPadOS. In fact starting with watchOS 9 the complications that you make for the watch can be brought over to the Lock Screen with minimal changes.

Let us briefly look at each of these families and where they can be used on their respective platforms.

AccessoryCircular

The accessoryCircular widget can be used in the area below the time on iOS 16 or in one of the small widget areas on the Apple Watch. On iOS 16 you can have up to 4 of these in the widget area below the time.

AccessoryRectangular

Similar to the AccessoryCircular, AccessoryRectangular can be used on the main widget area of the iOS 16 Lock Screen. If this is used on the iOS 16 Lock Screen you can put up to two of these in that area. On the Apple Watch it can be used in the main area.

AccessoryInline

AccessoryInline is useful for displaying a single line of text. This can be used in the area above the time on the iOS 16 Lock Screen or where one line of text might work best on an Apple Watch face.

AccessoryCorner

AccessoryCorner is a watchOS only widget that is used exclusively for the corners of Watch Faces. This widget has allows for both a small circular widget as well as a line of text.

As is the case with other widgets you can use App Intents to allow customization of the widget. There are a couple of tips that need to be shared. These are related to the system family, ViewThatFits, and ProgressViews. Let us start with system family.

System Family

When you are building a widget you may want to change the display for a widget based on the widget family. As an example you are not likely to fit a Rectangular widget into the same size an an Inline widget. Therefore, you will likely need to adjust the widget for each. You could create separate widget extensions for each, but this is unnecessary and duplicates code. Instead, you can use an @Environment property wrapper to get the system family. This would be done something similar to this:

```
@Environment(\.widgetFamily) var family
```

When you use this property wrapper you can then use a **switch** to define the view for each of the various widget families. Something like this:

```
switch family {
  case .accessoryCircular:
  case .accessoryRectangular:
  case .accessoryInline:
  case .systemSmall:
  default:
}
```

ViewThatFits

Even if you define views each of the various families, there may still be variations between individual devices, particularly when it comes to Apple Watch faces. Some watch faces will allow longer text, while others may not. For these cases you may need to provide a slightly different options. This is done by using the **ViewThatFits** struct.

You can use this just like any other view. However this will work a bit differently in that it will determine out of the options provided which one will first best, without losing any of the view. It can be used like this:

```
ViewThatFits {
  Text("\(entry.character.name) is healing, ready in \(entry.character.fullHealthDate,
style: .relative)")
  Text("\(entry.character.avatar) ready in \(entry.character.fullHealthDate,
style: .relative)")
  Text("\(entry.character.avatar) \(entry.character.fullHealthDate, style: .timer)")
}
```

By default the view that fits will be calculated for both the horizontal and vertical access. You can specify a particular axis by specifying the **in** parameter, like this: ViewThatFits(in:.horizontal) { }. For AccessoryInline options, it is not likely that this needed.

Progress Views

When you create a widget you may want to count down to a specific time. This may be for recharging a character or any other idea that you can come up with. Because SwiftUI does not allow constant updating this could be problematic. But, you can do this on a text field, using the "**style**" parameter. As you can see in the last entry of the ViewThatFits example above, it is specifying the type of Text as a timer. When you do this it will automatically update your view and show a timer given a provided date. This has actually been available since iOS 14, macOS 11, and watchOS 7, but it is a good thing to reiterate.

Rendering Modes

Widgets can come in a wide range of sizes and styles. New this year is the ability for Widgets to be shown Full Color, Accented or Vibrant. Full Color appears on some watch faces on the Apple Watch. Accented appears on Apple Watch faces with full color backgrounds, and Vibrant can appear on either the Apple Watch or on the Lock Screen of iOS.

There is a new WidgetKitRenderingMode struct that you can use to get the rendering mode from the Environment. When you do this you can then apply the proper look and feel to your widgets based on the current environment.

In **Full Color** rendering mode your widget content will be displayed exactly as you have it laid out in your widget.

In **Accented** rendering mode, widgets will be split into two different parts, and only the Views with a **widgetAccentable** modifier will be tinted with a color provided by the system or user. Alternatively, you can also switch out the view depending on the rendering mode.

In **Vibrant** rendering mode, your widget will be desaturated and then it will be appropriately colored for the background of the users's Lock Screen. One tip for the vibrant mode is avoid using bright colors. Instead, use darker colors or black.

To assist with this, there also the new **AccessoryWidgetBackground**() view that when used with a **ZStack** View, will provide a nice background to your Widget, based on what is being displayed by the system.

Closing Thoughts on Widgets and Complications

Widgets are now coming to the Lock Screen on iOS 16 . If you have existing watchOS Complications that are using the old ClockKit it might be a good time to rework them to use WidgetKit to be able to take full advantage of being able to easily bring the Watch Complications to the iOS Lock Screen.

There are some new Widget and Complication types, accessoryInline, accessoryCircular, accessoryRectangular, and accessoryCorner. The first three are available on both iOS 16 and watchOS 9, while the last one is only on watchOS 9. You can easily reuse your complications on the Lock Screen using the ViewThatFits view that will select which of the specified views will work best in the given context. All of these are great additions and things to consider for the future.

Closing Thoughts for Developers

All of these changes to the Users section of the book are made possibly through new features that developers can take advantage of through improvements to Swift, the addition of new APIs, and enhancements to Xcode.

Swift includes features like the enhancement for the @unavailable declaration which will allow developers to indicate that a particular method or function is not available for use in an Async/Await context. Beyond the changes for Swift there have been some enhancements to SwiftUI.

SwiftUI now provides a way of providing Auxiliary windows for your Mac apps, which can allow for more use cases for apps, and any auxiliary windows will appear on macOS. To go along with this is the new MenuBarExtra option, which means that apps can be written in SwiftUI even if they are just a utility app that lives in the Menu Bar.

One challenge that all developers face is how to display information and you have a new option with the new Swift Charts Framework. With Swift Charts you can add a variety of different types of charts right within your app and display information in a manner that makes sense for your users and their data.

While building your app you can take advantage of the improved Live Previews in Xcode, including being able to run the app right within SwiftUI Previews using the new Live mode. Beyond running your app live you can also look at variations of your app, like the Dynamic Type, Orientation, and even Color Scheme.

From time to time Apple adds new APIs for incorporating into your apps. Dark Sky is one of the services that Apple previously purchased has now been reworked into an entirely new Framework and API. If you need to incorporate Weather information into your app, there is the new WeatherKit framework. You can get a slew of information including daily or hourly forecasts and you can even get historical data as well. If you need to incorporate the weather on your website or for other means, there is also the WeatherKit REST API which you can access from anywhere.

Some programming problems require complex ways of extracting data. Often this can be accomplished by using regular expressions. These can be difficult to create and maintain. Luckily, regular expressions are now understood by the Swift compiler, which means that if you do create a regular expression it can be checked for validity, just like any other type. Beyond this Apple has created a new Regex type that will allow you to build regular expressions using a variety of methods that should allow you to easily follow what that regular expression is doing including capturing the results so you can use them elsewhere in your app. And these are just a few of the things that are new for developers.

Overall the changes for iOS 16, iPadOS 16, macOS Ventura, and watchOS 9 are big ones and there is at least one change that everyone will be able to use. Some of the features may not be available right at launch, but that is okay, it is better to have a fully working feature that is more bug free than to have it available right at launch.

www.ingramcontent.com/pod-product-compliance
Lightning Source LLC
LaVergne TN
LVHW081752050326
832903LV00027B/1914